Art and
ARGYROL

Art and ARGYROL

The Life and Career of Dr. Albert C. Barnes

by WILLIAM SCHACK

New York • THOMAS YOSELOFF • London

© 1960 BY SAGAMORE PRESS, INC.

LIBRARY OF CONGRESS CATALOG CARD NUMBER: 60-6835

THOMAS YOSELOFF, *PUBLISHER*
11 EAST 36TH STREET
NEW YORK 16, N. Y.

THOMAS YOSELOFF LTD.
123 NEW BOND STREET
LONDON W. 1, ENGLAND

The author wishes to express his appreciation to Crown Publishers, Inc., for permission to quote passages from: *William Glackens and the Ashcan School of Art* by Ira Glackens, copyright 1957 by Ira Glackens; *Appreciation: Painting, Poetry, Prose* by Leo Stein, copyright 1947 by Leo Stein; *Journey into the Self* by Leo Stein, copyright 1950 by the Estate of Leo D. Stein.

PRINTED IN THE UNITED STATES OF AMERICA

Dr. Albert C. Barnes, 1923 (United Press International Photo)

To my wife Sarah

Contents

7

Acknowledgments

SINCE THIS WAS NOT TO BE AN "AUTHORIZED" BIOGRAPHY, I did not know how much help I might expect from the inheritors of the Barnes Foundation. It turned out to be less than nothing, for they dissuaded everyone they could reach from providing me with any information, even information favorable to Barnes.

From William S. Howard, of the Narbeth Fire Company: "We have been instructed by Mrs. Barnes that any information released in connection with the late Dr. Barnes must first have her approval, and that she was not giving such approval at this time. Our connection with Mrs. Barnes is very close, and we honor her to such a degree that her wish is paramount. . . ."

From Kenneth Goodman, an organist Barnes befriended: "I assure you of my keen interest in the biog-

9

raphy which you are writing. . . . My recollections and
associations with Dr. Barnes are most pleasant and shall
always be greatly cherished. The late good Dr. Barnes and
I corresponded frequently. I have a number of these letters which may give some data. . . . I will clear with the
Barnes Foundation. You may expect to hear from me again
very soon. . . ." Miss Emily Buermeyer was disposed to
help until she heard that my biography of Eilshemius was
"a book of the cheapest type—appealing to the public by
way of sensationalism." I had got in touch with Angelo
Pinto in New York before I knew that he was still teaching at the Foundation. He replied: "Acknowledging receipt of your letter of October 10th, which states that you
would very much like to have the benefit of my recollections of Dr. Albert C. Barnes whose biography you are
working on, I assume that, since the biography you are
undertaking to do is to be, as you express it, 'a thoroughly
objective portrait,' that you knew Dr. Barnes intimately
and, consequently, that the 'objective' portrayal will be
based on your personal acquaintance with him and not on
hear-say information and 'recollections' from either friends
or foes." Evidently Mr. Pinto has never been near the
biography shelf in a library.

In *The Art in Painting* I saw an interesting reproduction of a painting by an artist I had not heard of: Luigi
Settanni. Assuming that he had had some personal association with Barnes, I asked him for concrete details. He
in turn asked me: "What is your purpose, your interest
in writing this biography of Dr. A. C. Barnes? Wherefrom
do you know me? Why do you want to have the benefit
of *my* recollection? What assurance do you have that the
person you write to for information is not a disgruntled
fired employee or a frustrated individual ever ready to

think up tales to see his name in print? Did you personally know Dr. Albert C. Barnes, or is it to be a 'biography' written entirely from secondhand, hit-or-miss, information?"

Evidently Mr. Settanni shared Mr. Pinto's notions of biography—and do I detect a fine feminine hand directing them both? "A disgruntled fired employee" comes straight out of a similarly suspicious letter of the master.

Finally, knowing what the answer would be, but for the sake of the record and having nothing to lose, I wrote the Foundation, offering in exchange for certain information to be specified in advance, to allow them to check my manuscript to correct errors of fact and to make what criticism they would, which, however, I did not bind myself to accept. I also stipulated that I would not credit the Foundation for its cooperation, lest it be held accountable for my misinterpretations, distortions or errors of judgment.—Did I say I knew what the answer would be? There was no answer.

The trustees are apparently as secretive with friends as with strangers, for Ira Glackens does not mention in his book, *William Glackens and the Ashcan School of Art,* what pictures his father bought for Barnes: it could not have been for want of asking.

Fortunately, the heirs of the Foundation lack the aggressiveness of the founder. Their sphere of control is as limited as their contacts with the world beyond their moat seem to be.

I must gratefully acknowledge my debt to the following persons and institutions for their experiences and other information: Lady Christabel Aberconway; Robert D. Abrahams; L. J. Atkinson; Alfred H. Barr, Jr.; Edmund R. Beckwith, Jr.; Bell Telephone Company of Pennsyl-

vania; Thomas H. Benton; George Biddle; Moncure
Biddle; Mrs. Brand Blanshard; Julius Bloch; Dr. Vitale
Bloch; Dr. Horace M. Bond; Jack Bookbinder; Miss Mar-
garet Bruening; Carlisle Burrows; Robert Carlen; Dr.
Roderick M. Chisholm; Andrew Dasburg; Dr. Elmer Field;
Georges Fieschi; Harry Fuiman; Fred Geasland; Miss
Emily Genauer; Waldemar George; Ira Glackens and
Crown Publishers; Dr. R. Göber; Miss Dorothy Grafly;
Dr. James Gutman; (the late) William C. Handy; the late
Edouard Herriot; Dr. Sidney Hook; Paul Jones; Mrs.
Irene Bland Jurix; Dr. Hans Krabusch; Jacques Lipchitz;
Jon D. Longaker; Miss Katherine E. McBride; Henry Mc-
Bride; James A. Michener; Darius Milhaud; Thomas
Munro; the National Archives and Records Service; Mrs.
Dorothy Norman; the Philadelphia *Inquirer's* Harold
Wiegand and Miss Eleanor Gaynon; the Philadelphia Mu-
seum of Art's R. Sturgis Ingersoll and Henri Marceau;
Mrs. Caroline Rohland; Bertrand Russell; Homer St.
Gaudens; Meyer Schapiro; J. F. Scull, Jr.; Gilbert Seldes;
Ben Shahn; Mrs. John Sloan; J. P. Slusser; Mrs. Eugene
Speicher; Mrs. Cynthia Stine and *Harper's Magazine;* Miss
Anne K. Stolzenbach; James Johnson Sweeney; Howard
Taubman; the University of Pennsylvania's Gaylord P.
Harnwell, Dr. Charles C. Price, Dr. Leonidas Dodson, and
Mrs. Flora D. Colton; Carl Van Vechten; the *Virginia
Quarterly Review;* Harry B. Wehle; Mrs. Sara B. Wein-
berg, Thomas Raeburn White; Yale University Library;
Miss Anzia Yezierska; the librarians at the Jefferson Med-
ical College; Princeton and New York Public Library art
department; and several persons who wished to remain
anonymous.

                                                          W. S.

Art and
ARGYROL

1

Obituary and Beginning

ON A JULY AFTERNOON IN 1951, A MAN SEVENTY-NINE YEARS old but still robust enough to drive his own car, was traveling along a country road in a suburb of Philadelphia. It was a road he had driven over for years, and there was a STOP sign where it met a through highway. He had often called the dangerous intersection to the attention of visitors, but on this particular day he himself drove past the sign without stopping: his car came onto the highway directly in the path of an oncoming trailer truck too late for him to stop or speed up or swerve. . . .

When the news reached his native Philadelphia that Dr. Albert C. Barnes had been killed in a crash, only a few among the many who knew him felt sorrow. More thought, How natural a death for a man who had crashed through red lights all his life! And in this thought there was no sorrow, hardly the sadness which one may feel for the death of any living creature, but rather a sense of relief

only a sigh removed from a sense of satisfaction. For
Barnes had hurt too many people in the previous quarter
century to be widely mourned, even if he had not died full
of years. More than one of his adversaries, if he had dared,
would have been delighted to hasten the act of an auto-
motive god which finally overtook him.

The malice which often attends successful men, magni-
fying their failings and belittling their achievements, had
an accomplice in Barnes's actual failings. These were great
and obvious enough to permit those who hated him to pass
over the virtue of his achievements, to ignore the versatility
which enabled him to pursue many different careers with
initiative, resourcefulness and energy. Even those who
uncritically admired other men's success stories did not feel
obliged to pay tribute to Barnes for coming up from a
harsh poverty to millionairedom and intellectual achievement. Perhaps he had been rich so long that some did not
know of his origins, or they may have believed one of the
rumors in circulation that he had made his fortune by
fraud. If they did not scoff at his art collection—the greatest of its kind in the country—they said that anyone with
a million dollars to spare could have its equal. There were
those who even questioned the sincerity of his love of art,
asserting that he was endowed with more irascibility than
sensibility. The gift which most impressed his enemies was
his talent for making enemies. Overlooking all his benefactions, they seemed to think that he was incapable of
kindness and alleged that he broke with every single person
he was ever friendly with, leaving a trail of "vile"—
obscene—letters behind him.

Unfortunately, it is impossible without offence to quote
many of his briefer paragraphs. We may track him through
thirty years of the Gazette by the smudgy trail he leaves behind him. His humor is coarse and his mood of mind Rabelais-

ian. . . . He out-Smolletts Smollett in his letters to young women at home and experienced matrons abroad.

This was written by Albert Henry Smyth, not of Barnes but of a more renowned Philadelphian, Benjamin Franklin, of whose collected papers the prudish Smyth was editor. One must take a Franklin—or a Barnes—as he was or leave him alone. Barnes did write offensive letters—too many of them—but there are only a few downright vile ones to be seen. Either they vanished at my approach or had been previously destroyed, for we have a deeper need to shed insult than to document it.

Even people who had no personal grievance against Barnes have thoughtlessly or casually slandered him, for a man who was so prone to do battle invited attack. A professor of philosophy noted for his careful thinking and writing told me that Barnes had written an anti-Semitic letter to a Jewish friend of his. The letter turned out to be hostile but without racial bias. To account for Barnes's aggressiveness, the same professor, without bothering to check the facts, asserted in a responsible magazine that Barnes had been a pugilist in his youth. In a reminiscent article which served as obituary notice, one of the few art critics not ill-disposed to him, whom Barnes himself admired, wrote breezily that he had driven an editor mad with his harsh criticism. Yet when I questioned the probability of his charge, the critic admitted that he knew nothing of the circumstances and could not possibly have written what had been set down in print.

The hatred of Barnes has not abated in the short time since his death. One well-known figure in the world of art did not even wish to associate his name in the pages of a book with that of Barnes because of "the rottenness of his actions. . . . I saw and heard such things about his treatment of art, his wife, his acquaintances . . . and all who did not toady to him. As one Philadelphia lawyer, who I am sure had no personal grudge against him, said, very simply, 'He was evil.' " Less theologically minded people have called him a son of a bitch; an artist among them said that he was at least a magnificent one.

Was he born one or was he made one by circumstance? If, from a single dream of Leonardo da Vinci of a bird pecking at his lips, Freud could spin out a monograph to prove that he was a homosexual, any amateur Freudian can, from the facts of Barnes's childhood, deduce the pattern of his adult life. But a life is more than a pattern, however much the pattern may dominate it; and to overstress the pattern is to lose the life. It is all the more necessary to fix the facts of Barnes's life because so much that has been written about him is either wholly wrong, partially true, or the half-truth which casts the shadow of a lie. Some of this misinformation may have been obtained from Barnes on the fly, speaking casually, and he was far from reliable even when he volunteered information deliberately. On several important matters his statements must be corrected or qualified. In bringing out the facts, so far as I have been able to obtain them, I shall not draw the pattern too tightly, but let every reader be his own Freud.

Albert Barnes once told a group of students that he would not want to see a biography written of him because it would portray him either as a devil or a saint. Even an authorized biography would have difficulty showing him with a halo. It would be much easier to make him out a devil, but this, too, is a task for someone else: I testify that I have seen his ten toes.

On February 1, 1864, President Lincoln ordered a draft of 500,000 men for three years or the duration, effective

as of March 10. The order made up many young minds in
conflict with themselves; the pending draft, and the lure of
a bounty in many states, brought the young men to the
recruiting stations. In Pennsylvania the bounty was $300,
the equivalent in purchasing power of about $1,000 today,
a sum large enough to have possibly influenced John J.
Barnes to sign up in Philadelphia on February 5. The
twenty-year-old youth was descended from one of the original settlers of William Penn's colony, and did not seem
likely to leave more of an imprint on the history of the
"green countrie towne" Penn founded than his forebears;
for when he joined the 82nd Infantry Regiment of Pennsylvania Volunteers he had left behind him only a butcher's
bench in a slaughterhouse. What he looked like to a recruiting sergeant—five feet four inches high, brown hair,
hazel eyes, dark complexion—hardly tells what he was
like. If he was as scrappy in his old age as the only written
anecdote concerning him indicates, he may have been a
lively, if not a scrappy, young man.

Enlisting for a three-year period, young Barnes saw action before his first year was half over, in the three-day
battle of Cold Harbor, Virginia. This was before the day
of machine guns, yet in its final assault on the strong
Confederate positions the Union army is reported to have
suffered 10,000 casualties within twenty minutes. Barnes's
company was all shot up, and he himself received such
a bad gunshot wound in his right arm that it had to be
amputated. Apparently infection set in, for he spent
nearly a year in government hospitals in Washington,
Baltimore and Chester, Pa. When he put in his application for a pension after his discharge from the army, he
signed it with an X. Either he was illiterate or, more likely,
he had not yet learned to write with his left hand. On

the basis of a disability rating of three-fourths, he was allowed a pension of $8 a month.

He was working as a letter carrier—perhaps a temporary one—when, at the age of twenty-three, he married Lydia A. Schaf (f)er, who was twenty-one, in a Methodist ceremony. Of the four sons born to their marriage in quick succession, one died within a year and another survived only two years. But their first-born, Charles, and their third son, Albert Coombs, were to be long-lived.

When Albert was born, January 2, 1872, the family was living in a small two-story house at 1466 Cook (now Wilt) Street, a narrow street in which two cars can barely pass each other. There was perhaps more wood and less brick when the Barneses lived there, but the general look is the same: house flanks house, roof level with roof and stoop level with stoop, the uniformity relieved only by a sharp-angled turn of the street. A block away, Kensington Cemetery still serves as a quasi park—a place of modest headstones where soldiers of Washington's army lie buried. A mile walk to the east and he could see living water— the Delaware River.

On Albert's birth certificate the space for "occupation of father" was not filled out. The omission could have been due to negligence but quite possibly was intentional. John Barnes was probably in and out of odd jobs. During his earliest years, the child was not aware of anything amiss. Usually parents are poor, not children. Give them something to eat, any old clothes, and a place to sleep, and, living in a poor neighborhood, they do not know that they are poor. But when Albert was six years old, things were so bad that he often went without the minimum something to eat; he knew what it was to be hungry to the point of pain.

Perhaps this contributed to his lack of interest in school;

and he got more pleasure from horsing around with the kids on the block, playing ball and hanging around the firehouse waiting for something exciting to happen. "Exciting" is a child's cover-all word for the abrupt breakup of daily routine. Consciously, all he may be aware of in the experience of fire is excitement. But a fire is also color, music, swift motion, conflict. When an alarm sounded, it brought the martial music of gongs, first solo, then clanging above the drumming of the hoofs of massively flanked horses. Bright red and gleaming brass streamed down the street to a house, commonplace ten minutes ago, now mysterious with smoke and the changing color shapes of flame, the field of a pitched battle between firemen and fire.

After the excitement is over, something, something different, endures. The red fire is dead; the triumphant red dragon is quiet in his stall. What is red? What is fire? A child does not have to pose the questions to which he seeks an answer. Albert takes up a piece of crayon and makes lines and they mean *red fire engine on way to fire.* He knows very well, though he makes believe he doesn't, that no fireman can leap on board, yet in a way the drawing is better than the real thing. The doors of the firehouse close; the engine disappears. Your own fire engine is always at hand, to look at whenever you like, to take wherever you please . . . even to follow to a dream fire more blazing than any fire in Philadelphia.

When Albert was eight years old, he discovered a more profound form of excitement in a Negro camp meeting. White Methodists had originated these religious revivals, some of which lasted for ten weeks and drew crowds every night. Most of the Negroes of the Philadelphia area belonged to the African American Methodist Church, and it was one of their camp meetings at Merchantville, just beyond Camden, across the Delaware from the city, which the boy attended. He could have made the trip by ferry and horsecar with companions his own age; more likely he was taken by his Methodist parents. The Barneses were apparently regular churchgoers and however little the service meant to Albert, he was responsive to the hymns. Now he heard songs, and singing, far more stirring. No doubt there were hymns conceived with passion, but they emerged in the spirit of their staid musical form.

The melodies and rhythms of the Negro spirituals, which the Fisk Jubilee Singers had only introduced to the North in the 1870's, were still shaken with the passion of their birth. And this was not a small congregation singing solemnly within confining walls, but an outdoor multitude as emotional as their songs. Between numbers they wandered about as the spirit moved them, waving their arms, dancing, shouting out of sheer exuberance or spontaneously eloquent in homely picturesque phrases.

Although he did not realize it at the time, the boy was having his first experience of religion. "I was switched suddenly from my everyday world to the realm of mysticism—a realm where nothing else counts except the ineffable joy of the immediate moment." He became "an addict to Negro camp meetings, baptizings, revivals, and to seeking the company of individual Negroes, who, I soon discovered, carried out in their daily lives the poetry, music, dance and drama which, when exercised by a group, gave the camp meeting its colorful, rhythmic, vivid and compelling charm."

In the next two years the family sank deeper into poverty. When Albert was ten years old, they struck bedrock. Unable to pay the rent of their home on Cook Street, they moved—for them, migrated—to the squatter slums in South Philadelphia known as "The Neck" or "The Dumps." This was one of the oldest sections of the city, part of an extensive area between the Delaware and Schuylkill rivers which had once been completely under cultivation but was gradually going over into marshland, sparsely spotted with piggery and distillery. A scattering of stone houses with some regard for design reflected the prosperity of a few residents. But the prevailing architectural style was improvisation; the best squatter houses were built of salvaged lumber and scrap sheet metal; the worst, of packing cases crudely joined.

The city of Philadelphia has by now razed the entire area, but as late as the fall of 1955 Dr. Charlotte Fleischmann, principal of the D. Newlin Fell School on its northern limits, wrote that many of the houses in The Neck lacked all hygienic facilities; the streets were unpaved; there were no sidewalks. One house—an extreme case— was without windows or heat. "The entrance to the houses is through dirt walks. Rats, dead and alive, are everywhere. The ground is littered with trash and the grass and weeds are so overgrown that in some places it is impossible to see the houses at all. The children disappear in the reeds when they are near home.

"There is no water in most of the houses. It is [drawn from hydrants and] carried in huge milk cans for more than a mile and is icy cold in the winter. On winter days, too, the roads are impassable and most of the children are non-attendant." Possibly conditions were not quite so bad when the area was more fully populated. The rodents may have moved in as the humans moved out.

A one-armed man and a mother with two small boys are not likely to have built their own home, however ramshackle. The family must have moved into an abandoned

shanty or one vacated for them for a token rental. Possibly
Mrs. Barnes, who was apparently of German descent, had
a friend or relation to help them locate a shelter.

The Neck was not a Hooverville or Bowery. Though
their homes were makeshift, the people, most of them
descendants of Hessian mercenaries who deserted from the
British army during the Revolution, were neither de-
pressed nor derelict. They were, Dr. Fleischmann observed,
completely satisfied with their neighborhood.

In a very few cases parents have expressed some dissatisfaction with their social conditions, but this is not the rule. They
refer to the section as 'Hollywood' or 'the suburbs' [one rude
house, in irony or pride, bore the sign: The Rementer Estate],
and they will tell you they like it because it is healthier than
in the city. The children marry and often settle north of The
Neck, but usually within a few months they move back and
settle comfortably in 'the suburbs.' Of course, too, their living
expenses are negligible. . . . They speak of themselves as
100% Americans and are resentful of any 'foreigners.'

Some of the people set out flower beds and truck gardens. At Christmastime they placed wreaths in the windows before fragments of curtains, and evergreens at the
doors: pathetic attempts to beautify their homes, Dr.
Fleischmann found them, but they could also have been
a robust gesture, like a ragged hat worn at a jaunty angle.

Among such people, whether or not the elder Barneses
liked them and associated with them, they had a chance to
recover from their dejection. Poverty was not their only
burden, for it must have been shortly before they moved
to The Neck or soon after they settled there that they lost
their two-year-old boy, George. Nowhere in print did
Barnes ever refer to his mother, which may or may not
indicate that it was she who ran—perhaps ruled—the family. Evidently she was determined to move back to civiliza-

tion as soon as possible. Charley, the older boy, must have gone to work at once, for Albert was selling newspapers the next year, when he was eleven years old. Perhaps he was following his brother's occupation. On bad winter days he must have had a hard time of it, for even if he stayed away from school with the rest of the boys, he still had to deliver his newspapers. To reach the nearest horse-car line meant slogging a long way through snow which lay where it fell until nature cleared it away.

Yet it was not the hard winters and the shabbiness of the neighborhood which most impressed the boy. At least, what the grown man remembered most vividly was the tough kids. He had always liked to roughhouse, but it was on more or less equal terms. At The Neck he met up with boys who did not observe the code of "hit a guy your own size." They saw him playing tops—they grabbed the tops. He couldn't believe his eyes. Those were *his* tops, bought with his own pennies, and he had to work hard for them. When he cried or protested, they didn't give him back his tops—they beat him up. The same thing happened again and again; sometimes they must have given him a licking just for the hell of it. Nor did the bullies spare Charley. The hurt went deeper than the flesh, and there came a day when the brothers decided not to take it lying down any more. They began to learn to box and to attend fights—as Albert said later, to pick up fine points, but also, no doubt, because they enjoyed, with other fight fans, the spectacle of one man (their champion) slapping down his (their) foe. In time the brothers became adept enough to stand off their former tormentors. Albert boasted later that he was never beaten up again, and one can believe that he did not get another shiner or bloody nose. But in vivid memory he was beaten up again and again. Long after the attacks on him were over, the sense of humiliation

remained. Blood stopped flowing within minutes; black
eyes and bruises healed within days; but his wounded pride
festered for years.

Despite the family's extreme poverty, Albert went on to
high school when he was thirteen years old. Perhaps his
parents wanted at least one of their sons to receive an
education; perhaps Albert had got over his early dislike of
school as kid stuff and himself insisted on further study.
It could be that he had become both curious for knowledge and aware of the fact that it was the only way to a
better future than selling newspapers. Of all the public
secondary schools in the city, Central High, the second
oldest high school in the country, was the only all-boys
school; and it had the severest entrance requirements. Rising to its challenge, Albert applied and was admitted.
The school was then located downtown, but that was still
miles from The Neck. Going to Central High was the
beginning of his spiritual departure from the squatters'
wasteland.

2

Doctor

THE RIGOROUS ACADEMIC STANDARDS OF CENTRAL HIGH (which gave, and still gives, an A.B. degree) put young Barnes on his mettle. Of the one hundred and twenty-five boys admitted in his class, more than ninety withdrew or were dropped by the end of the first semester. Among the survivors, Barnes ranked fourth. Pride in his scholastic achievement did not make him less self-conscious of the fact that he was wearing frayed pants or lessen his humiliation when some boys, as he bitterly felt, snubbed him for it.

He had the stimulating association of other boys, and especially of three who were interested in art: John Sloan, William J. Glackens, and Robert Preston. He was more intimate with the two who were to achieve a more prominent place in the world of American art. Sloan had to go to work after one term of school, but Barnes enjoyed the

company of Glackens for four years. They were soon "Al"
and "Butts"—Glackens' nickname from the childhood day
when he proudly called the attention of his playmates to
the brass buttons on his new coat.

Van Wyck Brooks has written that their common interest was baseball. This could mean that they were
merely fans, cheering on (at a distance) their favorite
Athletics or Phillies and pondering the tabular mysteries
of AB H R PO A E, or that they got out into the field themselves as well. Barnes was surely playing ball in those
years, probably on class or school teams, and Glackens
may have played with him.

But baseball was not their only common interest. Glackens had begun to draw when he was in the cradle. At
Central High he was more interested in sketching his
teachers than in listening or reciting to them. The drawing, Barnes wrote later, "was of what the teacher was in
reality, never what the teacher would have us believe
that he was." This seems the profundity of nostalgia, rather
than that of the drawing itself. Schoolboys do not know
what reality is, especially what adults are really like. Let's
say Glackens drew amusing caricatures. When they were
passed around they "made it impossible for the rest of us
to study." If the teachers had not succumbed to the artist's
good looks, his charm and his sense of humor, he would
have been expelled before he had traveled a hundred miles
into Gaul with Caesar.

Glackens had not yet had formal instruction in painting,
but he may have been doing canvases on his own, or at
least may have known more about painting than his friend,
for Barnes brought him his first pictures for criticism.
Glackens laughed at them. "I wanted to find out what he
was laughing at and I learned a lot from him."

During Albert's third year at school, the family got

away from The Neck. They moved into a small house, very much like the one they had occupied on Cook Street, in very much the same sort of poor neighborhood. This one was at 1331 Tasker Street, just off Broad, not two miles from the heart of the city. The Barneses did not rent the house—they bought it. Since John Barnes's pension was still only $8 a month, the down payment must have been made with pennies ruthlessly saved by Mrs. Barnes, in whose name the deed was recorded.

The improvement at home was not reflected in Albert's school work: his first term was his best. He fell from fourth place to somewhat above the median point, climbed again, slumped badly in the last two years. When he graduated in 1889, he stood twenty-fourth in a class of twenty-six. However, as Elmer Field, president of Central High, pointed out, those who were able to survive at all must have had good scholastic stuff in them whatever their ranking.

Barnes then registered for the three-year medical course at the University of Pennsylvania. Why medicine? After working all through his school years, Barnes was a hard-headed youth and he may have chosen the profession merely because it promised a good living. Doctors were then in such demand that fraudulent medical schools had sprung up all over the country; some of them handed out diplomas after a three-weeks' course of "instruction." At the same time, with the example of his father always before him, he may have felt a sympathy for the disabled and a desire to help them. Or he could have made himself believe this if he felt a need—despite his hard-headedness —for a motive higher than mere self-interest, or if he was not really sure that he wanted to study medicine.

To support himself, Barnes began to play semi-professional baseball. In addition, for his second year, he won a

Board of Education scholarship. Apparently under the existing rules, a college freshman was still eligible to compete with high school graduates. Nevertheless, the award was severely criticized. It should have gone, the dissenters thought, to a boy who stood second in the graduating class of Central High that year; and they accused the scholarship committee of favoritism in this and other cases. Unwittingly, it would seem, Barnes was thus involved in his first controversy. Was some member of the committee partial to him because he had known him as a newsboy in the past or, more recently, as a baseball player? More likely Barnes's good record in his first year at the university won him the award. The "examination average" of 94 he had in general chemistry and 96 in general pathology overshadowed the 52 he got in histology —the only low grade he was to receive in his entire course. In materia medica he rated "passed"—no figure was given.

Barnes told many people of his having played on a semi-pro ball team (he oddly neglected to mention what position he had covered) for $10 a game. If the season ran a full five months and he played in every game and it never rained on Sundays, his earnings would have amounted to some $200 a year—barely enough to pay for tuition, books, laboratory fees and personal needs. One can believe his statement that he went through college with a single suit of clothes on his back.

He managed to join a fraternity during his second year, but Phi Gamma Delta was evidently a poor man's frat. Established a decade previously, it had struggled along for a half a dozen years and died. It was revived, largely by a group of medical students, at the time Barnes joined it. Apparently he made no intimate associations with his fraternity brothers, for although he was to retain a close

frayed pants; this time it was cap and gown. It galled him
that he should have to rent them for commencement exer-
cises, from Strawbridge & Clothier for $2.25 when you
could buy a new outfit for $5 (and up). But as the owner
of a single suit, he could hardly afford to throw away an
extra $2.75 on regalia to be used for only one day. Actually,
the provost of the university had the power to excuse a
student from wearing cap and gown, but to advertise himself as a pauper before the assembled crowd was an ig-
nominy young Barnes could afford even less than the
rental fee.

He still had a year's internship ahead of him, which he
spent at an institution for the mentally ill somewhere outside Philadelphia. One can only speculate why he chose
to do his apprentice work in a field which was no further
advanced than it was in the time of Hippocrates, rather
than in general medicine, which could at least relieve
pain and diagnose some serious illnesses even if it did not
know how to cure them. If he was moved to become a
doctor by the plight of the disabled, he could have been
especially drawn to mental derangement, the most pathetic
of disabilities. He could even have been impelled toward
it, as many psychiatrists are, by his own deep-seated emotional instability, of which he need not have been aware.
Barnes did say, later on, that he had been interested in
abnormal psychology when he graduated. He may well
have forgotten by then whether the fact that he received
some small wage (interns in general hospitals, until recently, received no pay at all) had determined his internship. By the end of the year, he must have perceived the
hopelessness of patient and the helplessness of physician.
These could have been responsible for his decision to give
up medicine as a career.

He may have done so even if he had interned in general

ART AND ARGYROL

3

Chemist

THUS FAR THE ASSUMPTION HAS BEEN THAT BARNES DELIB-
erately gave up medicine for chemistry. In later years he
told of having a laboratory in the basement of his home,
presumably on Tasker Street. This may have been so or it
may have been an imaginative reconstruction of his career
as a chemist. The fact that the family was poor would not
be an argument against the probability of its existence,
for he could have got up a laboratory of sorts with a
saucepan from his mother's kitchen and a couple of test
tubes, a few lengths of tubing, a beaker, and pinches of
this and that compound from drugstore or paint store or
the school laboratory. His chemistry courses at the University of Pennsylvania are a matter of record.

In after years he used to tell an audience which could
be told anything concerning chemistry that he once
brought two compounds to his professor and asked him

35

what would happen if they were mixed. The professor didn't know; Barnes tried it and blew out a wall of the laboratory! Very picturesque, but it is unlikely that a professor of chemistry would not know the reaction between such compounds as were accessible to a student, or that he would allow him to make a possibly hazardous experiment without taking due precautions. If the story was not a pure gag, one could interpret it to mean that when he was in *high school* the boy, carelessly or ignorantly, played around with some chemicals whose identity he did not know in his *own* laboratory—if he had a laboratory—and that he blew out the wall of—oh, say a test tube.

We could be more sure that Barnes chose to go into chemistry rather than medicine if the record of the next half-dozen years were written plain. It is not, and must be reconstructed with doubtful accuracy from various sources conflicting in some details (Barnes himself added to the confusion) which cannot be reconciled. This understood, a course may be plotted with a minimum of conjecture.

After his internship Barnes went back to the University of Pennsylvania to take a course in philosophy and additional courses in chemistry ("I was a philosophical chemist"). This, on his own say-so. Since his name is not listed in the Graduate School or in the Auxiliary Department of Medicine which graduate doctors attended, he could have been enrolled only as a special student or in a kind of extension-school program. "The records are not sufficiently complete for us to feel that he was not so enrolled, but it seems a bit doubtful that he was," says Leonidas Dodson, archivist of the university.

If we give Barnes the benefit of the doubt, there is evidence to say that he supported himself for a year or two longer by tutoring beginners in chemistry, by playing baseball again, and by a job in an advertising agency.

Having saved up some money, Barnes set out for Germany. Not to waste any of his precious funds, he worked his way across the Atlantic, and continued on to Berlin. To study chemistry? It could have been simply to break loose, to travel for travel's sake. He was young and curious and had not been more than a hundred miles from his birthplace. It could also have been, in part, to get away from the family, from its disappointment in him. Giving up medicine did not entail as much loss then as it would today: three years against seven; and they were not truly lost for Barnes if he discovered a talent for chemistry in medical school. That is simple logic; so the young Barnes may have reasoned to himself. But it is not a thing which would go down with poor parents who had looked forward to his diploma as a symbol of salvation, banishing nightmare poverty forever. Could they imagine why he had thrown an honorable profession overboard, or understand any explanation he might have made? Whether they were outspoken in their criticism or left it unsaid, the youth could not have been insensitive to their dismay, and to their feeling that he was a failure.

If he was not yet sure of the extent of his interest in chemistry, he could have tried to mollify them, and convince himself, by saying that it offered great prospects. Even if he was sure of a desire for a career in this new field, he had no guarantee of making a quick success in it. The farther he got away from the scene of his first failure, the doubts of the folks, the visible signs of their present hardship and the fearful memories of the old poverty, the better his chances of success would be.

The fact that Barnes elected to go to Germany rather

than any other country in Europe is a positive indication
that his primary motive in going abroad was to advance
his new career. For he knew that in chemistry, "the off-
spring of the nineteenth century," the Germans were the
major pioneers. At college he had learned of Wöhler's
classical synthesis of urea which put an end to the generally held belief that organic compounds were produced
by a "vital force" in plants and animals. His imagination
must have been touched by Kekule von Stradonitz's realization in a dream of the structure of the benzene ring—a
problem which had long occupied his waking thought.
Barnes may not have known that Liebig, perhaps the most
far-ranging of the German explorers in chemistry, had
established the first systematic course of instruction in
that field, as he was the first teacher to present his advanced
students with ideas for research to develop their facility
in experiment, but Barnes was certainly aware of the result: the large number of American graduate students
taking their doctoral degree at German universities.
Wöhler, Kekule and Liebig were all teachers. Although
Barnes did not know enough chemistry to merit the company of the masters, where there were so many masters
there were competent men at every level. Above all, there
was an atmosphere stimulating for a beginner as well as
for an advanced student.

Departing for Germany in 1896, Barnes had enough
money to see him through a few months while he was
studying the language with the aid of textbook, newspaper
and café acquaintances. After that he made a living as
sales representative of an American stove manufacturer,
whom he may have met in Berlin or through his advertising agency before he went abroad—if he did work in
such an agency at this time. It is safe to assume that the
youthful Barnes sowed a proper acreage of wild oats, did

a little painting, and bought some small pictures he had in his possession ten years later. They were the kind of pictures anyone might have bought who had a feeling for art, small experience of it, and no money: pleasant little landscapes made by competent artists some of whose names are not even to be found in Thieme-Becker's thirty-seven-volume encyclopedia of artists. But the little pictures by Morten Müller, J. Haller and one or two others could have served to lighten the heavy Teutonic furnishings of his room and refresh him when he looked up from his heavy reading.

What was he reading? There were two institutions for advanced study in Berlin: the University of Friedrich-Wilhelm (later called University of Berlin and now Humboldt University) and the Technische Hochschule (now Technische Universität Berlin). As elsewhere in Germany, there was a sharp division between the university as a center of traditional learning and the humanities, and the latter-day technical institutes, the equivalent of our engineering colleges. The university required new students to bring Latin and Greek with them; the technical institutes, no more than a dozen letters of the Greek alphabet used in formulas and equations.

"I studied philosophy for a good many years, in Germany," Barnes testified, under oath, late in life. He could only have done so at the university. His name does not appear in the record of either regularly enrolled students or of those who took courses without credit (*Gasthörer*). Barnes could, however, have obtained permission from an individual professor to listen in on his lectures. The arrangement was exceptional but possible.

If Barnes was primarily interested in chemistry, one would expect to find his name in the registration files of the Technische Hochschule. Unfortunately and ironically,

its records of matriculated foreign students were destroyed
toward the end of World War II while those of domestic
students came through undamaged. However, the role of
foreign *Gasthörer* was preserved, and Barnes is not listed.
This would mean that if he took any courses at the school
he would, again, have done so with special permission. But
if he was clever enough to gain access to lectures, it is
impossible to imagine his being allowed to work in a
laboratory.

From what Barnes said twenty years later, one could
infer that he was selling stoves by the acre and that he
lived on his commission for years. From what he said
forty years later, he was dead broke after a year and a
half and had to solicit the help of the American consul
in Antwerp to get home. He was given a job on the tanker
Charleroi sailing from Rotterdam, but after he had sung
Negro spirituals the first night, the captain invited him
to dinner every night thereafter and his only task—and
it was a pleasure—was to sing.

Back home again, and determined to return to Germany,
Barnes worked for an advertising agency or as salesman
for a drug jobber or in the laboratory of Mulford's, a
pharmaceuticals manufacturer (later absorbed by Sharp
& Dohme, which is now a division of Merck & Co.). It is
possible that the reported "drug jobber" was Mulford's
and that Barnes could have had more than one job at this
time.

After all the doubts concerning the facts of his post-
medical years, we can at last say with certainty that he
was in Germany in the spring of 1900, for he was at the
University of Heidelberg during the semester May 9 to
August 6, taking a course of lectures in therapeutics under
Professor Rudolf Gottlieb, and a laboratory course in the
Pharmacological Institute, of which Gottlieb was director.

This was all the formal instruction in chemistry he had in Germany.

In a late letter he wrote that he went to Heidelberg to study chemistry "in accordance with the methods of science that *I had picked up by myself* [italics mine] and under the best instruction in the world." The last phrase could mean the instruction he obtained by following up his own driving curiosity, but most likely it refers to the instruction he received at the University of Pennsylvania, to which he remained loyal, in his fashion, all his life. But if his study of chemistry in Berlin had been confined to lectures and reading, it is remarkable that he was able to undertake laboratory work in Heidelberg, apparently above the level of routine experiments, nine years after his last, and limited, stint in a chem lab at the U. of P. It is significant, though, that he was enrolled at Heidelberg not as a student of chemistry but as a student of medicine. That he should have taken his courses in therapeutics, the same practical subject in which he had done so well at medical school, is an indication that he had some immediately useful end in view.

Still the philosophical chemist, he attended the lectures of Kuno Fischer, "the most brilliant expositor I ever listened to." One of the points Fischer stressed was that, in the age of science, Kant had staked out a proper field for philosophy in epistemology, the theory of knowledge. Having had so little experience in the laboratory, Barnes was naïve enough to think that a thorough grounding in epistemology would help him solve his problems in chemistry. "The actual result was quite the opposite." Pursuing the fine points of the theory of knowledge became a fascinating game, but an end in itself, without application to his own field; and he had to wean himself from it to pursue the empirical approach of experiment.

At some point in this pursuit he was joined by a fellow student named Herman Hille. The son of a merchant in a small Prussian town and a year older than Barnes, Hille shared his eagerness for knowledge. In the spirit of the German university tradition, he had roamed far more widely in its quest. After he had become a licensed pharmacist, he gave up the profession to travel in Germany and abroad (he studied English in London). His next position was an assistantship in physiological chemistry at the University of Würzburg. During the fall term of 1898-1899 and again the following year, he was taking a wide range of chemistry courses at the University of Heidelberg; at the time Barnes arrived he was completing his work for a doctoral thesis: "On the Primary and Secondary Symmetrical Hydrazines of Propionic and Valerianic Acids"—a title not much less baffling to Barnes than to the reader.

Both men knew of the use of silver nitrate for various medical purposes. In 1884, K. S. F. Credé had introduced an important new use, putting it into the eyes of newborn infants to prevent blindness from gonorrheal infection. This immediately led to a search for a form of silver which would be as effective therapeutically as silver nitrate without having its irritant quality. In other applications silver nitrate had the further disadvantage of sometimes causing discoloration of the eye and of the skin and membranes (argyria); and it coagulated the membranes to which it was applied before it could penetrate the deeper structures, so that its beneficial action was limited to the surface of a tissue.

In 1896 an investigator found the basic solution in a protective colloid—colloidal silver combined with dextrin. While Barnes and Hille were working on their research, several analogous "mild silver-proteins," as they are called, were created. While they were, like silver dextrin, nonirritant, they also lacked the therapeutic power of silver nitrate. Unlike it, they did not dissolve readily and therefore released only a small quantity of silver ions (silver atoms bearing a positive electrical charge), and it is only in this form that silver acts on tissue. Barnes and Hille were in search of a silver-protein compound which would release a substantial amount of silver ions on contact with an infected tissue. Since Hille had the intensive chemical training which Barnes lacked, he must have played a considerable role in planning the experimental work to be done.

In the end they decided to make use of the protein called vitellin, which occurs naturally in egg yoke and in certain plants; and it is possible that they made this decision after Barnes's preliminary experiments in Heidelberg. Their study then resolved itself into four parts: (1) to find a cheap source of vitellin; (2) to devise a means of extracting it; (3) to try out ways of combining it with silver and determining the properties of the compound thus formed; and (4) to test it on human beings.

It has been said that Barnes earned his keep while he was in Heidelberg by singing Negro songs in a beer garden. The story even names the particular song which got him the job—"You Can't Go to Heaven in a Rockin' Chair"—and only neglects to say whether Barnes did his repertoire in blackface. There is no doubt that he liked to sing, that he loved Negro songs, and that if he was going to sing them in public he could not have chosen a more charmingly incongruous place than a Heidelberg beer garden. If he did in fact sing there, and sang well, it was a very small advance payment for the bounty he was to receive from his brief stay in that city.

Where Hille carried out his part of the project is not

known, but we can trace Barnes's progress after his return home.

How did he get home? A hatful of pfennigs wouldn't buy a transatlantic passage. It seems that an American consul arranged. . . . Haven't we heard this before, or were there two different ships on which Barnes worked his way, entertaining passengers and crew as a vocalist? This much is true: he liked to sing and he loved those Negro songs.

4

Argyrol and a By-Product

ALTHOUGH HE RETURNED FROM GERMANY WITH A FIXED purpose, Barnes had first to look to his bread and butter even if he was living at his parents' home. Again he went to work for Mulford's, this time certainly in the laboratory. He was also ready to settle down, and was quite clear in his mind who was to be master of the household. Soon after his return he met Laura Leighton Leggett, simple, shy and intelligent and three years younger than himself, and decided that she would graciously fill second place. The daughter of Richard L. and Clara (Cox) Leggett, of Brooklyn, N. Y., she lived with them and a sister in a four-story brownstone house on a block of red brick and brownstone houses, at 281 Adelphia Street, a genteel neighborhood and conveniently close to downtown.

Barnes was so proud of his colonial ancestry (on his father's side) that he must have been impressed by that

of the Leggetts. The family migrated from Essex, England, to Barbados, B. W. I., in the early seventeenth
century. Gabriel Leggett went on to New York more than
a generation before a progenitor of Barnes set foot in
the New World. Two years before John Barnes enlisted
in the Union army, Laura's father had started a produce
business with a younger brother, Francis H., which broke
up after eight years. The Francis H. Leggett & Co.
which is a flourishing wholesale grocery today was
founded by Francis with a third brother, Theodore.

The Barnes courtship must have followed a well-
established pattern: the young—well, youngish—man
spoke ardently and at length about his ambitions; the
young woman listened sympathetically, wanting to believe him and believing him, and, if one source is to be
believed, having proof positive that he was not just talking: Albert performed some experiments with silver
vitellin on the kitchen stove of her parents. (This source
has Barnes beginning his research in the little basement
laboratory of his high school days, and at the same time
has him interfering with his mother's cooking on *her*
kitchen stove.) Though he had been raised as a Methodist,
Barnes no longer believed in any formal creed, so that
it must have been out of deference to his bride's parents
if not the bride that they were married, on June 4, 1901,
by the curate of St. James Protestant Episcopal Church
on Oxford Street, not far from the Leggett home.

The couple went abroad for their honeymoon, probably
courtesy of the Leggetts. Even then Barnes is said to
have "worked on" (thought of?) his invention, and, when
they rented a house in Overbrook on their return, to
have set up a laboratory in the kitchen, his wife staying
up nights with him to keep him in coffee. Mother's or
bride's or wife's—it is not implausible that Barnes did

some of his experimental work on a kitchen stove. It was a good steady source of heat; and if a housewife could prepare dinner for a family of eight on her stove a man could use it to set a few flasks to boil. Greater chemists than Barnes had performed more fundamental experiments on kitchen stoves. While he may have done some work at home, he also made good use of the more convenient facilities of Mulford. Whether his work was routine control analysis or new product research or a combination of both, Barnes found time, made time, to do his own research as well.

Even so, he was not satisfied with the progress he was making and farmed out some experiments to members of the chemistry department of the University of Pennsylvania. (Since he presumably specified just what he wanted, the credit, by accepted standards in scientific work, was his.) At the same time Hille must have carried out his part of the assignment successfully, for less than two years after they were in Heidelberg together they were able to prepare the compound which was their goal.

What Barnes and Hille had done was to extract gliadin, a protein found in wheat and other grains, and convert it to vitellin. To a salt solution of vitellin they added a concentrated solution of silver nitrate, causing a compound called silver vitellin to precipitate. When precipitation stopped, the solution was poured off and the precipitate dried in a vacuum. The resulting dark-brown powder was the "mild silver protein" which they hoped would supplant silver nitrate.

It was easy enough to find out that the substance was not caustic: the inventors could try it on themselves. But did it penetrate the tissues as silver nitrate did not? At the University of Pennsylvania, Dr. Edward Martin, with whom Barnes had studied clinical surgery, made a simple experiment: he steeped catgut in a solution of the new compound and found that it became impregnated through and through. The inference was that if the compound could penetrate so tough a substance as catgut, it would penetrate any body tissues it was applied to. To prove the point, Barnes had direct experiments made on tissues covered with mucous membrane.

Such a penetrating compound, the inventors reasoned, ought to be "valuable in the treatment of genitourinary diseases and in the various inflammatory affections of eye and nasal passages in which silver nitrate or one of its substitutes is [presently] used." In Philadelphia, Dr. H. M. Christian, surgeon in chief of the genitourinary department of the University Hospital, tried it out for the treatment of gonorrhea and cystitis, both by irrigation and injection. In New York, Dr. G. K. Swinburne at the Good Samaritan Hospital, and in Berlin, Dr. M. Wassidlo in his own clinic, also treated patients with gonorrhea. All three doctors reported that it was the best silver compound available for the treatment of that disease.

These facts were presented in a paper at a meeting of the American Therapeutic Society (which Barnes had joined) held in New York on May 14, 1902, and published in the *Medical Record* ten days later. Barnes's name was given first in the by-line: "M.A., M.D., late of Pharmacologic Institute, University of Heidelberg"—a rather pretentious claim of association for a two-course student; nor is it clear where he had got the M.A. degree.

The authors asserted that their compound contained 30 per cent of silver—twice as much as any other mild silver protein. In their enthusiasm, the young men used quite unscientific language, declaring (the italics are mine) that "the extreme solubility of our compound is *remarkable*. One ounce of it is freely and completely soluble in less than a dessertspoonful of water—a fact *which will be wondered at* by physicians who have been able, only with great difficulty, to obtain even a 5 per cent solution of other protein silver compounds."

The authors claimed further that a solution of silver vitellin could not have any coagulating or caustic effects on the mucous membranes. Reporting the clinical tests already performed, they announced that further studies were in progress at the Children's Hospital, Philadelphia, under Dr. A. G. Thomson, and at the Royal Westminster Ophthalmic Hospital, London, by Dr. Gustave Hartridge. These studies must have been on the use of silver vitellin in the eyes of newborn infants to prevent conjunctivitis, for this was to become one of its major applications.

One would have thought that Barnes, after dreaming for years of striking it rich, would have patented the product which potentially could make the dream come true. Instead, he and his collaborator published their researches. If he meant to exploit silver vitellin commercially—and he was intent on nothing else—why did he tell possible rivals what his product was and how it was produced? Barnes said later that he had not taken a patent because his exclusive rights to the product would have expired in twenty years. But they would have been only hypothetical rights if someone who read the article in *Medical Record* had also decided to manufacture silver vitellin.

Possibly the inventors were still so close to academic thinking that they could not resist the prestige of publication. More likely they were obliged to make public the tests carried out by the doctors, or thought it good publicity. As it happened, their failure to patent the silver vitellin process or even to register their trademark, Argyrol, did not cause them any difficulty. The existence

of half a dozen mild and strong silver proteins on the
market in itself limited further competition, and by its
quick success Argyrol was protected as a trademark in
common law. Even an identical product under another
name would then have been at a competitive disadvantage.

The initial tests on silver vitellin having proved successful, Barnes was eager to put it on the market. All he had
by way of capital was the family savings—$1,600 accumu-
lated by frugal living, for his salary at Mulford's must
have been a modest one. (The Leggetts either would not
gamble on a wildcat venture or could not afford to.) There
are no comparative figures on the value of a dollar of
industrial capital over the last half century, but it is
certain that $1,600 then was only a slightly longer shoe-
string than it would be now. Out of it had to come payment for all the initial equipment and supplies, a payroll
for six or seven employees for some months as well as the
partners' salaries, and raw materials to sustain production
if there was any considerable demand for the product.
Even if there were immediate orders, they would not be
paid for in spot cash. Barnes figured later that the capital
would not have lasted more than three months "if luck
had gone against us."

Planning to manage the business end of the enterprise,
he needed a chemist to run the plant. This man would
not be a run-of-the-mill laboratory man—he had to be
capable of adapting the process worked out on a laboratory scale to commercial production. Furthermore, he
would be working on the development of other new
products.

Barnes thought he had the right man in Hermann
Loeb, a somewhat younger colleague in the Mulford
laboratory. A handsome, easy-going German Jew, Loeb
had also studied chemistry in the Heidelberg school of

pharmacy. But Barnes was a tourist compared to him, for he had not only been there two years (after a turn at the University of Munich), but had been a member of a dueling fraternity: a real *Alt-Heidelberg* man. Presumably because Barnes was not in a position to pay him adequately, he offered Loeb a partnership in his venture. But Loeb believed that he should have turned over to their employer, Mulford's, the research performed in their laboratory, and refused the partnership. Barnes turned to another colleague (a Scotsman—his name has been lost), who also rejected his offer on the same ethical grounds.

Whether Barnes disclosed the entire story of his and Hille's researches in an effort to make them change their minds, I do not know. The effort would probably have been wasted on Loeb, who didn't care for the American way of life and might already have been thinking of returning to Germany (as he eventually did, marrying a rich widow) when Barnes approached him. It was Hille who finally became Barnes's partner.

Why didn't he ask Hille in the first place? The simplest explanation is that Barnes had agreed to pay his German collaborator for his work as he had presumably paid the chemists at the University of Pennsylvania. Possibly Hille himself had preferred to stay at home, where, with his excellent training, he could look forward to a rewarding future. After all, there was no guarantee that even if they succeeded in inventing a silver antiseptic it would be successfully marketed. Again, Hille might have been more interested in research than in operating a plant. This is all purely speculative; and so is the notion that Barnes, thinking that one of his Mulford associates would make a more congenial—a more submissive—partner, had tried to doublecross Hille.

In the fall of 1902 the Barnes & Hille company started

to manufacture Argyrol at 24 N. 40 Street, Philadelphia.
The plant consisted of eight rooms in a hotel or what used
to be a hotel, for this was now a poor Negro neighborhood. Rent was cheap and so was local labor; though he
needed only a few men, every penny counted.

The company had to get business in a hurry, but how?
According to Barnes, it never had a salesman, inside or
traveling, and never advertised in the trade journals, "because we found in the psychology of William James
principles which enabled us to dispense with these lux-
uries. From his and similar books we developed a business plan which in two years was financially profitable."

Whatever James's contribution was, the fact is that the
company promoted its product by direct mail, using
doctors' testimonials for copy. Apparently Dr. Martin
supplied the first statement on the value of Argyrol, allowing Barnes to distribute it throughout the country to
doctors and drug jobbers and wholesalers. In 1903 Barnes
went to London, Glasgow, Dublin, Paris and Berlin, giving other doctors test samples and getting their endorse-
ments. The following year the company opened offices in
London, England, and in Sydney, Australia. In effect,
these were sales offices and Barnes himself was the company's traveling representative if not, strictly, its salesman.

Orders—sizable orders—poured in. Handicapped at first
by inadequate working capital, the company could hardly
keep pace with them: unable to expand either its facilities
or its labor force, it operated on a hand-to-mouth basis.
It was in 1923 that Barnes wrote that the company became financially profitable in two years. Many years after
that he said that in its first year it made $40,000 profit
and in its second year $100,000—more than a 6,000 per
cent return on its initial capital. He is said to have become a millionaire at thirty-five (in 1907).

From the change in his style of living in the middle 1900's, there is no doubt that he had become wealthy. Year by year the company's sales increased at an accelerated rate; the demand for Argyrol became world-wide. Eventually it was packaged in two, five, ten, and at one time twenty different sizes for various markets; the one-ounce unit selling for fifty cents proved to be the most popular. A very large part of that fifty cents must have been profit, for the price of Argyrol remained unchanged for fifty years; that is to say, even when over-all costs rose, it could still be sold at a worthwhile margin. Yet for Barnes to have been a millionaire at thirty-five would mean that his share alone of the company's profits averaged nearly a quarter of a million dollars four years running, aside from Hille's share and earnings used to increase capitalization. "A millionaire at thirty-five" seems to have been struck off for dramatic effect. How much less impressive is "a millionaire at forty-two" or even "a millionaire at thirty-eight." It can safely be said that Barnes grew very rich very fast.

Soon after putting Argyrol on the market, Barnes & Hille brought out a second product, called Ovoferrin. This was an iron tonic different from earlier types in that its iron content was, like the silver in Argyrol, in a colloidal state. The assumption was that the human body could assimilate colloidal iron more readily than the iron held in stronger chemical union in such compounds as iron sulfate. While Ovoferrin did not have the sensational success of Argyrol, it was a profitable item. The fact that Barnes did not refer to it later as his invention probably means that it was Hille's work, though it could mean that he did not especially care to boast of a product lacking the prestige of Argyrol.

The success of Barnes & Hille did not strengthen the

partnership. Whatever the reason—personal differences, conflict over management policies, the dissatisfaction of each with the other's share of the profits—they resolved to separate. But neither would sell out to the other. "Barnes & Hille, chemists" was listed for the last time in the Philadelphia telephone directory of October, 1906. The partners must have wrangled fiercely before Hille agreed to withdraw, for its successor, the A. C. Barnes Company (a corporation), did not appear until the May, 1908, issue of the directory. That the company was able to get along for a year and a half without a telephone indicates that its business was largely out of town; a few personal calls took care of the local wholesalers. Nor did the internal quarrel affect sales, for soon after he took over, Barnes needed more space and bought the building in which the plant was located, for $8,000.

What happened to Hille? Thirty-five years later, Barnes said that he had bought out his partner for "several hundred thousand dollars." If true, this would dispose of the rumor that Hille committed suicide though it might lend shaky support to another rumor that Barnes had him deported during the First World War as an enemy alien— nine years after the dissolution of their partnership!

In June, 1908, he finally got around to registering the trademarks of his company's two products. By this time Argyrol at least was so well-known that his right to its exclusive use would have been recognized in common law. The registration of the name, however, simplified legal procedure in case of infringement. Four months later he in fact brought such a suit against a Brooklyn jobber named Pierce.

Three customers were his witnesses. One of them testified that when he asked for Argyrol he was given another mild silver protein called silver nucleinate and his receipt called it Argyrol. On Pierce's price list, too, his silver nucleinate appeared as "$1.20 oz. Argyrol." The second witness testified that a clerk told him that the two products were identical; the third, that a clerk told him he didn't know whether they were identical, "but we have the right to call it silver nucleinate 'Argyrol.' Argyrol is $1.85 and this is $1.20, and you will save money. If it isn't right, you can bring it back."

The court issued an injunction restraining Pierce "from placing Argyrol on his price list and supplying customers who called for the same with a different and cheaper preparation in its place."

Barnes was represented by the prominent law firm of Robinson, Biddle & Benedict. Possibly his next lawyer was John G. Johnson, who was called the most celebrated lawyer in the state of Pennsylvania and who shared with Barnes a strong interest in art: Johnson had already acquired an important collection of old masters.

The Barnes lawyers must have been largely occupied with protecting Argyrol, for they are said to have brought suit "all over the world" to prevent infringement. The decision in the Pierce case set a precedent for New York State. Similar decisions in other states made it a simple matter to prevent further infringement in those areas. A copy of the court order shown to the offender was usually sufficient to make him desist and no prosecution was necessary.

If the world-wide policing of drug manufacturers and jobbers was an immense job, it paid off handsomely, since the infringers could have drained off a substantial share of the company's business if they had not been restrained. Yet, if Barnes had a direct hand in this work, as is not unlikely, he could have paid a high moral price for his success. This constant suspicion, surveillance, ferreting out

and pursuit became a habit of mind—in a mind prone
to suspicion—which tended to carry over into his personal
relations.

At the same time the factory produced a wholly un-
premeditated by-product which was a more bracing tonic
for Barnes than a vat of Ovoferrin. He had hired Negro
labor because it was cheap, but there is no abstract labor,
only human beings, and these colored human beings gave
him trouble. Almost every morning at ten he would receive a telephone call from the magistrate's court telling
him that one of his men was being detained for disorderly
conduct, assault and battery, or some similar charge—
nothing (Barnes said) more serious than that. What could
he do? As a law-abiding citizen, as a responsible employer,
he fired the man. He fired two, three, five . . . men.

It was virtuous, but continual personnel turnover can
be more demoralizing in a plant with eight employees
than in a plant employing a thousand. Predisposed to be
sympathetic with Negroes from his attendance at camp
meetings and his love of their music, Barnes came to feel
that understanding might be more useful than righteous-
ness. He knew those boys who were getting into trouble
with the law. Others might call them "low-down niggers"
and let it go at that. (It was not many years ago that the
operating personnel of the Philadelphia streetcar system
struck when the company tried to upgrade Negroes to the
rank of *motorman*.) But Barnes knew they were perfectly
good human beings who were getting into trouble because
they had nothing better to do.

"In 1908 we reorganized the business on a cooperative
basis," he wrote fifteen years later. This did not mean that
it became a profit-sharing business, but that a good deal
of time was spent "to unify to a common purpose the
diverging temperaments of the principals": three colored

men, five white women and one white man, himself. (Is
this perhaps an indication that Barnes had clashed with
his partner over employee relations?) "We all lived together as a family," he said elsewhere. If he had said
"*happy* family," one would have suspected him of sending
his employees birthday greetings by card file, or treating
the men to beer at Saturday closing time. He did a great
deal more than that, even if "cooperative basis" was a
euphemism for paternalism. But it was not a cold, mechanical paternalism. What he tried to do was to give his
employees, especially the colored men, an interest in their
work and in each other, and to show them that the boss
("the business never had a boss and has never needed one")
that the white man was genuinely concerned for their
well-being, in and out of the plant. Convince them of
that in action, not words, and—Barnes was confident—
they would not do the foolishly mischievous things which
landed them in jail.

What he meant by the business not having a boss was
that "each participant has evolved his or her own method
of doing a particular job." That was the "cooperative
basis" he fostered. If a man was doing a job which was
not interesting in itself, going about it in his own way at
least gave him the satisfaction of apparently doing what
he wanted. It was not always that simple. One man aspired
to be a chauffeur but was loath to give up his job at the
plant. Barnes resolved the dilemma by letting him service
one of his personal cars. One middle-aged woman was too
full of energy to be content with her job of labeling and
wrapping bottles; she became "a disturbing factor."
Barnes put her in charge of stock and shipping, where "a
new motor coordination is necessary nearly every minute,"
and where she had a chance to mother the younger girls.

This was intraplant "adjustment," anticipating the

sociology rather than the efficiency experts to come. Barnes went beyond that. Take Johnny White—there was a boy who liked to use his fists, not on his neighbors, but in the ring. Johnny liked to fight, but he could think of no better way of doing it than to take part in the "battle royal" at "Diamond" Lew Bailey's Broadway Athletic Club. This was a form of pugilism invented by Bailey in which three or four men slugged each other at will and at random trying to knock each other out. The rounds lasted two or three minutes and their number was unlimited. The last man standing on his feet was the winner.

Most states banned the battle royal. In some places where it was permitted, management added to the fun by blindfolding the contestants. Bailey, like another Barnum & Bailey, put on a bigger and better show. He put ten men into the ring at one time, ten "giants," the posters proclaimed. One of these was Argyrol Johnny (who was only a featherweight). As an old fighting man himself, Barnes went down to Lew Bailey's to see him in action. He got to the club late, and Johnny was still in there on his feet. But he had taken terrific punishment and he went down before long. For his performance Johnny, like the others, received fifty cents.

Barnes advised him to quit that kind of brutal slugfest. At Bailey's Thursday night bouts (admission 25¢), boxers were paid from $15 to $25, and the fight was limited by law to eight rounds and no decision. That was fighting man to man, like a man. Johnny didn't know if he could make a go of that, but Barnes assured him that he could and offered to train him. Johnny finally took him up. Barnes gave him pointers drawn from William James's *The Principles of Psychology*, and also put on the gloves with him. After the battle royal, Johnny could take anything he dished out, and he felt free to let go with some pretty stiff wallops, which the old man took like a sport. In due course Johnny was signed up for a match.

The record is a bit blurred at this point. According to Barnes and his disciples, Johnny won this fight and a whole string of fights after it, to become a contender for the title—and all without losing a day at the plant, though one fight paid him more than a week's work. Johnny was nervous before that title bout. He said he didn't feel fit. But his trainer encouraged him and the boys said he'd do all right, they wanted to see him featherweight[1] champ. And Johnny went forth to do battle and was knocked out in the first round. For years the local sports writers— here is the other version of Johnny's career—got a laugh with an allusion to the prizefighter trained on psychological principles who was kayoed in his *first* professional bout. By their account, Johnny had won his preliminary victories over amateurs.

Johnny's defeat didn't matter. The point was that Barnes had given him a chance to bring out the best fighting that was in him; he had gone far enough. Now take the case of Jake. Jake was a good man in the factory, "worth a little bit more than anybody else, so we gave Jake more money." The other men became jealous and probed for Jake's weaknesses. Sure, he's all right on the job, but look at him at home: he beats his wife, don't he? Barnes said,

[1] The transcript of the court record from which this story is taken contains many errors. It refers to William Penn as "William Payne"; it has Barnes living on Lex's rather than Latches Lane, and attending the University of "Ireland" instead of the University of Heidelberg. It has the question put to him: "Have you spent any part of your wife in the study of art?" It could be, therefore, that the court stenographer had heard "featherweight" for *heavyweight,* since Johnny took part in the battle royal. But elsewhere he is said to have been a bantamweight, so that he must have been in one or the other lighter than heavy class.

"We won't bother about that. He does his work." Well, one day Jake doesn't show up for work—he'd been jailed for beating his wife. Barnes had someone look into the case, who reported back that Jake had been arrested, not on the complaint of his wife, but of other women "because the wife hollered too loud. And so I took the boys together and I said, 'If Jake wants to beat his wife, if she likes it and she doesn't complain, we don't approve of that, but we don't think it is any reason for you boys to hold him up to scorn.' And then I told them that Jake was a sadist and his wife was a masochist, and it was a perfectly natural explanation to them, and when I said that, they got interested in psychology. We took [out] books and got right down to tacks and found these boys absorbed it."

The white women in the plant were engaged in clerical and light factory work. In retrospect Barnes called the black and white staff "a pretty interesting thing to make an experiment with," but it seems transparently a management device to minimize the distraction potential between the sexes. Later on, as Barnes carried further what is now called "human relations," some of the women were given ample opportunity for self-development, though within his great shadow. As their number increased, these Negro laborers remained his children, never to be coddled, but to be helped when they were in trouble and guided when they were not. As a thoughtful but domineering father, he sent his married men's wages to their wives. As a kind father, he took up the mortgages on the homes of several men and paid them off.

If the by-product of the factory could have been an antidote to the poison of suspicion and surveillance which the defense of his main product induced, it would have been worth as much to Barnes as his millions. But he could be freely beneficent only within the "one family," within the domain of which he was overlord (not boss). In the larger world he was not so sure of himself; his fortune could not open every door, nor reopen the accessible ones which closed against his temperament; but it did lead, to begin with, to that area of enjoyment which money can buy.

5

The Fox Hunter

As BARNES BECAME RICH, HE THREW OFF AS WITH A SINGLE
gesture the habit of poverty he had worn so long. He
moved out of a rented house in Overbrook into a home
of his own in nearby Merion. In short order he bought
paintings and horses, cultivated a taste for fine food and
liquor, hired groom and cook and butler. In the outer
trappings at least, he had become one with the best people
of the Main Line, as the suburban area west of Philadelphia is called.

The house was built on Latches Lane, on a tract of land
to which Mrs. Barnes took title in 1905. It was a somewhat swampy, undeveloped neighborhood, and Barnes
had the land drained and filled in order to build half a
dozen large houses, each with substantial grounds. His
primary aim was not to make a profit from their sale but
to protect his flanks from possible encroachment of small

homeowners. He was moving up fast, up the social scale which is simply calibrated, in dollars.

Barnes and his wife took riding lessons at George McMenamin's academy in Port Kennedy. Before long he developed a stable of his own and hired Charles Funk as groom. When Charley told his cabby friends about it, they laughed and predicted that the job wouldn't last long. The way that man treated his horses, riding one until it was wringing wet and then jumping on another until it was in a steaming sweat, how could a groom keep up with him, that is, if there were any horses left for him to work on? They were wrong. Barnes's horses survived his hard riding and Funk was with him for some ten years. At Merion he had four horses to take care of, and Barnes boarded two or three more at Valley Forge, pleasant rolling country where, usually with his wife, Barnes went riding on Saturdays and Sundays.

Having learned to ride, Barnes went on to ride to hounds: he joined the Rose Tree Fox Hunting Club. It is possible this was not the most exclusive club of its kind along the Main Line, but then no fox-hunting club is exactly plebeian.

As a fox hunter, Barnes showed great courage, according to a man who was allowed to tag along with his father in the club's hunts. What did "courage" mean in this case? Obviously the pursued was no danger to the pursuer, and it takes skill rather than courage to ride a horse. But Barnes rode by balance alone, as he had been taught by McMenamin, and those who know say that the proper way to ride to hounds is by a combination of balance and grip. "When Dr. Barnes endeavored to ride by balance alone he was lacking the necessary grip to save himself if the unexpected happened." The unexpected happened almost every time he went hunting.

Each time, he suffered a fall. And his courage consisted in his always coming back for more.

But why did he go in for fox hunting, and, before that, for riding? Barnes's passion for this sport could have been kindled in part by a desire to play the gentleman. McMenamin's was patronized almost entirely by socially prominent people. But it is hypothetically possible, in the absence of certainty, that Barnes simply loved to ride a horse. It is still not an exotic animal; and in those days a horse was as much a part of the cityscape as it was of the countryside. If the city boy did not have even a plow horse to mount, he could at least take pleasure in the sight of a team of full-flanked Percherons hauling a fire wagon or beer truck: in his eyes as admirable as the noblest steeds of Araby of romantic story. Grown up and able to afford them, the poor city boy might well take to horses.

At McMenamin's, Barnes struck up an acquaintance with the patrician clientele. With most of them, as with Moncure Biddle, an investment broker and collector of rare books, it amounted to no more than a casual greeting and exchange of pleasantries. Only with his brother George Biddle, the artist, did Barnes sometimes jump or ride together, but then, by virtue of his occupation, *he* was partly *déclassé*. And it was only this Biddle of the aristocratic Biddles that Barnes was either sufficiently interested in or perhaps dared to invite to his home, and the artist was there, several times, primarily to see the collection, not to pay a social call.

Once Biddle brought his mother, who was an art lover and whose interest in the Barnes collection was aroused by her son's account of it. Although the conversation was amiable, it was without social consequence. In his Argyrol suit in 1908, Barnes's lawyers were Robinson, Biddle &

Benedict (Robinson was related to the Biddles). Later on Barnes's lawyers were also his friends outside of office and court; this early he may have retained the prominent firm simply to have the advantage of its prestige and the relationship was strictly business. On the scant evidence available, it cannot be said fairly whether Barnes went to McMenamim's for the people or for the horses.

Grant that he learned to ride because he enjoyed riding. Did he also take up fox hunting because he loved to hunt foxes? Unlike riding a horse, that could hardly have been a poor city boy's ideal. Foxes don't steal chickens from butcher shops. To street gamins like Al and his friends who never saw a fox outside of zoo or picture book, fox hunting was decidedly an eh-wot-dontcher-know pastime. Perhaps in the grown man the primal lust to kill asserted itself as it did in other men, outwardly less aggressive than himself, who festively masked the primal impulse in bright red and brass and did not stay to see the carcass. But one must suspect that Barnes wanted to show the upper-class gentry that he was as good as they were.

It was very real upper class. According to Struthers Burt in *Philadelphia: Holy Experiment,* some three hundred families, "many of whom have been in the city since the time of William Penn, still exercise . . . a power far in excess of their numbers. They control Philadelphia's wealth, and their power and traditions are understood by all other Philadelphians, and either looked up to or resented." Which way was Barnes likely to have felt, when his ancestors were also contemporaries of William Penn?

If the upper class were merely a money class, Barnes might conceivably not have been greatly interested in mingling with them. But they were not, and they did not accept newcomers on the basis of money alone. P. A. B.

Widener, son of Joseph E. Widener, whose father before
him (a fellow worker of John Barnes in the slaughterhouse) had made a fortune, has written that Philadelphia
society is the most high-hat in the country, giving his
generation of Wideners something of a hard time socially.

In all the country, and for that matter in all the world,
[Burt declares] there are no finer men and women than
Philadelphia's best; none more charming, more simple, more
dignified, more interesting, more good-looking, more cultivated, and more intelligently liberal. And they are depend-
able in a way that a great many otherwise fine people are
not. In all the world there are no houses where you could
find better talk, or better thought, than in certain Philadelphia
houses.

Surely one or two of these paragons, and possibly three
or four on the next lower rung of excellence, must have
belonged to the Rose Tree. If they admired Barnes's
courage in coming back after every fall, indulging in a
little gentlemanly laughter at his obtuseness in not modify-
ing his style of riding, they could only look askance at his
manners. He acquired the reputation of being a thruster,
a man who pushed his way in ahead of other people, out
of turn. The Philadelphia aristocracy, says Burt, "intimate
and interrelated, have their own ways of life, and their
rules and taboos, and their own ways of enforcing the
latter." They did not look with favor on thrusters. Indeed,
they might very well have overlooked all his virtues for
the one breach of manners.

Barnes told Charley Funk, however, that several members had approached him but that he had not cared to
cultivate them socially. It is significant perhaps that he
had to tell this to his groom. And was he not being
ostentatiously democratic when, having lunch at the club
with his wife, he did not relegate Charley to the out-of-

sight servants' room but had him right at their own table?
Nor did he just let him sit there symbolically. It was, "Did
you have enough to eat?" and "How about a second portion of dessert?" Touched as he was by the master's
solicitude, the young man couldn't help observing Mrs.
Barnes's irritation: her husband devoting to their servant
the attention he should bestow on her! But she was only
his wife, playing only a passive role in his double demonstration for all the aristocrats to see: Barnes the democrat,
brother of his groom, and Barnes the democrat, scorning
their disapproval. And didn't Charley (only Barnes called
him *Edward* at the club—not Eddie but Edward—to distinguish him from an employee named Charles Funk) want
to see the members' loving cups and other trophies? Barnes
threw his overcoat, with his membership badge pinned to
it, over Charley's shoulders, so that no one would question
his right to be there.

To account for Barnes's later apparent hostility to
people of higher social status, it has been assumed that
in these years, whether at the club or elsewhere, some
society person snubbed him. Though Barnes's own denial
is not proof to the contrary, a simpler explanation is that
he himself did not feel at ease with the upper social
class. These people were too sure of themselves to need
to put an upstart—if they considered him such—in his
place. It was enough that, even if they were polite to him,
he would feel uncomfortable in their presence.

Even this may be too strong an assumption, for when
Barnes left the Rose Tree it was to join another group in
organizing an informal pack near Phoenixville. But he
soon gave up fox hunting altogether. When the group
became a recognized pack known as the Pickering Hunt,
they asked for permission to cross his property, and he
refused it. If he had had a personal quarrel with them,

they were not likely to have approached him. Perhaps by that time he had decided that the sport was exclusively for the rich and highborn and did not care to have any association with it.

If he gave up his pleasure of the rich, Barnes continued to get far more pleasure from baseball, the pastime of all Americans. When he wasn't home from the factory by three o'clock, they knew he was out watching the Phillies or Athletics. As a connoisseur of the game, he especially delighted in the teamwork of the "A's," guided by their manager Connie Mack. Possibly he had not been aware of it in his playing days, but he knew now that baseball was not only a game but also an aesthetic performance, felt as such by people who did not know the meaning of the word.

Since Mrs. Barnes was not in the least interested in baseball, Barnes would sometimes take Charley Funk with him when an especially exciting game was in prospect and it was pleasant to have a companion to swap enthusiasms with. On such an occasion, Barnes would have his wife drive Funk to the railroad station, where Barnes would meet him in his car. Mrs. Barnes didn't like it one bit, being a servant of a servant.

On the other hand Funk was resentful of Mrs. Barnes's sending him to the station to meet every train when she was expecting some package from town. Otherwise he had no fault to find with her as mistress of the house. Years after her marriage, she was still going to her home in Brooklyn to pick up some of her things, taking Funk with her to pack and ship them.

It was the master of the house to whom Funk was attached. Barnes did a great deal more for him than take him to ball games. He was interested in Charley's family, looked in when the children were sick, spent a lot of time

Dear Fay & Gang,

Finally, some good Govt. travel — to Heidelberg for a week, instead of K.C., D.C., or Ft. Worth. I took a week's vacation afterwards and visited Mainz, Trier, and a few places in Rhine vicinity. A highlight was a day in Deidesheim, meeting up with my friend Richard Smith who has corsibed with [illegible] river — to drive and are active in the big cooperation there. I hadn't been in Germany since my army days of '72–'73 — few changes in Trier and Mainz? I drive [illegible] noted most in Frankfurt, Grosse, Allijn

The Beauchamps
4424 Larchwood
Philadelphia, PA
19104

Trier, Porta Nigra

Traben-Trarbach, Grevenburg

Bernkastel-Kues

Die liebliche Mosel

Kröv

trying to buy a house for him. And he found a couple of good ones. The trouble was—and it is odd that a man who had been so conscious of his poverty should not have been aware of it—they were too expensive. Barnes did not take it amiss when Funk turned them down. When Funk himself came on what he considered a satisfactory house in the adjacent town of Narberth, Barnes looked it over. He found it substantial and well worth the asking price of $2,300. Funk had $800 in the bank and Barnes took a mortgage for the balance at 5 per cent. The Funks have been living in the house for over forty years.

The $800 Funk had in the bank had been deposited, not by himself but by his employer. Funk never received his full wages, but only what Barnes thought he needed to live on: the rest was compulsory savings. Funk didn't like the idea, and Mrs. Funk, a woman with common sense and a mind of her own, liked it still less. But they knew his intention was good, as the deal with the house showed. They were to receive further substantial proof of his benevolence.

The Funks remember Barnes as a man more sympathetic to the poor than to the rich. Joel Rubincam, a member of the volunteer Narberth Fire Company, feels the same way about him. Some years after he settled in Merion, Barnes satisfied one of his childhood passions by joining these Narberth firefighters (who also serve part of Merion). Though he was not on active duty, he faithfully attended the monthly meetings of the company as a director. Once, a fire broke out in an apartment house. The chief took the engine out, and Barnes went along for the ride and got a big kick out of it.

Every year the forty men of the company and their guests—about a hundred people all told—sat down to a catered banquet at headquarters. Barnes paid the bill. The guests often included Ross Davis, chief of the Philadelphia Fire Department, whom Barnes warmly admired.

The privilege of footing the bill was the only one the company allowed Barnes. At the firehouse he was not a rich manufacturer but just one of the boys, whatever their calling, whatever their fortune. Joel Rubincam, who knew him for some twenty-five years, thought "he was a regular feller." An employee of the Railway Express Company, Rubincam was out with his truck early one morning and saw a figure humped up on the steps of the barbershop. Who the hell was that, sitting out there at eight o'clock in the morning? Was he a salesman, a customer waiting for the place to open, or what? Oh, it was Doc Barnes! Rubincam had a whimsical idea. As he came even with the steps, he stopped his truck, got out and handed the man a dime. Barnes looked up in surprise. "Oh, it's you," said Rubincam. "I thought is was a bum sitting there." That gave Barnes a big laugh.

Yes, said Rubincam (despite what happened later on), Doc Barnes was a real democrat, always taking up the fight for the little feller. He wouldn't let him be pushed around. Understandably, Barnes was at home with plain folks. No matter how far money and education had taken him, he was one of them as he could never be with people who rode to hounds as a matter of course.

Not mingling in society, the Barneses did not go in for conventional entertaining and being entertained. Perhaps Mrs. Barnes missed it, but her husband did not, or not nearly as much. For he did not sharply divide his life at home from his life in the factory, and the factory was also part of his social life. Trying to make a boxer out of Johnny, looking into the psychology of Jake the sadist

and his masochistic wife, were more interesting than
making conversation with elegant people you didn't give
a damn about. In one way the factory was an annex of
his home. When he had filled the walls of living room,
dining room, bedrooms, study, bathroom, with paintings,
he began to hang them in the offices of the plant—for his
employees to enjoy. Maybe it was an afterthought, but the
pictures *were* in the factory and they stimulated one of
the men, Theodore, to try his hand at drawing.

One day Barnes said to him, "Theodore, that is a good
copy of what you have there, but what is the use of copy-
ing? I would not want to copy somebody else. Why don't
you try something of your own?" This comment, Barnes
said, aroused the interest of the other men in the paintings
and they studied them. Well, if they looked at them
closely, that is, from close up, a fond foster father and
art collector might well suppose they were "studying"
them. However, his intention was sound and his interest
sincere: this was certainly a part of his social life. And
he was augmenting it with an intellectual activity around
which he was soon to create a new social life of his own.

Correlated with the exclusion or self-exclusion of the
Barneses from society was their failure to participate in an
activity as mandatory as fox hunting: charity work. In
their early years of affluence the Barneses did not go in
for philanthropy. Barnes could put his hand in his pocket
for a man at the factory; he would not contribute to an
institution. When his college fraternity, Phi Gamma Delta,
was soliciting alumni for contributions to a building fund
for a new chapter house, Barnes wouldn't give anything:
he just wasn't interested in the fraternity. He *was* interested in the Philadelphia Symphony Orchestra, yet he
was not among the annual donors until the Seven Year

Endowment Fund was formally established in the season of 1916-1917, after which he and Mrs. Barnes were regular contributors.

Some time after Barnes gave up fox hunting, one of the members of the Pickering Hunt called to ask for a contribution to the Community Fund. "Mrs. Barnes opened the front door three inches and refused him entrance or conversation." She is said to have changed, and Barnes was to continue to give, but always to individuals. A personal benevolence has a dual advantage for the donor: a smaller amount goes a longer way, and he receives his gratitude plain.

6

A Student Again

As soon as the factory began to prosper Barnes resumed the cultivation of his interest in painting. This too was high living, of a private kind, and closer to his heart, one must suppose, than the conventional forms at which he was also having his fling. Perhaps one of the reasons he gave up fox hunting was to devote more time to the pursuit of art. Late in life he said that he "gave five years of 'grinding study' to art and tried painting again."

One day or one week he looked over all of his pictures with as much detachment as he was able to, as other men turned thirty review their youthful verses, wondering how they could have written such obviously sloppy stuff, glowing with pleasure at a sparkling line or two in all that dead rhetoric. Going through the canvases he had painted over the years, Barnes may have found a pleasing

73

passage of color or a neat composition or at the least a reminder of some charming landscape (whose charm he had failed to capture in paint), but he realized, he was dismayed to realize, that his work was without merit. The spark of life he thought he had infused in them was like the spark springing brightly from a fireplace only to fall, before it reaches the flue, dead dark.

He counted up his pictures as other men total up their verses, for even the creator of disappointing works can be ruefully proud of their number—he counted up his pictures, one hundred and ninety of them, and burned them up. From now on he would buy the quality he had himself failed to create. By this act, whether he was aware of it or not, he freed himself from the jealousy, only poorly concealed at best, which most artists feel for the work of another. Even to a rank amateur, Rembrandt is unconscious competition. Once Barnes had freely confessed that he was no artist, he could devote himself wholly to the cultivation of true artists and acknowledge merit wherever he recognized it, until even collecting became a quasi creative thing.

By this time he must already have been buying paintings, but he did not know what quality was. If he had not picked up his first pictures during his stay in Germany, he could have bought them at this time, since his knowledge and taste had remained static. The paintings he bought now surely were not too different in spirit. For the prices he was now able to pay, they were larger and by more reliably famous artists.

Undoubtedly he liked these new masterpieces, yet in a sense they represented his personal taste less than his small pictures by modest unknowns, for as he patronized the best art galleries in New York and Philadelphia he was limited in his choice to the conservative paintings which they had in stock and naturally promoted. The chances are that Barnes knew nothing about Alfred Stieglitz's Photo-Secession Gallery at 291 Fifth Avenue, where, in 1908, the first works of Matisse ever seen in this country—they were drawings brought back by Edward Steichen—were exhibited. Barnes had most likely not even heard of Matisse. There had been several revolutions in French painting since the Barbizon school flourished. The only French revolution Barnes knew about was that of 1789. He was buying Barbizon paintings, together with Henner's red-headed pin-up girls.

It is possible that Barnes had some worthwhile Rousseau, Diaz or Daubigny; it is probable that his Millet was one of the sentimental scenes rather than one of the vigorous portraits; it is all but certain that his Corots were the feathery spring landscapes—charming in one, two, five . . . canvases, after which the formula becomes so familiar that a second look at them is as boring as a repeated hearing of Ravel's *Bolero*.

Some time in 1910 or 1911 Barnes decided to look up his high school classmate, "Butts" Glackens. In his recent book *William Glackens and the Ashcan School of Art*, Ira Glackens, his son, does not say why. Perhaps, as in their school days, Barnes was again coming to him "to learn a lot" about art. Possibly he wanted to buy some of his old friend's work, or at least to see what he was doing. Glackens had already made his reputation as an illustrator and was beginning to achieve prominence, if not too much recognition, as one of the ashcan painters.

Barnes wrote Glackens and there was no answer. He wrote again—again no answer. He sent a telegram, addressing him by his old nickname, to ask him why he did not answer the letters. That reminded Glackens of the envelopes in the pocket of his smock. Habitually absent-minded, he may also have felt that a letter twenty years in coming did not call for an immediate reply.

Once the two met, they quickly re-established their old intimacy. It was Barnes who pressed it, for the likable youth he had known had matured without distortion into an admirable man, his sense of humor intact, his generosity unimpaired. Few other artists so habitually looked for the good things in another man's painting as Glackens did, even when he did not like the work as a whole.

Glackens had married two years later than Barnes, in 1903, and married a very different kind of woman. Edith Dimock had studied with William Chase, who admitted that he could not understand her but thought she was a genius. Certainly she was a woman of spirit and wit, as Barnes was to find out, and these qualities were reflected in her water colors. One critic, reviewing an exhibition of the American Water Color Society, decided that, rather than "tear innocuous paintings to pieces," he would devote the whole of his article to some one fresh work, and it was the work of Mrs. Glackens he singled out. Happily, too, she had an income which enabled her husband to cultivate his obsessive passion for painting without thought of sales, without loss of his inborn serenity.

Whatever Barnes's motives may have been in resuming his old friendship, he found more than he had come for— not only a true artist but also a harmonious family. To the two Glackens children, Ira and Lenna, he became Uncle Albert and his wife Aunt Laura.

At their first meeting, Barnes had only begun to talk of his collection when Glackens interrupted to tell *him* exactly what kind of pictures he had—an utterly conventional collection. The dealers had taken him in as they had other rich men. The thing to do was to stow his pictures in the attic and make a fresh start at collecting, with modern art.

It was not easy advice to take. Barnes had put a sizable sum into his pictures; he liked them; and he could not at once assume the point of view of a practicing artist whose own art, under the influence of Renoir, had emerged from a dark palette into jeweled, sunlit color. But Barnes did not repudiate the advice—he took time to think it over.

Meanwhile the Barnes and Glackens families were seeing a good deal of each other. In the summer of 1911 the latter rented a summer cottage at Bellport, Long Island, on Great South Bay. Mrs. Barnes's mother took a cottage at Blue Point, not far away, and when her daughter and son-in-law visited her they took the Glackenses along. (Barnes's parents had continued to live in their home on Tasker Street. His mother died the following May, approaching her sixty-sixth year, of lobar pneumonia and a contributory brain tumor. Though his father presumably continued to live on at the house, Barnes himself took title to it.)

The summer passed, and the fall, without Barnes acting on Glackens' advice: he had not put his pictures into the attic.

Some time after his first visit with Glackens, Barnes paid a call on his other artist classmate. John Sloan had got off to a late start as a painter in his early thirties; Sloan was then, at the age of forty-two, still making a living as an illustrator and printmaker. He had yet to sell a painting. It was Barnes who made that first purchase, of a reclining nude; he also bought two prints. If Sloan had had any ambition to live from the sale of his paintings (which he knew was impossible), he would have been disillusioned by the transaction with his first customer: his old friend "drove a very hard bargain." In further payment, Barnes invited Sloan and his wife Dolly for a weekend. But he did not become intimate with Sloan again as he did with Glackens. Perhaps he did not like Sloan's paintings as well, or Sloan, who was as scrappy as himself, unlike the gentle Glackens. That weekend was their last meeting.

It was probably while Barnes was puzzling over the new French pictures that Glackens introduced him to other outstanding American painters—Maurice Prendergast, Ernest Lawson, Charles Demuth, Alfred Maurer—and Barnes bought their work as well as that of his old friend. These may have been the transitional pictures which helped him to reach a decision, for they derived from the French masters. Early in 1912 Barnes made up his mind to have the masters themselves. He gave Glackens $20,000 to go to Paris, with a free hand to buy what he liked.

As traveling companion Glackens had his friend Maurer, and when they reached Paris, which they both knew well, Maurer also accompanied him on his round of the galleries. Before long Glackens wrote his wife that Barnes was not going to get as much for his money as he expected. "You can't touch a Cézanne under $3,000, and that for a little landscape. His portraits and important pictures range from $7,000 to $30,000." And later: "Hunting up pictures is not child's play. Poor Alfy is worn out." On February 21: "I am mighty glad it is finished and I am sick of looking at pictures and asking prices."

The first painting Glackens bought was "a fine little Renoir" of a girl reading, for which he paid $1,400; the twentieth was a Degas. This he saw after he had used up his letter of credit, cabling Barnes that it was a good buy. His other purchases included a Van Gogh (*The Postman*), and probably examples of Cézanne, Monet, Gauguin, Pissaro, Sisley and Seurat, possibly a Matisse.

About the middle of March Barnes saw the pictures, mounted in beautiful antique frames—saw them with dismay. Disliking the unconventional frames, he thought he would find the pictures more agreeable in a familiar kind of setting, and had them reframed.

In 1912 the Impressionists were not household names in America, not even in France, and Barnes knew only the household names. Henner's coy females, sweetly painted, had not prepared him for a vigorous Van Gogh portrait, harshly painted, or the austerity of Cézanne. And to step out of the woodland scenes of the Barbizon painters, with their restrained light pattern among dark masses, into the Impressionist world, in which the woods were cut down to let in sun-drenched color, was a blinding experience. At first glance the shattered colors in a Renoir or Monet looked chaotic. The change of frames did not lessen Barnes's dismay. Glackens suggested that he live with the new pictures for six months to become familiar with them. If, at the end of that time, he still did not care for them, he, Glackens, would take them off his hands.

Within six months Barnes was himself on the way to Paris; and he had not sold out to Glackens. Had the artist's prescription worked and Barnes come to like the pictures? Or was he enjoying the pleasure of being in the vanguard of a triumphant modern art? It could be that from seeing and liking Glackens' work (influenced no doubt by his liking for the man), Barnes came to like Renoir. This would not mean that the rest of the twenty canvases appealed to him just as much. But he was predisposed to like them, and he was determined to understand them and the modern movement which begot them. Where could he get to know them better than at their source?

The Paris of 1912 was not full of galleries dealing in modern art. It was easy to see all their exhibitions and back rooms and have time left for the old masters in the Louvre. And everything that Barnes saw, with alert mind and senses, was instructive. For a man at the beginning of his development, however, it was important to meet with people who already had the knowledge and taste he was trying to acquire.

After their tiring round of the galleries on behalf of Barnes, Alfred Maurer had brought Glackens around to some stimulating people living at 32 rue de Fleurus; now he introduced Barnes to them: Gertrude Stein, who had gone straight to Paris after giving up the Johns Hopkins Medical School in 1904, and her bother Leo. He being a bachelor and she being a bachelor, they shared an apartment in conversation and altercation. (Gertrude Stein wrote "Two," which is about herself and her brother, "two" being one and one, she was one and he was one makes two, though "Two" really and truly tells nothing at all about Gertrude Stein or Leo Stein. The longer they lived together, the less conversation, the more altercation, the reason being that Gertrude Stein became famous and Leo did not, not nearly as famous, and he did not know he was furiously jealous. They had to part company.)

There were two more Steins in Paris: Michael, the brother of Gertrude and Leo, and his wife, Sarah. Soon after the four arrived in Paris, Gertrude and Leo Stein had bought a Cézanne—an unpopular artist; in 1906 Leo Stein bought *Joie* (or *Bonheur*) *de Vivre* by Matisse, another unpopular artist; and all four Steins together bought the same artist's daring picture *Femme au Chapeau* in 1908. Thereafter the Michael Steins became his first steady —and lasting—patrons.

When Barnes paid his first visit to their apartment, it was densely hung with Matisses illustrating his development year by year. They had also had a Renoir, a small Cézanne and two Picassos. Leo and Gertrude Stein's apartment was crowded with the work of a more diverse group of advanced artists. Gertrude Stein, and Leo more so, loved to talk about modern art. Albert Barnes would have loved to talk about modern art but he did not yet know anything about it, so how could he open his mouth when Gertrude or Leo held forth? Picasso had not painted a portrait of Albert Barnes and he had painted fascinating portraits of Gertrude Stein and Leo Stein before Albert Barnes had ever heard the name Picasso. And how could he tell whether or not Clive Bell was right in thinking that neither Gertrude Stein nor Leo Stein had a genuine feeling for visual art and that Leo was at best a theorist?

For Barnes theorizing was useful, too. He listened to the Steins for any scrap of insight they could give him. No doubt he bought his first Picasso (for ten or twenty dollars) under the influence of Gertrude and Leo and his first Matisse (unless Glackens had bought it for him) under the influence of Michael and Sarah Stein. On this first trip he also bought a Renoir (for $800), perhaps on his own initiative.

From Paris Barnes went to London to study the National Gallery, and to Berlin to study the Kaiser Friedrich Museum (which was under construction when he was last in the city); and wherever he went he was "quite humbly asking for guidance in his reading."

7

The King

IN HIS COLLEGE YEARS BARNES HAD BEEN TOO POOR TO
attend concerts. But he must have had easy access to music
while he was a student in Germany and cultivated his
taste for it. Now at home and at ease financially, he satisfied his pleasure in music in a princely way.

Young Leopold Stokowski became conductor of the
Philadelphia Symphony Orchestra in the 1912-1913 season.
One day he received an invitation from a Dr. Barnes to
attend a recital at his home to be given by Fritz Kreisler.
Stokowski had not yet heard of Barnes, but of course knew
the great violinist and was glad of the opportunity to hear
him in the intimacy of a private home. As the conductor
was approaching the Barnes house at the appointed time,
he was surprised to find the street empty of cabs or cars.
Could he have made a mistake: was the recital scheduled
for another day? He didn't think so; since he was already

there he thought he might as well go in. There were no hats or coats in the vestibule, but he was expected, it seemed. He was shown in and told that Dr. Barnes would soon join him. A few minutes later the violinist came in, accompanied by a woman and a big man with a strong, a granitic, face, and proceeded to give a recital just for Barnes, his wife, and Stokowski.

In his book, Ira Glackens tells of other recitals at which the audience was composed of the Barneses and the Glackenses, "one of whom was not in the least musical." There were clocks all over the house, all set at precisely the same time. When one struck four, all struck four; and their clanging in unison would have ruined a recital if, before it began, Mrs. Barnes did not go from room to room to make time stand still. Then the four listened on various occasions to Stokowski himself (playing the piano?), Guiomar Novaes, Misha Elman. Mme. Novaes had her hosts worried when she made her entrance exclaiming, "I'm angry!" What had they done, or omitted to do, that she was offended? Nothing; nothing at all: it was only her Portuguese accent which made "I'm hungry" sound like "I'm angry."

In February, 1913, Barnes attended the first international exhibition of modern art held in this country, at the 69th Regiment Armory in New York. (Glackens was chairman of the committee selecting the relatively tame American group.) He did not buy anything, it is said, because he felt he had better pictures. This would indicate that he was, for a collector of a single year's standing, either extraordinarily arrogant or making extraordinary progress. But it would not be remarkable if his carefully chosen, bought and paid for Cézannes, Renoirs and other older masters were superior to the hastily gathered exam-

ples on view; and he was not making such rapid progress
that he dared take a chance on *Nude Descending the Stairs*
or other such bold or wild paintings by younger men.
Boston and Chicago invited the show, but not Philadelphia. Barnes himself was apparently not ready to take the
initiative to bring it to his native city.

In the summer of 1913 Barnes again visited the great
museums of London, Berlin and Paris. Day after day and
all day long, he went through the huge galleries systemat-
ically, determined to get at the qualities of great art.
Always he had with him a volume of Berenson to guide
him among the Italian paintings. On his own, he was
buying more Renoirs and Cézannes.

The following summer he made the same dogged
rounds, still with Berenson in hand. By this time he was
beginning to think that Berenson excelled as a detective
in the art field but that he did not provide the criteria for
judging the merits of the artists, famous or obscure, with
whom he dealt. Barnes's own ability to perceive the
quality of other kinds of painting was deepening. If he
could not yet attempt to define great art, he was at least
learning to recognize it on sight.

As his confidence in his taste grew, and by now it was
growing rapidly, he stepped up his buying. Within three
years of the Glackens purchase, he had acquired *fifty*
Renoirs. The high prices of Cézanne reported by Glackens
went higher. That was no deterrent: Barnes had fourteen
of them. His collection included also some Picassos and
examples of virtually all the leading French moderns, as
well as the Americans previously noted.

Briefly, in October, Barnes became a doctor again,
when Glackens underwent an operation at the Jefferson
Hospital in Philadelphia. Barnes donned white smock and
mask, and stood by to make sure that all the sponges which

went into the patient came out again. On the twenty-third, Glackens wrote to his wife: ". . . Mrs. Barnes was in this afternoon and Barnes in the morning . . ." On the twenty-fifth Barnes brought his friend a gift, not a fancy package from a high-class gift shop but something far more precious to a patient in a hospital. "Barnes brought in some home-made soup this morning and I had some for dinner and [the] rest will keep until supper. It was quite a different thing than the hospital variety." And he informed his wife that Mrs. Barnes would have a room ready for her when she arrived. On November 2 he wrote his wife again: "Dr. Stuart tells me that I can go on Thursday. I think I shall go out to Barnes and shall probably stay five days or so. I think Barnes counts on my staying that long at least . . ."

Although Argyrol had found a ready market, independent researchers continued to test it and other silver compounds under many variable conditions. The original Barnes-Hille claims were not all sustained. It was found, for instance, that long-continued use of Argyrol could cause argyria. Its effectiveness in treating infections of the nose and throat was not considered positively demonstrated. Nor was there any substantial basis for using it in the treatment of venereal diseases—an application for which it is still employed in certain foreign countries.

However, in the 1916 edition of a standard textbook, *Diseases of the Eye,* George E. de Schweinitz wrote that Argyrol was used to treat various disorders, including ulcer of the cornea and conjunctivitis, particularly in the newborn (conjunctivitis neonatorum), in whom, in extreme cases, such disorders could lead to blindness. According to that author, "within the last few years Protargol [a strong silver protein] and Argyrol have largely replaced

silver nitrate in the practice of many surgeons," several
of whom had worked out a systematic treatment with them.
On the other hand, some doctors reported Argyrol to be
effective only in comparatively mild nose and throat
infections. For home use Argyrol had the drawback of
staining the nostrils (and hence the bed linens), which
frightened off some customers, but the nasal discoloration
was temporary and the linens could be washed clean. The
demand for the product continued to increase.

When the First World War broke out, the government
bought out the entire production of the plant, which, it is
said, was then doing research on gas masks for the Army.
So small and limited a plant could only have carried out
some phase of a larger program. In the files of the Chemical
Warfare Service, there is no published credit to the Barnes
company.

Relieved of sales promotion duties, his paper work taken
care of by three capable women—Miss Laura Geiger and
the sisters Mary and Nelle E. Mullen—Barnes was free
to spend most of his time with his paintings and to read
and reflect on art. In the April, 1915, issue of *Arts &
Decoration* he made his first venture into art criticism.
"How to Judge a Painting" is written straightforwardly
and fluently; sometimes discursive, it is always lively. If it
contains one of the most barbarous English sentences ever
committed to print (one forbears to quote what the
editors were too awed to edit), the article also contains
some trenchant statements. However, it is not as a piece
of prose that the piece is significant but as a reflection of
Barnes's forthrightness (which could become cruel) in
judging other people's opinions; his own mingled honesty
and evasiveness, plainness and pretentiousness; and his
incipient pursuit of a rational understanding of art.

Crediting a "lifelong" friend "who combines greatness

as an artist with a big man's mind" as the most valuable
single influence in his art education, Barnes has Manet,
Renoir, Monet and Degas, in the one fancy passage in the
article, acclaim Glackens as close kin: this was the praise
of friendship.

How should one judge a painting? Like the amateur
writer and critic he is, he begins with a quotation of a
quotation, but a choice one—George Moore quoting
Degas:

Do you think you can explain the merits of a picture to
those who do not see them? I can find the best and clearest
words to express my meaning, and I have spoken to the most
intelligent people about art and they have not understood;
but among people who understand, words are not necessary.
You say 'humph-he-ha'—and everything has been said. Public
taste has not been advanced one jot by writing about art. I
think literature has only done harm to art.

From his own experience Barnes found that "books,
the usual means of acquiring elementary knowledge, fail.
A textbook on art is an impossibility. The standard so-
called authoritative works are, for the most part, compila-
tions of the traditions and accretions that surround art,
barely touching it, written by antiquarians, experts, bad
painters, professional writers or plain dunces." He conceded, however, that "even when such books seem to fail,
they probably help" us to appreciate an artist's work by
compelling us to give his paintings themselves our closest
attention. So, with a Cézanne or Van Gogh before him,
he had spent months wading through "the verbosity and
froth" of a Meier-Graeffe. In the end, he wasn't sure but
that it was his close scrutiny of the picture rather than the
book which made him see the light.

If books were of little help, newspapers and magazines
were none at all. Of the artists who wrote for the important

monthly magazines he singled out two of the most prominent for attack.

The principal offender is Mr. Kenyon Cox, who is a teacher of
art students, a painter of the lifeless, a writer of sophisms
about art, a thoroughly conventional respectable man. He is,
if he may be judged by his paintings, an artistic cripple
hobbling through the present on the tottering crutches of the
dead past. . . . Another publicist-painter who is doing his
best to resuscitate the dead, in the form of academic art, is
Mr. William M. Chase. . . . Mr. Chase's personality is lovable,
but as a painter and artist he unfortunately stands for traditions in art, rather than good art.

For a moment the businessman in Barnes confused
aesthetic and cash values, taunting Chase for having spent
a fortune in his youth on dead paintings rather than on
the French Impressionists, which would now be worth
millions; but he redeemed this lapse with his comment
on Chase's recent statement that "Matisse does the best
he knows how, but Cézanne never knew how." Said Barnes:
"It is my opinion, based upon the fourteen Cézannes in
my collection, that Cézanne knew almost exactly how."

Nor did he think the champions of the advance guard
too reliable a source of information. He didn't jump
through every hoop Picasso sailed into the air. Although
he had the highest praise for some earlier Picassos he
owned, he was not afraid to risk the judgment that, in his
current Cubistic phase, the artist was just "having fun
with the public."

Barnes acknowledged his debt to two writers. George
Moore's books "will give a man more insight into art essence than all other books on art ever written"—a venial
exaggeration if he meant that Moore had a fine perception
of what his Impressionist painter friends in Paris were
doing; a gross exaggeration if he implied that Moore was

a thinker in aesthetics. He was always "raising the fringe" of a subject, but he could only pursue a girl, not a thought, to a conclusion.

The book Barnes found most helpful was Clive Bell's *Art,* published in 1914. He was honest enough to confess that, if it had appeared five years previously, he could not have understood it. He must have been thinking especially of a concept which was Bell's chief contribution. People talked freely but vaguely in praise of form in art. To define it, Bell conjured up a magical adjective: *significant.* Only significant form mattered, and it was achieved when lines and colors were combined in an aesthetically moving way.

Still, when he looked around at the collection of his friend and lawyer, John G. Johnson, and at the Frick, Widener, Havemeyer and Altman collections, he made value judgments. These collections, he said, are "all superb, with Havemeyer [now part of the Metropolitan Museum of Art] easily first in importance in art rather than in names. . . . One could study art and its relations to life to better advantage in the Havemeyer collection than in any single gallery in the world." (Incidentally, he spoke of these as millionaires' collections, as if he were not in their class. While he didn't question the pleasure they got out of their "pedygreed [*sic*], really great paintings," which represented a dealer's or expert's choice rather their own—he was discounting his own forced start—he knew men of more modest means who enjoyed a deeper aesthetic pleasure in picking their own way through the broken field of art.) Superb as the millionaires' collections are, if Widener offered him his $700,000 Raphael Madonna for his own Renoir bust, he "would refuse to be cheated." Altman's Rembrandt (*Woman Cutting Her Nails*) [also in the "Met"] "would be an inadequate swap for my greater Cézanne's portrait of his wife." Nor would he exchange his "colorful Sisley" for a "gloomy Ruysdael." The experts would not agree with him, he knew, but he asserted that his judgments were based on the only valid criterion, that of intrinsic quality.

But what are the criteria of intrinsic quality? He was not yet able to apply Bell's concept of significant form and in the end admitted that he didn't know how to judge a painting. Like George Moore before him, he was simply educating himself in public.

But it will surely help indirectly if the seeker for light learns not to judge a painting by the many accepted standards. . . . Pinned down to a working formula, no man can do more than express his own opinions and recite his experiences. Mine has been to buy a painting for what I think is in it, to have honest painters in my house and talk to them about my pictures, to lose no opportunity to look at paintings anywhere, to read books on art and not to be discouraged at how little they give to make an artist's work more enjoyable and understandable.

In sum, this meant little more than "I don't know much about art, but I know what I like." Unable to help the reader "understand" art, Barnes compensated him with some insights and incense on the art of collecting. He wrote as if he had been at it for years and years; and note how benignly, in the first sentence, he assimilated the criticism of Glackens:

Every collector who studies his paintings soon learns to accept his own discarded pictures as the necessary milestones on his way to the destination. . . . To discard an expensive but bad painting by a famous artist hurts me less than to put in the attic a picture by an unknown painter that I thought was good when I bought it. But mistakes are inevitable and that makes for interest. As years go by, the mistakes occur less often, but never entirely cease, and sooner or later one gets a collection that is quite as personal as its owner's face. Then, and before then, comes the pleasure one gets from living with them as friends, children, objects of worship, diversions, serious mental occupations, whichever role chooses to fit the mood of the moment.

What are some of the pleasures? The least is the mere possession, the best, the joy that one can feel but not express to others; between these two extremes are pleasures that may be compared to the notes of a piano, limited in what can be produced only by the performer's skill and knowledge. Good paintings are more satisfying companions than the best of books and infinitely more so than most very nice people. I can talk, without speaking, to Cézanne, Prendergast, Daumier, Renoir, and they can talk to me in kind. I can criticize them and take, without offense, the refutation which comes silently but powerfully when I learn, months later, what they mean and not what I thought they meant. That is one of the joys of a collection, the elasticity with which paintings stretch to the beholder's personal vision which they progressively develop. And that is universal, for a painting is justly proportionate to what a man thinks he sees in it.

As a substitute for other pursuits, collecting, living with and studying good paintings—the enthusiast believes—offers greater interest, variety, and satisfaction than any other pleasure or work a man could select. It is more difficult to get a personally chosen good collection than it is to make a big fortune. . . . It is more laborious to learn to recognize quality in painting than to write a popular novel. . . .

A man with a house full of good paintings needs no subterfuge of excessive heat or cold to drive him north or south, to get away from his own wearying self. Golf, dances, theatres, dinners, traveling get a setback as worthy diversions when the rabies of pursuit of quality in painting, and its enjoyment, gets into a man's system. And when he has surrounded himself with that quality, bought with his blood, he is a King. . . .

Barnes did not exactly sacrifice all the minor pleasures of life for the pursuit of art, but the exaggeration suited the mood—let it pass. A King: in this mellow mood it was the royalty of the fairy tales he conjured up, monarch of all he surveyed. In reality, the head that wore this crown, too, was to lie uneasy.

At this time, however, there was nothing to disturb his sovereign enjoyment. When he got home from the factory at three o'clock (if he did not go to the ball game), he would have Charley Funk in from the stable to help him rearrange his paintings. They transposed the big pictures on these walls, shifted the smaller ones on those. Hour after hour they wrestled with heavy frames so that each picture might show to best advantage, according to its size, its theme, its importance . . . and more than once, after they were finished with their labors, all the pictures were back where they were in the first place.

It was not only for his own pleasure that Barnes indulged in this scene shifting. Although he had made his latest purchases with considerable self-confidence, he was far from sure of himself every time, and he was glad to have visitors discuss them freely. Among the "honest artists" he welcomed were Franklin Watkins, George Biddle, Charles Sheeler, Arthur Carles and others who were not as widely known, such as George Harding and Henry McCarter, whom he liked personally and respected as painters and teachers at the Pennsylvania Academy of the Fine Arts, the oldest art school in the country.

He enjoyed hearing their praise doubly: for admiring what was deserving of admiration, and for complimenting him on his choice. But these young artists were not all praise. They were feeling their way, not only in the whole world of art, as lovers of art, but also in an obscure corridor of that world, as creators of art seeking a style of their own. It must be supposed that they could and did comment sharply, sometimes with unswerving precision, sometimes wrongheadedly, but always to their own edification and to Barnes's education. He listened intently to their artist talk for shortcomings he had not perceived, for suggestions of basic aesthetic values, for the fragment of truth in their brash statements. Their adverse criticism hurt, but he could take it for the sake of education: after all, they were not criticizing him, but other men's paintings, of which he happened to be the custodian; and it was in his power to terminate that criticism at any time—very much in his power. . . .

Among the famous visitors was Bernard Berenson. Barnes was miffed when Berenson intimated that he might have included some old masters in his collection, though he contended that he had listened to Berenson with "a sense of compassion" (not quite daring to say "a sense of superiority"), "for what I thought was his lack of appreciation of good art. That sounds egotistic and smug, but is really intelligent and honest." If Barnes meant by this that a critic should be able to judge the art of his own time as well as the art of the past, he was making a sound point more recently developed by Lionello Venturi. But he did not know that Berenson had been ahead of him in appreciating at least one of the moderns, having written a spirited letter to *The Nation* in 1908 in defense of the exhibition of Matisse drawings at Stieglitz's gallery. It was only when Berenson "showed his admiration for a very few of my Renoirs, Gauguins and Glackenses" that Barnes stopped commiserating with him.

Leo Stein was another visitor to Merion; probably Gertrude Stein also. Leo Stein was still a great talker, no doubt talking out many of the ideas which were one day to appear in his book. Now Barnes was beginning to be a talker whereas he had been all listener during his first sojourns in Paris. Respecting Stein's ideas, he still enjoyed

listening to him; but Stein was like a vaudeville monologist and his act ran, not for eight minutes, but for the duration of his visits. Barnes wanted to have his say, too, such
as it was, but he could not get a word in frontally or edge-
wise; Stein just kept talking. One day it was just too galling;
Barnes said, "It hurt like hell." He couldn't take it and
made it plain that Leo Stein was no longer welcome. He
stayed on in the States until the war was over, but he did
not come to Merion again, not even to say good-by.

There was one more visitor from Paris who was seeing
the war through in this country—Jules Pascin. Although
he already had a reputation in Paris, particularly as a
superb draftsman, Pascin was virtually starving in New
York. His purpose in going to Merion was not to see the
Barnes collection but to add to it. If he had any paintings
available, he did not try to "impose" them on Barnes—
he brought with him only a portfolio of drawings. Un-
accountably—for it is difficult to imagine that none of
then. were of sufficient merit—Barnes did not buy a single
one.

While Barnes became friendly with a dozen native
artists, he was never as intimate with any of them as he
was with Glackens. He often had the artist and his wife
down for weekends. When he was in New York he dropped
into the studio on Washington Square and the Glackens
home to see the rest of the family. He gave Ira, on his tenth
or eleventh birthday, a gift of a $50 Liberty bond.

Ira Glackens has given us some pointed anecdotes concerning his elders. Though he believed his easy-going
father never had an unpleasant moment with Barnes, he
knew the case was different with his mother. She was not
as content as her husband was to take him on his own
terms. Particularly as an "emancipated woman" (still a
fighting phrase then), she resented Barnes's old-fashioned

notion of the status of man and wife, and his treatment of
Mrs. Barnes (whom George Biddle found "pleasant, a little
timid and self-effacing"). Once, while Barnes lay comfortably on the sofa, he called out sharply, " 'Laura, my pipe!'
and Laura's feet could be heard in the silence pattering
up the stairs. The silence on this occasion was particularly
deep with E.G. in the room. She believed in object lessons.
From her chair she tossed her handkerchief ostentatiously
in the middle of the drawing room rug and said in the
same peremptory tone, 'William, my handkerchief!' "

The object lesson had no other result than to antagonize
Barnes. Mrs. Glackens was prepared for that; she could
take it, for a good blow delivered for "the cause." It was
not the only time she came into conflict with Barnes. During another visit at Merion, they all went out for a ride.
Mrs. Barnes, who had learned to drive only a short while
before, was at the wheel. Suddenly a dog leaped into the
path of the car. Mrs. Barnes swerved sharply to avoid it.
The passengers were only "slightly jolted," but Barnes
was furious, not at the dog, but at his wife. Why, they
could all have been killed! And he kept repeating it and
harping on his wife's bad driving. Mrs. Barnes became
more and more nervous and Mrs. Glackens, observing her,
more and more angry. Suddenly Mrs. Glackens popped
around and cried out, "Shut up!"

It gave Barnes a greater jolt than the jerked car. *Shut
up!* No one ever talked to him like that. He kept quiet
all right, but so did everybody else. The excursion was
spoiled. Afterward no one enjoyed the dinner. That night
Glackens said to his wife, "I guess we won't be invited
here again in a hurry."

He was right, yet Barnes did not include him in his
resentment. Though he kept away from the Glackens
home, he still dropped into the Washington Square studio.

This kind of split relationship was not to the liking of the
artist. He bided his time. One day he invited Barnes to
lunch at home. Edith, he assured him, would not be
present—she was away. So she was when they arrived.
They had lunch alone. Barnes left the table, taking his
cut of apple pie in the palm of his hand, and went downstairs. It happened that Edith was there now, and wouldn't
it be doubly ridiculous for a man already ridiculous with
apple pie in his hand to make a show of anger? They
were reconciled, but Barnes had to take Edith Glackens
on her own terms and these were that she would be as
forthright with him as she—and he—was with everyone
else. That was as good as a guarantee of sporadic friction
between them.

8

An Experiment in Adult Education

WHEN THE CASE OF JAKE THE SADIST GOT THE BOYS AT THE
Argyrol plant interested in psychology, Barnes guided them
as best he could with the help of the textbooks of the day.
John Dewey's *Democracy and Education*, which appeared
in 1916, inspired him to try a much broader experiment.
One reviewer predicted that "the twenty-first century will
study three great stages in educational theory—Plato,
Rousseau and Dewey," while another declared that in spite
of Dewey's espousal of individualism "his moral ideal is
really that of the 'good mixer' "—a concept now called, in
the jargon of sociology, "adjustment." Siding with the
majority which found Dewey's method supreme for developing an individual's potential, Barnes tried it out in
an experiment under the guidance of Miss Mary Mullen,
herself the bright beneficiary of Barnes's program of employee self-improvement.

At this time the factory may already have had the maximum number of employees it was ever to require—some twenty persons, of whom perhaps a dozen were Negro men. It was this group which Miss Mullen brought together for an hour several times a week, as she wrote ten years later, for a "systematic study of problems intimately related to the Negro's life, both business and personal," based on Dewey's teachings. (Much later, Barnes said that the study period was 12:30 to 2:30, thus reducing the nominal eight-hour working day to six.) Miss Mullen planned the program and directed the discussion.

An associate has described her as a sweet woman without a sense of humor, and her account of the project, interesting as it is, would have benefited from a leaven of humor. She made the straight-faced statement, for example, that although attendance at the factory "seminars" was voluntary, everyone turned out for them—as if the men could possibly have knocked off work for any other reason but to improve their minds.

The discussion, she wrote, was informal, "but not haphazard or desultory." The first topics were psychological, "presented without any unnecessary technicality, and simply as a study of the impulses, the instincts, which constitute the ultimate sources of behavior, the organization of these impulses into habits, and of habits into the personality as a whole. . . . The meaning of intelligence as the method of organization, both of the personality and environment, was explained." Besides Dewey's book, important new books which were relevant to the course were discussed—Bertrand Russell's *Why Men Fight* (1917), H. G. Wells's *The Outline of History* (1920), and the like.

Such books took the class beyond purely Negro problems. They analyzed art, music, poetry and drama on the basis of aesthetic principles. In particular,

a large collection of pictures . . . provided material for un-
ending comment and debate. . . .

At first the discussion was dominated rather by feeling than
intelligence: imagination constantly tended to encroach upon
the sphere of reflecton. The leader of the group did not re-
press feeling and imagination but analyzed them when they
intruded in the wrong place. . . . Thanks to the keenness of
their interest, and to their powers of picturesque expression,
the discussion retained a color, a vividness, and intensity which
visitors to the class, men who occupy chairs in colleges and
universities, declared to be a welcome contrast to the dullness
and perfunctoriness characteristically found in the ordinary
academic classroom. [Unfortunately, Miss Mullen does not
quote from the discussions.]

We do not mean to convey the impression [she concluded]
that we have developed a crowd of savants, or art connoisseurs, but we are sure that we have stirred an intelligent interest in spiritual things. . . .

Barnes had written, three years before, that there were
rarely less than a hundred pictures on view at the factory,
and that they were sold at cost to interested employees.
"Four of the group have collections of modern paintings
varying in number from a few to several hundred." The
four must have been Mary Mullen and her sister Nelle,
Laura Geiger and—Barnes himself!

He had occasion to think of what he would eventually
do with that "large collection of pictures" in the factory
and the growing collection at home when his lawyer and
friend, John G. Johnson, died in 1917, bequeathing his
1,280 paintings to the city of Philadelphia.

Barnes also had a decent concern for the welfare of his
domestic employees. Charles Funk had been with him
some ten years when Barnes decided to give up horses for
automobiles. He asked Funk whether he was not interested
in some more promising line of work for the future. Hav-

ing a slight knowledge of auto mechanics, Funk thought he would like to try that expanding field. As it happened, Barnes was a friend of the president of the company producing a car locally. Instead of giving Funk a letter of recommendation, Barnes called on his friend in person to see that Funk got a job. (No fool, Funk realized that this hiring from the top would prejudice the men in the shop against him, and he took pains to let the foreman know that he was under his orders.)

As an apprentice, Funk received a low wage, but his pay check remained the same as he had received from Barnes, for Barnes made up the difference from the compulsory savings he had enjoined on his groom. As a parting gift, Barnes gave him several small pictures, but Funk treasured more deeply the memory that Barnes had never spoken a harsh word to him. And his wife agreed that they "never saw a good-hearted man like him."

The horses gave way to Pierce-Arrows and Packards, and the groom to a chauffeur, Albert Nulty. Just as the cabbies told Funk he wouldn't last long with Barnes, the taxi drivers gave Nulty a month. They, too, were proved wrong, by eleven months and thirty-nine years. After he had been with Barnes some time, Nulty began to build himself a garage and driveway for his house. He did this in his spare time and the work proceeded slowly. Sunday mornings Barnes went walking with his dogs and week by week he watched Nulty's progress. When the job was finished, Barnes asked him what it had cost, and wrote out a check for the amount. The car that went into this garage was also Barnes's gift.

While Barnes was applying Dewey's principles of education at the factory, he sought a direct contact with the philosopher, not merely for personal-social purposes but to understand his ideas more thoroughly. He therefore enrolled as a special student in Dewey's seminar at Columbia University in 1917-1918. The late Irwin Edman, who was also a member of that seminar, wrote many years after that they all "felt in Dewey the mark of the true teacher, one who did not lay down dogmas but cooperatively helped to elicit from his students fresh hypotheses and also helped them both to develop and discipline these. He was a master of initiating independent thinking in his pupils."

As a student of science, Barnes already had a disciplined mind and the capacity to think independently. But in thinking along new lines he was fortified by the example of Dewey. As Edman wrote further,

It remains indeed one of the sociological paradoxes of American culture why and how a technician among philosophers should have influenced thought so much more widely than in philosophical circles and why a man, by the usual outward, visible signs not a good—and indeed by all conventional criteria a poor—teacher, should have so deeply inspired and remade the thinking of crucial individuals in all the professions, teaching above all.

The answer to this apparent enigma is not too hard to find. The fact is that Dewey, as those of us who were his pupils remember vividly, in his very hesitations, his very ignoring of the demands of an audience—that they be entertained, kept in suspense—these very things emphasized what his discourse positively displayed: the phenomenon of a man patiently thinking, exploring, suggesting, developing and testing ideas. In a seminar this was even more striking. . . .

If this hesitation, this exploring, this testing of ideas, was so attractive to groping youth, how much more deeply appealing it was to a man of forty-five, who, having attained the threshold of one profession and creativity in another, and with all the assurance that money can buy to fortify him, was voluntarily a student again. If his intellectual idol, after producing a masterpiece like *Democracy and Education,* was not pontificating but still exploring, he too was sustained in his exploration of the means of fully applying Dewey's ideas to the study of art.

It was a gifted group who were assembled in that seminar. Besides Barnes and Edman, who was to become head of the department of philosophy at Columbia, there were Brand Blanshard, now head of Yale's department of philosophy; his twin brother Paul Blanshard, who was to become the author of *American Freedom and Catholic Power* and other books on social themes; Margaret Frances Bradshaw (later Mrs. Brand Blanshard), who was to write *Retreat from Likeness in the Theory of Painting;* and Anzia Yezierska, who was soon to achieve popular fame with her first book of stories of immigrant life, *Hungry Hearts.* In that class, Barnes, much older than the rest and with solid achievement behind him, seldom spoke. Probably young Irwin Edman, whom Barnes "worshiped," according to Miss Yezierska, did a good deal of the talking.

Barnes was friendly with all the members of the class except herself, she felt. One would suppose a bond of sympathy between the man risen from the slums of Philadelphia and the young woman from a Polish ghetto, who looked back on herself as the "little immigrant girl who never had a birthday," and who was now striving to get away from factory work to become a writer. But Barnes stood aloof from her, "did not even regard me as a human being." Miss Yezierska believes it was because she had no academic status, was not, like the others, studying for a Ph.D. This hardly seems credible. She may still be echoing her youthful hypersensitivity: she was agonizingly self-conscious in the presence of all the members of the seminar as beings of a higher social order, of which their formal education was only one sign. If Barnes disliked her, it could have been for this very self-consciousness or some other personal trait. Nonetheless, when at the end of the year he proposed a project for the group, he included her at Dewey's request.

The problem he placed before them was to find out why the Polish element in Philadelphia was not assimilating. Not only did they live in a neighborhood of their own (most foreign-born groups did), but even the children of the second generation were clinging to the language and customs of the old country.

Why did Barnes choose this of the many urban problems which called for study? Possibly it was suggested to him, if only indirectly, by the author of *The Americanization of Edward Bok* (widely acclaimed when it was published two years later), who must have been working on his autobiography at this time. Or he may have been uneasy at the foreign invasion of an area sacred to his memory: Little Poland was only about a mile from his birthplace.

Whatever his motive, the members of the seminar were delighted with the prospect of a field study under the direction of their master, Dewey; and those who had not yet earned a nickel in their lives, as well as Miss Yezierska, who had made her living in sweatshops, were equally delighted with the bounty of the paymaster—$100 a month.

To become intimate with the people they were to get the lowdown on (in three months), they looked for living quarters among them. When they were unable to find suitable (desirable?) flats in the houses Poles lived in, Barnes rented a house for his protégés at 2007 Richmond Street, along the waterfront, which was one boundary of Little Poland.

It happened that Dewey could not get to Philadelphia at the beginning of June. While the project marked time, Barnes drove down to the house in his big car to visit the group, and he gave them a list of books to read. In addition to *Democracy and Education* he recommended W. Trotter's *Instincts of the Herd in Peace and War,* the thesis of which was that psychology can become an effective guide in everyday life. A sociologist who reviewed it said: "The worst and the best that can be said about a book of this kind is that it is suggestive. It entertains, it enlivens, it starts a flock of ideas, but it settles nothing." The book appealed to the rationalist in Barnes, as did his other recommendation: F. M. Alexander's *Man's Supreme Inheritance* (with foreword by Dewey), which laid down the principles and techniques of a system of re-education in which the mind may achieve perfect control over the body.

In the continued absence of Dewey, the group felt restive. Paul Blanshard therefore "persuaded them," as he wrote to me, "to undertake a rather amateurish little social survey of the neighborhood by submitting questionnaires to the people who lived there. I felt that we needed some sound factual basis for the conclusions that we were groping for in the philosophical realm."

About a month after the project started, Dewey arrived in Philadelphia and Blanshard departed. At this late date, Blanshard cannot recall why he was dropped. In general, his point of view was different from that of both Barnes and Dewey, but he cannot say definitely that Barnes, whom he remembers as "temperamental and a bit crotchety," was responsible for his dismissal. Possibly, he thinks, Dewey took umbrage at his spoiling his fellow students' fresh, innocent approach to the subject.

With one month down and two to go, the investigators selected converging paths. Edman undertook to study the influence of the Polish press; Miss Bradshaw, Polish children in the schools; Miss Yezierska, the role of women in home life; and Brand Blanshard, the influence of the Catholic Church on the Polish group.

While they were pursuing their tentative exploration of the Polish-Americans, the Polish-Americans were investigating them. Who were these people anyway? Why were they all living in one house, a house with typewriters in every room? What about that big car which drove up to the house mysteriously every so often? Was this the master mind of the group, and were they pretending to poke into the affairs of ordinary, unimportant folk as a blind for espionage? We were at war; the Cram shipyards were only a short distance away: a word to the wise. Someone wrote the word to the police department. A detective came around to investigate. . . .

One Sunday Barnes invited the group to his home. There was music by three members of the New York Symphony Orchestra string choir; there were the pictures all over the place, including the bathroom. At this time Barnes was freely admitting almost anyone who cared to see them. Miss Bradshaw came away with the impression that he hid behind the draperies to listen to visitors' comments, and if he heard some such remark as "What's the picture all about?" he was deeply resentful. She thinks it was a defensive reaction, because he was himself unsure of the value of his paintings. It is hard to believe that this was wholly true. Still, it was only a half-dozen years since Glackens made his first purchase and seven more years were to pass before Barnes committed himself in writing to what he considered the basic values in art.

Monday, it was back to the project again. . . . In the end, the earnest young people agreed that the Church, in whose parochial schools there were children of seven and eight unable to speak English, was the main factor in retarding the assimilation of the Polish community. When Miss Bradshaw intimated as much to Dewey, the philosopher smiled wryly as if to say, And what are you going to do about it? Edman, Blanshard and Miss Yezierska departed, leaving Miss Bradshaw to clean up the house.

Later on, Brand Blanshard wrote a pamphlet, *The Church and the Polish Group;* Miss Yezierska drew on John Dewey and her fellow students in a novel, *All I Could Never Be;* and Dewey himself became interested in the struggle for power in this country between Paderewski's conservative party and a so-called "popular" Polish party in anticipation of the restoration of Polish independence after the war.

If the project itself was less than earth-shaking, the resulting friendship with Dewey shaped Barnes's whole future. At first, he was the mentor, not only showing Dewey his paintings but trying to give him a sense of aesthetic values to supplement his vague philosophical notions about art. A few years later Dewey became friendly with Thomas Benton through his then controversial murals at the New School for Social Research. Dewey was "interested" in them, [Benton wrote me], "but he never 'responded' to them in favor or adversely, as people who 'see' paintings do. Dewey never had a judgment of his own with regard to specific works. I have talked with him on the subject of art and could never believe that he had ever really *seen* any one work of art."

In the fall Barnes and Dewey went down to Greenwich Village to see the Provincetown Players. Like every intelligent theatergoer of the time, they were immensely impressed by the achievements of that dedicated band, mounting imaginatively in a tiny theater, without funds, stimulating plays which the Broadway producers would not touch. On this particular night the offering was Eugene O'Neill's *Where the Cross Is Made* (which reached Broadway in expanded form as *Gold*), with Ida Rauh in the leading role. After the performance they went backstage— more accurately, upstairs—to the little room where the actors had coffee with their friends, and the two visitors had a long talk with Miss Rauh. The company had been haled to court by the fire department when they knocked down the wall between front and back parlor to make their theater, supporting the ceiling with beams. As a former law student, Miss Rauh argued their case and the judge condoned the violation committed in such a good cause. If she told Barnes the story, it would certainly have delighted him. But the fact that she was a fine actress and that the company was devoted to regenerating the shoddy commercial theater was sufficient to elicit his help. The next day he sent Miss Rauh a check for a thousand dollars.

Shortly afterward he invited her to have lunch with him and Glackens. She expected to be taken to some swanky place frequented by the well-to-do, but he went instead to a little Italian spaghetti restaurant on Mc-Dougall Street. He was making a display of unconventionality, she felt, *pour épater les bourgeois*. It could be, however, that Barnes (and Glackens) knew their spaghetti and took it where they found it.

Barnes attended several performances at the Provincetown, sometimes alone, sometimes with Dewey. In the next two years, without formally registering for the seminars, he came up every week from Philadelphia to sit in on them.

Perhaps it was his association with Dewey that led

Herbert Croly, a founder of the New School for Social Research in 1919, to invite Barnes to teach psychology there. Dewey urged him to accept, Barnes wrote in a late letter, "because he was convinced at that time that any real progress in education must come from outside the universities." But he was too busy to consider it.

9

The Explorer

IN THE 1920'S, IN THE FIFTH DECADE OF HIS LIFE, BARNES
was engaged in the most numerous and diverse activities
of his career. If they were not strung together in a neat
sequence like beads, it was not because he went from one
thing to another haphazardly. To begin with, his prime
interest was in expanding his collection on a grand scale.
This led logically to the problem of where to house it.
Then, having decided to build a public museum, he
began to consider, as his slowly developed ideas on art
finally crystallized, whether his museum should not be
something more than a public museum. At the same time
his buying became more purposive; he was not merely
expanding, he was *developing*, his collection. And while
this was in essence the rationale underlying his own
movements, events outside his control intervened to de-
termine his future course. To tag after him strictly chron-

ologically through these intermingling activities would be to re-create the chaos of life without achieving the fusion of experience.

Although the School of Paris was his major field of interest, Barnes continued to give considerable attention to American art. In September of 1920, Barnes spent a weekend in the art colony at Woodstock, New York, then the most vigorous of the American art colonies, certainly in the East. The news of his coming stirred up great excitement: was there a single artist who did not hope to sell to the famous collector? On short notice, he had asked Eugene Speicher to reserve accommodations, which were scanty then, for a party of three, and he was guided by Speicher through the studios of George Bellows, Henry McFee, Andrew Dasburg, Paul Rohland, and perhaps a few others.

Caroline Rohland recalls Mrs. Barnes as "a quiet, homey sort of person, conventional and pleasant," and Barnes as "genial and charming." Both of them showed a genuine interest in the charming stone house of the Rohlands and in the beautiful garden in which it stood, far back from the road. On Sunday the Speichers threw a party for Barnes, at which the Rohlands and several other artist couples were present. It was a gay evening; Barnes laughed heartily at Rohland's humorous sallies and at Speicher's stories of his boyhood, especially of how he had once played hooky from school.

Barnes is said to have asked prices at the studios he visited without committing himself to purchasing anything. Possibly the third member of the Barnes party, a young man, was a secretary to whom Barnes dictated notes on the precise location of the pictures which interested him, for after he had been home several days he wrote some such order as: I want the still life hanging beside your wife's dresser in the bedroom.

Apparently not very many artists received such notes. Barnes bought a small Dasburg. If he was interested in the work of Bellows, he may have been put off by the artist's independent manner—no truckling to art patrons for him. From Rohland he bought five monotypes: it is a reflection of his growing insight that he should have chosen these rather than the artist's flower paintings in oil, which he also liked, for the monotype medium subtilized their broadly decorative quality. On receipt of the pictures, Barnes sent Rohland a check with a penciled note saying that they "successfully competed in cheerfulness and charm with a bright crisp day. You ought to do more canvases and show them. You're saying something."

Though he could ask Speicher to get a room for him and use him as a guide, Barnes had expressed so little interest in his work that the artist did not bother to take him to his own studio. Soon after his visit, Barnes wrote him that he would never get anywhere as a painter until he threw off the influence of Henri and his school. Whether his criticism itself or his manner of stating it was disagreeable, Mrs. Speicher, fearing that it would upset the artist, did not show him the letter until he had finished a landscape he was working on. Speicher replied that Barnes would regret having sent the letter. There is no way of knowing whether he did. But it must be said that in refusing to buy the work of Speicher, whom he liked and whom readers of *The Arts* a few years later voted the outstanding American artist, Barnes showed an ability to set aside personalities in making aesthetic judgments.

The following spring Barnes attended an auction at the Anderson Galleries in New York and bought four works by Marsden Hartley for all of $175. He had them sent to his factory address.

At an exhibition of contemporary American painters held in the Pennsylvania Academy of the Fine Arts in 1922, Arthur Carles brought to his attention the paintings of Thomas Benton. Barnes bought three and persuaded his friend Maurice Speiser, the well-known lawyer, to buy another. Barnes was also interested in a Dasburg painting and asked Carles to wire the artist that he would take it if the price were reduced. He got the painting.

But it was to Paris that Barnes turned for his major explorations. After the war he was generally able to take a winter as well as his usual summer trip to Europe. Each time, he sought out artists, dealers and other collectors for possible purchases. A crop of new dealers were his chief source of supply, along with Vollard and Durand-Ruel, who still had a few good Cézannes, Renoirs and Impressionists to sell—Bernheim-Jeune, Barzansky and, above all, Paul Guillaume. Independent as he was becoming in his art judgment, he still seemed to need to lean on someone, not exactly for advice, but for leads and sometimes for confirmation of his judgment. An art dealer is the last person in the world one would have expected him to consult for a disinterested opinion, and Barnes often expressed his contempt for their kind; but of course the art dealers whom *he* regarded with favor were not mere merchants. Witness Ambroise Vollard, who had bought Cézanne when no one would look at him; witness young Paul Guillaume, who, as far back as the turn of the century, as a mere youth, had done pioneer research in African Negro sculpture.

Now he had amassed a wonderful collection of carvings and bronzes and was a pioneer in diffusing appreciation of them, i.e., selling them. And Guillaume had no trouble in selling himself to Barnes, for he was not only intelligent and enthusiastic about art but also personable, well-mannered, soft-spoken and conscientiously flattering; and he had a beautiful young wife. Nor was that all. Writing of the gallery a few years later, when he had visited it "a hundred times," Barnes called it a temple, a place where all kinds of creative people and connoisseurs met "to worship works of art and communicate with kindred spirits." Here he came face to face with "six chiefs of African tribes, besides four *chefs de ballet russes* [*sic*]. . . . In a single week I have met . . . English, Japanese, Norwegian, German, American and Italian painters, sculptors, composers, poets and critics—men whom I had known only by name." This is where Barnes casually met Stravinsky, Satie and the six French composers associated with him, and came to know more intimately some of the leading French painters. (Curiously, Barnes never met Renoir, who died in 1919. Years later he told friends that he had not looked up the artist he so highly prized for fear of being disillusioned—an odd, immature attitude for a man in his forties, who must have known, from the gifted artists he did meet, that although they seemed to be quite ordinary away from their easels, they had in them, if it was not always obvious, some mark of the dedicated man.)

One summer afternoon when the heat was intolerable outside, I called at the temple and found Roger Fry and Paul Guillaume discussing Negro art. I listened for a while and then took possession of Roger Fry and had a talk on Renoir and Cézanne which I shall remember for the rest of my life.

The atmosphere of the place is imperturbably peaceful, for no matter how keen the discussion it is never desecrated by a personal quarrel between artists of even widely diverging opinions. One instinctively and always respects a sanctuary."

In Paris in 1920, their differences having been composed at the peace conference, Barnes and Leo Stein met amicably again. He probably also saw Gertrude Stein, with whom he had no quarrel. All through that year Stein was worried about money. Although he was a clever talker, he was only an innocent in the world. If he had had to make a living, Gertrude Stein knew, he just couldn't have; he would just have lain down and died. He was lucky to have a father who was rich and had set him up with an income. He was lucky now to have a friend like Barnes. Two days before the end of the year, he wrote Barnes, asking his advice on what to do with the Renoirs he had in storage in New York. "Apart from a painfully small property which has been enjoying some shrinks recently," these paintings were his "principal possession," and he didn't know "where to strike the balance between the rise in Renoir prices and the fall in francs. If you don't mind giving me some counsel in the matter as to whether there is a practicable market now or whether one had better wait; whether selling at auction gives a fair return or whether some other method were more judicious . . ."

On March 8 the lamb asked Barnes to look at the pictures:

Do about them whatever you think advisable. I'm afraid that you think of them as more important than they are. Most of them are small and slight, and one very lovely nude I cracked by foolish handling in the old days of my pathological impatience. . . . Anything that you think advisable to do about them would suit me, as I have much more confidence in your judgment than in mine.

What went through Barnes's mind when he read: *you think them as more important than they are?* That Leo was a good honest soul? or that he was remarkably naïve— plain, a damn fool? And what did Barnes make of the fact that it was only in a footnote that Stein remarked that there were "some other things" with the Renoirs—a Delacroix, Cézanne water colors and an oil, a Daumier, and a bronze by Matisse! That his friend was a holy innocent or a sucker?

Apparently Barnes reported that he could not find a satisfactory customer for Stein's things, and offered to buy them himself. . . . Friends of Stein asserted that Barnes's "purchase" was a steal, that instead of being generous to an impractical friend Barnes acted on the principle, Never give a sucker a break. If Stein himself was aggrieved, there is no mention of it in his published letters.

By 1922 Barnes had so many pictures and was thinking of buying so many more that he had to have a building in which they could be properly seen. Nor was there a doubt in his mind about who was to see them. Quite simply, he had often told the Glackenses that he intended to establish a museum which would be open to everybody, "the only rule being the rigid one that no guided tours, lectures or critical examinations whatever were to be allowed: the public could come and look for itself." Evidently, when he said this (Ira Glackens quotes him without a date), Barnes still had no more confidence in art critics and criticism than when he wrote his piece in *Arts & Decoration*, and had himself not made any progress in how to judge a painting.

Nonetheless, what he envisaged now was not a conventional museum but an educational institution, to be known as the Barnes Foundation. Although his plans for it were not worked out in detail, he applied for a charter, and on December 4, Judge J. F. Miller of the Court of Common Pleas in Montgomery County granted it. By this time Paul Phillipe Cret, a Philadelphia architect of French birth, had long been working on a museum-type structure

together with an administration building which were to
constitute the home of the Barnes Foundation. They were
designed in French renaissance chateau style rather than
modern perhaps because Cret felt that the relatively simple
traditional French style would be more compatible with
the vivid paintings inside than would the then severely
stripped modern style which he had himself used elsewhere.

That same month Barnes went off to Paris on a three-
weeks' buying trip to help fill the museum—it turned out
to be the headiest single spree in his collector's career.
He had been reading up on Greek and Egyptian sculpture:
in Paris he had the good luck to meet a Greek ready to
join his ancestors, who was loaded with antiquities, and
parted with *forty* of his bronze and stone reliefs and
figurines on the best of terms. Elsewhere Barnes bought
two Dutch and one Italian painting of the fifteenth century.

In a private collection he discovered a Claude Lorrain
as good as any in the Louvre and an El Greco finer than
any which had been offered for public sale in his lifetime.
Heavy layers of dirt concealed the true worth of these
pictures from the owner and his visitors. Barnes bought
them. To be granted the privilege of making these discoveries, he facetiously wrote Glackens, was divine compensation for the saintly life he had led. How are we to
understand his claim of being a discoverer? Did he mean
that his eye was able to penetrate the grime and see the
pictures in their true colors? More likely he bought them
because they were cheap, and after he had had them
cleaned, the contrast between the refreshed and the be-
grimed paintings was so great that he thought they were
masterpieces. Perhaps they were.

Barnes made his greatest strike in the modern field.

Having turned down Pascin's drawings when the artist visited him during the war, Barnes redeemed himself now by buying several of Pascin's paintings. He bought some Kislings, not yet become too slick. He bought fine early works of Picasso and Utrillo, and the Matisse *Joy of Living*, which Leo Stein originally owned. He bought Segonzac and Derain, Laurencin and Gritchenko, Lotiron and di Chirico, Kars and Perdriat and (in sculpture) Zadkine.

Here was work by ranking artists not yet widely accepted, as well as work by a few artists whose reputations never reached this country and have waned in France. Having bought so much African sculpture from Guillaume, Barnes readily agreed to his proposal to look in on a young sculptor in the front rank of the advance guard, Jacques Lipchitz. Guillaume was not Lipchitz's dealer, and he had had a violent quarrel with him, yet he did not allow his pride to stand in the way of serving his client. The rest of the story is given here as Lipchitz recalls it.

Despite his reputation, he was not making a living at this time. He had just broken his contract with his dealer, Léonce Rosenberg; he was in arrears three quarterly payments on his rent; and he had no immediate prospects of a sale. Staring glumly out of the window one day, he saw a stranger approaching in the company of Guillaume, whom he considered an "enemy": it didn't improve his spirits. He was quite prepared to turn Guillaume away, but his wife reminded him that they could use a customer.

The two men came into the apartment and Lipchitz was so cold to Guillaume that he did not even introduce his companion. The man looked at the few pieces in the room and asked if that was all he had to show. Lipchitz led him to a small studio downstairs, but that, too, contained only minor pieces. "Is that all?" said Barnes. "No," said Lipchitz, "there's more in my big atelier, but it's quite a way from here." Barnes and Guillaume followed him silently down the four blocks to the studio.

There, Barnes quickly showed his interest. He pointed to one piece, asked the price, and wrote it down. He pointed to a second piece, asked the price, and wrote it down. These were both stone sculptures, but the artist was so anxious for ready cash that he set a low price on them. Now that the rent was paid (if the man bought the two pieces), Lipchitz's native shrewdness asserted itself, and he raised his price on the next one. He would be losing money on the transaction if he didn't and—"How much for this one? . . . How much for that one?" And what could he lose by asking higher and higher prices? The man was probably just shopping around. . . .

Barnes priced eight or ten bronzes and stone figures. Toward the end Lipchitz's prices were higher than those he would have dared ask from a dealer or collector in Paris. He watched the man tot up his figures, himself doing the same job mentally, and waited for the offer. It was only about 10 per cent less than the sum he had asked, and Lipchitz, stunned, mumbled his satisfaction and thanks. The visitor handed him his card. Lipchitz insists that he had never heard the name before.

He was therefore somewhat worried when Barnes, instead of waving the checkbook, casually asked him to ship the pieces to Merion, transportation collect, and promised to send a check on their arrival. Lipchitz was in a dilemma. "Albert C. Barnes, Merion, Pennsylvania" meant no more to him than "John Doe, Niles, Indiana." Should he part with so much of his work to a total stranger in a far-off country? . . . He shook hands on the deal and they all went to a café to celebrate it. Barnes could not yet speak French (Guillaume commanded a fluent English): he matched his half-forgotten German with the sculptor's three-quarters Yiddish-German.

Artist friends were looking on, and when Barnes left rather abruptly they mobbed Lipchitz. They didn't let him tell his story—*they* told *him* all about Barnes: what they wanted was an introduction. Anxious to get back to the apartment to tell his wife the good news, Lipchitz took the whole gang along. With his last francs, he got some bottles of cheap wine and they drank toast after toast "to Dr. Barn-ès of Merion, Pennsylvania." While the party was going on, the doorbell rang and a woman left a note from Barnes inviting Lipchitz to dinner. They were to meet at Paul Guillaume's gallery at 5 o'clock.

When the artist arrived, everybody bowed to him and kowtowed to him, for although the slogan "nothing succeeds like success" was made in America, it is very good French, too.

Barnes was sitting on the floor of the back room studying Cret's blueprints of his museum. Pointing to twelve niches in the plans, he asked Lipchitz to give him an estimate on stone sculptures to fill them. The artist's new-won wealth had gone to his head and he allowed himself the luxury of saying honestly that he thought his style would not be compatible with that of the building. If he had had the opportunity of discussing the project with the architect before construction had started . . . "No matter!" said Barnes. "By ten o'clock tomorrow morning I want you to give me your estimate; and now we will go out to dinner."

It was a fabulous dinner—the first of many fabulous dinners the artist was to have with his patron. And every course tasted more wonderful because of that slip of paper in his pocket, for when they had left the gallery

Barnes said, "I was foolish to tell you to wait for payment until your things arrived in Merion," and handed
Lipchitz a check in full payment.

Afraid that he had angered Barnes in hesitating to
accept his commission, Lipchitz swiftly changed his tack.
He would undertake the work, he said, if he were allowed
complete freedom in choice of subject and style—a condition Barnes immediately agreed to, as he had given Cret
a free hand in the design of the building. That night
Lipchitz stayed up late, figuring, with his wife, the size
of his pieces, the cost of stone, the hours of labor required. . . . The next morning he had a contract. It was
arranged that as soon as a piece was finished, Lipchitz
would send it on to Merion and receive payment. (It must
have been a year or two later that Mrs. Barnes had Lipchitz create several "garden pieces," a genre almost
monopolized by conventional sculptors.)

On the same day that he received his commission,
Lipchitz believes, Barnes was struck by a painting they
saw in Guillaume's show window: *Le Patissière*. The
pastry cook was portrayed by a disintegrative but not un-
sympathetic eye. The drawing was distorted but strong;
the color was subtly applied in vivid inlays. Barnes had
never heard of the artist, Chaïm Soutine; outside of a
small circle of advance-guard artists and critics, few people
had.

Barnes was eager to see more of Soutine's work. According to Lipchitz, he and Pascin and perhaps Guillaume
accompanied him to the Zborowski Gallery. According
to the French critic Raymond Cogniat, who has written a
monograph on the artist, it was Guillaume who took him
there. According to Abraham Walkowitz, it was Alfred
Maurer. How many cities aspired to be the birthplace of
Homer?

Cogniat specifies that it was on the first of January, 1923, that Barnes appeared at the gallery. The artist had recently come up from Ceret, in the south of France, with what Cogniat, a *friendly* critic, called "hallucinatory baggage"—a hundred of the most despairing landscapes, *"exaspérés comme un délire."* It was these, and other, canvases which were exposed to Barnes's view. None of the paintings he owned, not even the Van Goghs, could have prepared him for the work of Soutine.

Did Barnes perceive the powerful art underlying the torment, or was he in part influenced by one or more of those present that this was a talent of a remarkable order? Lipchitz accompanied Barnes on many of his purchasing expeditions in the next few years, and he says that Barnes made up his mind quickly, knowing just why he bought or rejected a painting. Yet he implies plainly enough that Barnes observed him as he expressed his enthusiasm for, or remained indifferent to, the masterpieces the dealers brought out. "Although the Doctor never asked and I never gave advice, I assume that he found me useful or he would not have had me as his constant attendant."

Barnes may have seen something unusual in Soutine (not all the pictures were really hallucinatory); he respected the high opinion of the artist entertained by those close to him; and he decided to take a flier when he saw that he could do so at bargain-basement rates. He put in his bid not for one or three or five but for the lot. How many did that include? Cogniat says one hundred canvases, but Robert Carlen, the Philadelphia art dealer, says that Barnes told him he bought sixty of them at $50 apiece. At any rate Cogniat agrees that the purchase came to $3,000.

Leopold Zborowski was not a shrewd dealer—he was neither shrewd nor a dealer by choice, but a poet who

shared his meager income with his friends Soutine and
Modigliani, and had their pictures on his hands. He was
willing to sell cheap because he had yet to sell a single
Soutine; and the artist was willing to sell cheap for the
same reason and because he needed a sign of recognition
as much as he needed money.

At the rate of exchange then, $3,000 amounted to
60,000 francs, and Soutine, normally half-mad from ulcers,
could have deliriously imagined them to be prewar francs
when Zborowski handed them to him. What in the world
could he do to celebrate? He ran into the street and
hailed a cab. "Where to?" said the cabby. "Where to? why
not the Riviera? Nice!" said Soutine. "That's a long way
from here," said the driver dubiously. Soutine flashed his
roll; the taxi dropped his flag. Mile after mile Soutine
luxuriated in the thought of his good fortune, and when
the six-hundred-mile trip was over he parted with the
$100 fare with pleasure. When he came back to Paris
he began to sport ties which cost, he bragged, 300 francs.
These and the taxi ride were, like his patron's fox hunting, flamboyant gestures of farewell to poverty and ob-
scurity. Barnes's purchase set an example for other collectors. With his pictures selling quickly and a more steady
patron than Barnes to sustain him, Soutine was free to
live out his fevered life painting in unquiet peace.

Zborowski had also not sold any of his Modiglianis up
to this time. Not even the artist's sensational life and his
death at thirty-six from tuberculosis brought on by dis-
sipation, nor the suicide of his mistress when she learned
of it, had aroused interest in his painting. The tempestu-
ousness of the Russian and Russian Jew was evident in
Soutine's work; in Modigliani's, the discipline of Italian
and African Negro art was in firm control. His stormy
life went on outside of it; the Sephardic Jew in him was

submerged. This work, poles apart from that of Soutine, also appealed to Barnes, and he became one of the discoverers—some say *the* discoverer—of Modigliani, the first buyer of his paintings.

For good measure Barnes bought fourteen pleasant little water colors by Alexis Gritchenko from Zborowski and Guillaume. (The artist was traveling in Greece at the time, but he was present the following summer when Barnes bought three more of his sketches from Guillaume. As Barnes spoke in English, Gritchenko asked Guillaume what he was saying. The dealer answered, laughing, "Oh, he says that you have no talent.")

In January and February, Guillaume held an exhibition of seventy-five modern works purchased by Barnes on that trip. Although it might have been only a shrewd dealer's way of flattering his client without seeming to, the show was—it is easy to see now—a splendid group of paintings and sculpture worth any gallery's space. Barnes wrote soon after that it aroused "extraordinary interest . . . among artists and the public" and became "a matter of international news." That is to say, Philadelphia newspapers received two cables about it—not, one may guess, from the Associated Press but from one who had a keener sense for art news. Neither Barnes nor Guillaume could have anticipated that the exhibition was to have a profound effect on his life.

10

The Prophet at Home

"DR. BARNES HAS JUST LEFT PARIS," GUILLAUME REPORTED
in the January issue of *Les Arts à Paris,* a magazine which
had some notable contributors writing on art generally
but which was essentially his house organ. "He was here
three weeks, spending every minute of it not in social
calls, parties, official receptions, but only as this man
knows how to make the most of his time—this extraordinary, democratic, ardent, irresistible, unbeatable, charming,
impulsive, generous, unique man."

On these wings of song, Barnes arrived home late in
January, and an exhilarating time lay ahead of him. His
cables had been read, and now his artist friends Arthur
Carles and Henry McCarter asked him to bring the
Guillaume exhibition intact to the Pennsylvania Academy.
As a loyal Philadelphian, avid for the approval, for the
applause, of his fellow citizens, Barnes agreed.

124

He had meanwhile given Forbes Watson, editor of *The Arts,* permission to make the first public announcement of the establishment of the Barnes Foundation: this appeared in the January issue of the magazine. *The New York Times* picked it up; *The New Republic* asked Barnes to do an article on the Foundation. In his letter to Watson, he amplified, awkwardly, what he had said before to the Glackenses: "Primarily the hope is that every person, of whatever station in life, will be allowed to get his own reactions to whatever the Foundation has to offer, that means that academism, conformity to worn-out conditions, counterfeits in art, living and thinking, can have no place in the intended scope of the Foundation."

Watson played up the event for all that it was worth. In the January and February issues he wrote and profusely illustrated two articles on the collection. In another article Cret explained the design features of the museum: it was to have twenty-three exhibition rooms of moderate and varied size to avoid monotony, grouped around a large central gallery. In April there was a study of Glackens based on the little-known pictures Barnes owned, which included many of his best. In his comment on the collection as a whole, Watson wrote:

Many of these paintings are of a sort that are not generally taken for granted by the large public. . . . The fact that many people are likely to be nonplussed, on their first introduction to this collection, only shows how much we need such a museum as the proposed one at Merion. And it is not at all a bad scheme to have this just a little off the beaten track. It gives people a chance to show a little energy in their desire to enjoy art.

In the well-considered foreword Barnes wrote for the catalog of the Academy exhibition, he took note of the first point in this passage. First he explained that most of the works on view were executed by

artists now living in Paris but who were born and spent their youth in other countries—Russia, Poland, Italy, Spain, Bulgaria, Lithuania, Belgium. The work is a product of the influence of the French environment upon cultures and endowments racially and radically foreign to France. Perhaps that explains why the exhibit differs in certain significant phases from any held previously in this country. All of the artists represented, except Modigliani, are living, and all are under thirty-five years of age, except Picasso, Matisse and Derain.

All fresh art, all art in a new idiom, seems strange, he went on, citing the case of a Schönberg piece which outraged press and public when it was first played by Stokowski and the Philadelphia Symphony Orchestra and was applauded by much the same audience and critics eight years later. The change was effected by a process of education, by hearing other new music until the ears and minds of the listeners were prepared to hear something different from the idiom of Mozart and Beethoven. He anticipated therefore that "both the paintings and the sculpture will probably seem strange to most people."

To loosen their prejudices, he assured them that the painters they were looking at all knew the great artists of the past

through enraptured, assiduous studies in the galleries of Europe [and that], these moderns are as individual in their expressions of what they believe constitute the essentials of plastic art as are any of their predecessors. That entitles their work to respect and attention. . . . These young artists speak a language which has come to them from the reaction between their own traits, the circumstances of the world we all live in, and the experience they themselves have had. . . . To quar-

rel with them for being different from the great masters is
about as rational as to find fault with the size of a person's
shoes or the shape of his ears. If one will accord to these
artists the simple justice of educated and unbiased attention,
one will see the truth of what experienced students of painting
all assert: that old art and new art are the same in fundamental principles. The difference lies only in the degree of
greatness, and time alone can gauge that with accuracy.

As time goes, 1923 is only a middle-aged man's remove
from his youth. In the American art world, it is antiquity.
Ten years had passed since the Armory show, but the
Museum of Modern Art, which now seems to have always
been with us, was not yet in existence. It was only in
1921 that the Metropolitan Museum of Art had given its
first exhibition of modern French art—a brilliant show,
but it had met with sharp criticism. The year before,
Philadelphia had seen a similar exhibition of Impressionists and Postimpressionists drawn from private collections
in the city. Some of these collectors were also helping
young artists, and there were many exhibitions in the city.
"Philadelphia, or at least a charming and delightful part
of Philadelphia," R. Sturgis Ingersoll has written, became paint-conscious. On Friday and Saturday nights
parties were given in various homes at which "the painters,
the musicians, the Museum people, and amateurs of one
sort or another, mixed in a cheerful belief that something
was happening." The 1920 exhibition was an expression
of that belief.

For the time and place, it was a "modern" show. What
Barnes was bringing to the Academy was, by comparison,
ultramodern. Barnes's careful, reasonable statement was
lost on the people who walked into the exhibition on
April 11 and every day for four weeks thereafter. Lacking
all previous experience of the sort of painting and sculp-

ture to which they were now exposed, they received a
shock which mere words of explanation could not relieve.
The newspaper critics were hardly more understanding.

In the *Inquirer,* C. H. Bonte referred to "the frequently
indescribable curiosities" in the show and in particular to
Soutine's "seemingly incomprehensible masses of paint,
known as landscapes. Some of the pictures of alleged human
beings might serve as illustrations to Gorky's gay and
optimistic masterpiece of dramaturgy, *The Lower Depths.*"
Dropping his irony, Bonte summoned up enough "educated and unbiased attention" to be able to find that "in
a vague way Matisse here [in *Joy of Living*] does not
seem very far removed from Botticelli," that the Picasso
Composition (also known as *Peasants and Oxen*) was
"only moderately bizarre" and "by no means unattractive,
especially in color and design," and that there was something good to be said, with reservations, for Utrillo, Pascin,
Derain and Kisling. Oddly, Bonte awarded his greatest
praise to Hélène Perdriat's *Idyl,* an arrangement of two
dressed and two nude female figures which at this remove
seems chicly mannered.

The task of Miss Edith W. Powell, of the *Public Ledger,*
was a painful one. Not only had she seen the collection
many times—she also looked on Barnes himself almost as a
father. But there had not been any Soutines in Merion
before and it was his paintings which outraged her most.
Concurrently with the Barnes works, the Academy was
holding an exhibition of the paintings of Charles Willson
Peale, Rembrandt Peale and James Peale. Unimagina-
tively, Miss Powell took the obvious tack of wondering
what the Peales would have thought about the Soutine
portraits "of the dregs of humanity," the alleged portrait
of Joseph Pennell (she knew what he really looked like)

or the self-portrait. Not that the landscapes were not also puzzling. . . .

"To us, Soutine represents the falling to pieces of old concepts. He may be mad, he may be an outcast, and being a Russian he may be morbid, emotional and un-literal, but he presents life as he sees it. . . . The question is, Are we willing to look at the world with his eyes . . . even if it seems to us diseased and degenerate? Is it a good thing to visit morgues, insane asylums and jails? Even if we know what is inside?" Though Miss Powell found the Perdriat canvas "undeniably gratifying as de-sign, pattern and line," she believed that Charles Willson Peale, broad-minded as he was, "could not have under-stood how even a Parisienne could paint this canvas with the insidious in its exquisiteness." What she was troubled by in general was "the unabashed presentation, and even flouting, of the unmentionable," which in the Perdriat work in particular was the pubic hair. "Is it desirable? We do not encourage every impulse to self-expression."

In *The North American,* Dorothy Grafly had one word for "the art of the rabid modernists"—uncleanness.

It is as if the room were infested with some infectious scourge. . . . The fevered passion [of the artists] for unclean things! In landscape or figure study, the same uncleanness persists. The vivid colors used by Matisse, clean in themselves, are in the hands of others deteriorating, rotting, becoming muddied with filth.

The sculpture Miss Grafly found "less revolting," but, sharing the taste of her sculptor father, she could not but feel that it was a blind alley, "with its emphasis upon problems" and disregard for the realistic representation of the human figure. In general, she declared, "The modern-ist lacks subtlety, delicacy, or finesse."

Before the critics had written their reviews, Arthur Carles had tried to explain that *Joy of Living* was interesting for its rhythm and color arrangement. Miss Grafly quoted him, but she could not accept the reduction of the human figure to a rhythmic element, just as Bonte missed "plausible human beings" and did not realize that the color and design he praised in the Picasso canvas were not incidentals but the artist's central concern. Nor did the critics follow him when, to illustrate the point that any subject could be the motive for a work of art, he said that he could appreciate the beauty in the massing of freight cars after a wreck. That, said Miss Grafly,

is the clue to the situation. The modernists appreciate a wreck, human or otherwise. It is the "modernist" in us which will draw us to see blood stream into the gutters after an accident, or watch the parts of a mangled human being gathered into a basket. We may not go home and paint our sensations. It requires courage or bravado for a man to exhibit his depravity in public.

Did a mere layman without diploma cry *depravity*? A group of doctors, psychologists and alienists headed by Dr. Francis X. Dercum stated publicly that

the artists who painted such things were either crazy or moral degenerates. . . . The works represent . . . ghastly lesions of the mind and of the body. . . . The work of insane persons who lean toward art . . . are far superior to the alleged works of art I saw at the exhibition. . . .

The innocent paintings of the Impressionists a generation before had been branded by Dr. Max Nordau as "degenerate." Critics, like other people, have always missed the point of a new idiom in art. Barnes must have known that even Leo Stein had at first viewing disliked

the *Joy of Living,* and Edith Glackens said right out loud
that she found Soutine repellent. (Probably agreeing with
her, Glackens did not express any opinion, observing his
own dictum that "artists say the silliest things about
painting.") And in his foreword Barnes himself had fore-
seen the probability of the adverse reaction to the exhibition. Yet, when it came, he could not take it in stride.

The exhibition was not a failure. For the moment, it
had more to say to young artists, who returned to the
show time and again, than to the general public, but it
was also a necessary, if painful, primer for the education of
critics and public. Instead of taking pleasure in having
performed this useful function, Barnes chose, or could
not help choosing, to take offense at "his" detractors: he
behaved, not as if he merely owned the pictures, but as
if he had painted them. In an artist, anger is a natural
defense of the pride of creation; in a collector, it is only
the hurt pride of possession.

Barnes threatened to drive the critics out of the city.
Especially angry with Miss Powell, he wrote her a letter
which unnerved her. She would never be a real art critic,
he said, until she had had relations with the iceman, and
he went into explicit details. Having a high regard for
him still ("he has such big psychology books"), Miss Powell
said to her sister critic and confessor, "Do you think there's
something in the iceman idea?" She left soon after for a
long stay in Paris. Miss Grafly was made of sterner stuff:
she is still active in Philadelphia art journalism, and no
doubt smiles at her youthful judgment.

To "answer" the statements of the doctors was futile:
the foreword to the catalog had said everything that an
intelligent man could say. Barnes could only resort to
ad hominem thrusts. He offered to give the Philadelphia
Symphony Orchestra $100,000 if Dr. Dercum could prove

that his criticism was not evidence of the very abnormal qualities he read into the paintings. Further:

Who, pray, seriously interested in the science of normal and abnormal psychology has ever heard of them? I have one of the most complete libraries in this country on normal and abnormal psychology and nowhere can I find any of their names recorded. If any of them will qualify, say, at the next meeting of the American Psychological Society, as grounded in the fundamentals of psychology or aesthetics, I shall give to the city of Philadelphia my entire collection of paintings and a suitable gallery to house them. [Failing to submit to this test, they should be content with] the inevitable of fireside, slippers and silence.

But irony and ridicule were not cathartic. Irony was the falsetto voice of disappointment; ridicule the leashed voice of fury.

What had provoked them still rankled, demanding stronger action than words. If he could not physically reach the critics of the press, he could drive the critical out of his own temple. "To have honest painters in my house and talk to them about my pictures"—that came to a sudden end. "Along with several others," one of the best-known painters wrote me, "I received out of the blue a number of vilifying letters." Barnes seems to have been paying them off for past candors.

At the same time he excluded newspapermen as a class, though his hostility to them antedated the Academy show. Three years previously, when she first became a reporter, Miss Grafly had had a letter of introduction to him from Glackens, who was a friend of her father's. Barnes received her in friendly fashion, showed her the pictures hung all over the house, including the bathroom: she had a pleasant, stimulating time. Hardly had she reached home when a special delivery letter caught

up with her. It was from Barnes, warning her not to
write a line about what she had seen or heard. Trivial in
itself, the incident suggests Barnes's attitude toward the
press and gives point to the statement of Harold Wiegand,
editorial writer of the Philadelphia *Inquirer:* "He soon
developed into quite a pest in the newspaper offices because of his frequent and unprintable letters to the editor
and his assertions that he was being misquoted."

Rejected artists and rejected newspapermen formed the
"Barnes Club"—a symbolic club without initiation fee,
dues or headquarters: the only requirement for membership was that one be *persona non grata* to Barnes. Miss
Grafly says that "almost anyone who was anyone in the
art world of the 1920's and 1930's belonged to it."

But the greatest consequence of the harsh reaction to
the exhibition at the Academy—Barnes's drastic revenge
—was not to become apparent for another year, when the
Foundation opened—half-opened—its doors.

11

Preparations

SINCE THE FOUNDATION WAS GOING TO BE AN EDUCATIONAL institution, Barnes was seeking the criteria which his article, "How to Judge a Painting," had failed to provide. While his ideas were crystallizing, he had begun to think of a staff. Perhaps on impulse, as he read an article by Francis Hackett in *The New Republic,* then in the first lively decade of its existence, Barnes got in touch with him at the end of January or early February, 1922. He was one of the many admirers of Hackett's brilliant book reviews and essays and was delighted when the editor-writer agreed to come to Merion to listen to his offer.

Hackett did not come alone. With him was his Danish-born wife, Signe Toksvig, who was also a writer.

Barnes took to Hackett personally and made all the greater effort to persuade him to join him. He unfolded his plans for a great educational center which would bring a true understanding of art to the whole country. The Foundation was going to spread its ideas in its own journal and books, so that the opportunities for a gifted writer would be unlimited.

While the men were having a lively and amicable discussion, the wives were engaged in flat desultory talk. Miss Toksvig tried to leaven it, but she found Mrs. Barnes unresponsive and she was not used to being a monologist. The silences became oppressive. Resentful in the first place at having been shunted away from the company of the men, and feeling that Mrs. Barnes had been completely suppressed, Miss Toksvig wondered how *she* would get along with the master. Barnes is said to have subscribed to the notion that marriage is a cheap and wholesome substitute for prostitution. Miss Toksvig didn't have to know that to hate him.

By the end of the visit Hackett was very much interested in Barnes's proposal. As a matter of form, he said he would sleep on it. Barnes thought he was as good as signed up. But Hackett's wife went to bed with him on the proposal, and she made it plain that if he joined Barnes he was inviting divorce proceedings. Being very much in love with her, he turned the offer down.

It is said that Barnes did not accept the answer matter-of-factly as one of two possible answers. When he made a man a good proposition, the answer should be yes; and he angrily declared that he would turn loose the four hundred "detectives" of his company (agents checking infringements on Argyrol?) to investigate the private lives of the editors of *The New Republic*. If they were caught with the goods, the magazine would come tumbling down. The implication was that in self-protection they should throw out Hackett. . . . The picture must be slightly caricatured, for Hackett broke abruptly with the magazine within weeks while Barnes published an article in it a year later, shortly before the exhibition at the Academy. (This described the Foundation as an outgrowth of the educational project in the factory. It was a sober straightforward piece, except for this statement: "No dealer, expert, or similar person has been consulted in the choice of any of the works in the collection." Concede that he had not "consulted" Guillaume: what of the purchases Glackens had made, with an assist from Alfred Maurer? One can only suppose that if the question were raised, Barnes would have said that an *artist* was not similar to a dealer or expert.)

At a banquet many years after, a man who had known Hackett intimately sat next to Barnes. "I tried to take him into my establishment," Barnes told his neighbor. "I'd have made a man of him. But he had a wife, a bitch, a man bitch, who yanked him around by the balls. It was a shame and a sin, a real man yelling with a clutch on his balls."

Having failed to sign up Hackett, Barnes turned to John Dewey, who was to become educational director of the Foundation, for recommendations among his former graduate students. Laurence Buermeyer, who had been instructor in philosophy at Princeton for several years, was his first selection, for he was well grounded in the general field of aesthetics.

Barnes himself was more immediately concerned with painting. By this time he was seeing paintings more steadily for their aesthetic values rather than their pictorial content, and he was trying to arrive at their basic elements. While he was still uncertain about them, he was eagerly investigating other people's ideas. Having bought three of Benton's paintings, he invited the artist to Merion, and he was impressed by his intelligence.

Benton was not only articulate (he found Barnes halting in oral disputation) but had some original notions on the analysis of paintings: concepts such as rhythms of surface and rhythms of depth; convexities and hollows; and a single viewpoint in extended space organization. These were tentative ideas for developing a system of teaching and comparative analysis of the structure of paintings—Barnes's major interest at this time. Whatever the value of his ideas, Benton expressed them clearly, without pretension or obscurantism, and related them directly to the pictures before them. Barnes was so impressed that he commissioned Benton to prepare analyses of certain paintings in the collection.

The artist was delighted. Finding Barnes friendly, even kindly, he looked forward to a long pleasant relationship with his enlightened patron, began to hope that his struggle to make a living was at an end.

In late spring, just before Barnes left for Paris, the two met again and parted on the best of terms.

About a month later, Benton received a harsh, insulting letter from Barnes. Why? The artist had seen him blow up (interpreting this as compensation for his inarticulateness in argument with his intellectual equals—he was fluent enough with inferiors). But the explosion had soon spent itself and Benton could regard it indulgently: who else had bought and paid for three of his paintings? He had never seen Barnes nurse his anger as he did in that letter from Paris. Benton never discovered why Barnes wrote it. It contained no explanation; it simply told him off.

Possible explanations depend on a date. Benton thinks he last saw Barnes in the spring of 1922. In that case one must suppose that, in talking freely and frankly to Barnes as he did, he said something which Barnes did not at once realize ran counter to his own beliefs. But it is as hard to believe Barnes was so obtuse as it is to discover what that offending opinion might have been. The trouble with supposing a difference of opinion is that it requires us to assume that, after breaking off personal relations with Benton, Barnes would have been capable of praising his work as he did in the Academy exhibition catalog *the following year:*

Corot has never revealed to me a composition as satisfying to a critical analysis as is the composition in a painting by a young American, Thomas Benton. But to compare Corot at his best with Benton would be an offense to the exquisite sense of values, the fine intelligence which created the forms in Benton's picture.

In the early 1920's, in reaction to the unjust underrating of American art which had long prevailed, even discerning critics were overpraising every new promising artist, particularly those who were exploring new geographical areas of the country rather than new areas of painting. Many people shared Barnes's high opinion of the Missourian Benton, considering him, in his use of high color and distortion for purposes of design, an advance-guard artist. In the perspective of Paris, however, his stature diminished.

Barnes's change of mind was probably not self-starting. At Paul Guillaume's temple, where, Barnes wrote, he had an unforgettable conversation with the English critic Roger Fry, he also had a "memorable argument" with the French critic Waldemar George which "lasted an entire afternoon. Before it was finished I had learned something about one phase of modern painting that I had never been able to understand from volumes of writing." (This was still Barnes the Explorer, generously acknowledging his intellectual debts.) Thereafter he spent a good deal of time with George, and most likely showed him (and Guillaume and some of his artist friends) the catalog of the Academy show, and they probably read those two sentences about Corot and Benton with astonishment.

Apparently Barnes had still been thinking of Corot as the painter of the feathery landscapes he knew from his pre-Glackens collecting days. His friends must have made him aware now that modern painters and critics had re-evaluated Corot on the strength of his architectonic Italian landscapes and of his figure paintings, in which beautiful drawing and color were infused with all the warmth of his generous nature. Guillaume in fact sold Barnes a fine Corot figure piece on this trip. At the same time, Barnes was made aware that his high opinion of Benton was unwarranted.

Shocked that he had been so wrong in his comparative evaluation, Barnes could have—should have—kicked himself. Instead, feeling that he had been taken in (doubly taken in if he had changed his mind about the value of Benton's analyses as well), he followed a form of behavior antedating its description in his "big psychology books"—he chose to kick Benton.

Furious himself, all that Benton could do by way of retaliation—and it was only partly that—was to write an article, "Form and the Subject," for *The Arts,* in which he deplored insignificant subject matter, such as Cézanne's apples and napkins. Barnes was at about the same time writing, apropos of a Cézanne composition of bathers, that "the subject is not essential." Benton declared that Cézanne, Renoir and their followers had nothing to give the younger generation of artists. They would seek larger conceptions, "more compelling themes, and these will demand a better and more intense form . . ."

Barnes read everything; he must have read this article;

and like many others he may have thought that Benton was belittling the whole art of the French masters, which was very far from his intention. Even if he understood that Benton meant that their painting idioms were not suitable for the oncoming generation of artists, one can readily imagine that he felt justified in breaking his short-lived relationship with his protégé.

He had made one—no, two mistaken judgments. But he was learning—he was still learning.

Waldemar George has written me an account of a typical day they spent together. At nine o'clock in the morning George would pick Barnes up at his hotel—the Mirabeau, on the Rue de la Paix. Often there was a crowd of artists and courtiers on the sidewalk hoping for a sign of his favor.

We would take in five to ten museums and private collections, going to the Louvre, the Musée Guimet (which houses the art of the Far East), the Musée Ethnographique (which displays pre-Columbian, African Negro and Oceanic art, and the Musée Cernuschi, perhaps to study archaic Chinese sculpture. We would then make the rounds of antique dealers like Malban, who specialized in Chaldean and Egyptian art, and galleries and studios, visiting especially Louis Marcoussis and Lipchitz. In summer we would dine at the Pré Catelan in the shade of the century-old trees of the Bois du Bologne.

Paul Guillaume and his young wife were always with us. Towards eleven o'clock at night Barnes would ask them to open up their gallery on the Rue la Boëtie, which had long been closed and which we got into via the service entrance. We stayed there till a late hour of the night looking at the African Negro sculptures and the paintings of Soutine. Sometimes Barnes asked Guillaume to call up some young artist and have him come over to explain his picture, to justify

certain color relationships or some linear rhythm. I didn't care
for his pedantry, but I did admire his boldness.

Barnes was also learning from the printed page. There
were now magazines of a different order from the ones
he had criticized in his *Arts & Decoration* article. In particular, he was a close reader of *The Dial,* the most
sophisticated magazine of arts and letters not limited to
one issue which had yet appeared in this country. *The
Dial* published a great deal of art criticism and reproductions of a wide variety of paintings, sculpture, drawings and other mediums, with a frontispiece in full color.
It was wonderfully receptive to new talent.[1] It was a
source of leads for new artists and fresh ideas, and Barnes
read the magazine thoroughly; and as a constant reader
he ventured to write sharply to the editor, Scofield Thayer,
when he did not like some article or reproduction.

In the spring of 1923, Thayer was in Paris, and Barnes
called on him at the Ritz, perhaps by appointment. In
any case, he barged into the room without having himself
announced and, foregoing preliminary pleasantries with
either Thayer or Gilbert Seldes, then managing editor
of the magazine, who happened to be there, he began a
loud and vigorous tirade against the critical writing in
The Dial.

Seldes, who gives me this story, thinks he concentrated
his fire on its art criticism. Thomas Craven was writing
most of the articles on art subjects; Henry McBride was
doing a monthly article on art developments in Paris; and
that year Roger Fry had been a contributor. Seldes is

[1] The author once walked into *The Dial* office cold, unknown to
the editors, with some woodcuts by a foreign artist unknown in
this country. In a few minutes they said they would reproduce one
of the pictures; in a few days they sent a check for the artist.

not sure, however, that Barnes mentioned any of them, though he was later to attack both Fry and Craven. The one man Barnes denounced, Seldes positively recalls, was Paul Rosenfeld, who was then writing a monthly "Musical Chronicle" for *The Dial*.

Apparently Barnes disliked this as much as the art criticism Rosenfeld was to write, and for the same reason —its impressionistic lyrical style, which was poles apart from his own analytical approach. The precise nature of Barnes's diatribe at the Ritz is perhaps less important than his climactic exclamation: the trouble with *The Dial* —whose contributors that year included Sherwood Anderson, Van Wyck Brooks, Benedetto Croce, T. S. Eliot, David Garnett, Knut Hamsun, Bertrand Russell, Edmund Wilson—was that there were too many Jews in it! Barnes had made the exciting discovery of Soutine and Modigliani; he was seeing Lipchitz constantly; he was on the best of terms with Kisling, Pascin and the Steins—all Jews. Was he really anti-Semitic or had he, in his intemperance, merely reached for the nearest weapon, an ancient but still serviceable poisoned arrow, suggested by the name Rosenfeld?

Seldes heard of an unusual episode in Barnes's collecting career which took place at this time in the studio of Nathalie Gontcharova and Michel Larionov.

Even before World War I, not in Paris but in Moscow, these two artists had been experimenting in an abstract idiom. In the 1920's Gontcharova was well-known in Paris for her stage settings and other decorative work; *The Dial* had reproduced her *Espagnole* in the August, 1922, issue; and it was her things which Barnes wanted to see. Larionov, who had been ill for several months, was present but took no part in the conversation. Barnes looked over many pieces, setting aside a few for possible purchase. But he forgot them all when he caught sight of "something special"—Seldes thinks it may have been a painted screen—and asked Gontcharova what she wanted for it. She said she had made it especially as a gift for Larionov and couldn't sell it. Nothing daunted, Barnes made a handsome offer. The couple needed the money badly, yet Gontcharova's pride held firm. Barnes doubled his price. She repeated that it was made for Larionov and she wouldn't sell it. Barnes raised his bid. Larionov couldn't stand it any longer and ran out of the room. "Barnes kept piling up offer on offer until Gontcharova drove him out of the studio."

Jacques Lipchitz recalls a very different kind of story. As noted before, Barnes often had the sculptor with him on his buying expeditions. He would inform Lipchitz of his coming in advance, and Lipchitz would look forward to another holiday among the great Renoirs, Cézannes and Matisses Barnes was still acquiring. They had become such good friends that Lipchitz ventured to suggest that he ought to supplement his collection with old masters; Barnes did not take umbrage at the suggestion as he had when Berenson had made it. But that had been more than a decade before and Barnes had come a long way since then.

Lipchitz was with Barnes the time he bought a great many fine and high-priced paintings at one gallery. At the end of the session, the sculptor was thinking of the fabulous dinner to come, for Barnes always took him to some superior restaurant which he, for all his long years in Paris, had never heard of. Wanting to relax after the long day of concentration and confinement, Barnes proposed that they walk back to his hotel. As they were pass-

ing one of the Potin stores, a quality food chain, Barnes
decided to buy some honey for his wife. They resumed
their homeward walk; the hotel was almost in sight when
some fearful emotion, the cause of which he was perhaps
not aware of at first, stopped Barnes. He must return the
honey! They walked back to the store, where he exchanged the tin of honey he had bought for three francs
25 centimes for a carton of honey costing three francs.
The tin would only be thrown away—why waste a penny!

The early wounds of poverty had suddenly begun to
hurt again, like an amputated leg, and he told Lipchitz
bitterly of his having had to rent cap and gown for the
commencement ceremony at the University of Pennsylvania.

To run ahead of the story: shrewd as he was, Lipchitz
did not press his advantage with Barnes. He made no
effort to sell him more of his work, and he did not introduce him to any artists except those Barnes himself
asked to meet. Lipchitz had many friends, and acquaintances who tried to become his friends, if only to get
such an introduction. These he found it easy to refuse.
No matter what show of anger they might put on, he
knew—and they knew—that they would be just as chary of
introductions if they were in his place. But one day an
artist approached him whom he could not put off so
easily.

This man and his wife were both intimate friends of
the family. The wife had been ill, and at this time she
needed an operation. It was, her husband told Lipchitz,
literally a matter of life and death. Wouldn't he, just this
once, ask Barnes to look at his paintings? If he did not
buy anything, nothing was lost, but if he did buy there
would be enough money for the operation.

Lipchitz felt like a heel insisting that it would be use-less for him to approach Barnes, but his friend persisted and Lipchitz finally told him that he would sleep on it and give him a decision in the morning. He did not sleep on it—he was unable to sleep at all: he had no alternative but to take the risk of alienating Barnes. After they had spent a day together, Lipchitz put the question to him and Barnes wasn't pleased.

"Is he a good painter?" he asked.

"He is an honest painter."

Barnes grew angry. "You know what good painting is!"

Lipchitz replied that his friend's work was not unworthy of inclusion in his collection.

Barnes stayed angry; he kept on rebuking Lipchitz for trying to foist a friend on him and ascribed false motives for his act. Now Lipchitz grew angry and threw aside discretion. He pointed out that he had never asked Barnes for a single favor before. If he refused this one, he would be less than human and the sculptor's faith in him would be damaged beyond the possibility of repair. Barnes yielded. Reluctantly and ungraciously, he agreed to look at the friend's paintings. But not at his studio—let Lipchitz select four canvases and take them to his own place. Barnes promised to be there in the morning at ten.

The next morning, punctually at ten, he called on Lipchitz. The sculptor had set up the pictures in the most favorable light, and put a price tag on each one. Now he stood aside, mute, allowing Barnes to make his own decision. Looking them over in silence, he abruptly chose two, and handed Lipchitz 4,000 francs ($200). He gave instructions for shipping the paintings and left without saying another word. The next day he sailed for home.

Lipchitz was glad that he had forced Barnes's hand.

With the 4,000 francs his friend was able to arrange for an operation, and his wife went through it successfully. It saved her life.

Some six months later Barnes was in Paris again. This time, contrary to his usual custom, he had not informed Lipchitz in advance of his coming. Nor did he get in touch with him after his arrival. It was only through a dealer that Lipchitz learned that he was in the city. Standing on his pride, the sculptor did not try to look him up.

Barnes called on him eventually. Without having made an appointment, he burst into the studio and shouted, "I'll never forgive you for what you made me do! You made me confound art with philanthropy! I never want to see you again!" And walked out.

Although Guillaume, in January, had marveled how usefully Barnes spent his three weeks in Paris, avoiding social calls and public receptions, Guillaume, in October, was modestly bragging of how he had recently persuaded him to fall in with certain social conventions. He had often urged Barnes to call on the American Ambassador to France, Myron T. Herrick. Even a J. Pierpont Morgan, who could ignore conventions and governments too, had paid his respects to his country's representative. One day that fall, when Barnes arrived at the gallery in good humor, Guillaume said, "The Ambassador is expecting you in five minutes." Barnes took a cab right over. A corporation lawyer and former governor of Ohio, Herrick had been Ambassador to France when the First World War broke out and was an active participant in its reconstruction. He received Barnes so cordially and informally that Barnes told him his life story; Herrick in turn told Barnes *his* life story: they both had a good time. And as a tribute to the major interest of his guest, the Ambassador made him a little drawing on the spot.

Next, Guillaume was able to get Barnes to pay a call with him on Paul Léon, the French government's director of fine arts. Since they were to attend a formal affair later, they were dressed for that occasion, to save time, when they called on Léon. Apparently taking Barnes for some American yokel, rigged out as he was for this informal call, the director was properly bored and hardly listened to him as he told about the Foundation and its work. Léon began to yawn. Before Barnes should say something rash, Guillaume diplomatically interjected that M. le Directeur was of course thoroughly familiar with the great work being done in Merion, and hustled his friend out of the pompous presence.

The spat with the editor of *The Dial* in Paris had put the fear of God and Barnes in Scofield Thayer. When McBride in his Paris Letter included an anecdote about Gertrude Stein, Braque and Barnes—Thayer asked the writer to delete it, for fear of offending Barnes, though the magazine usually allowed its authors complete liberty. In the November, 1923, issue, he reproduced *Joy of Living*, with credit to the Foundation. In the February, 1924, issue, he published an article by Buermeyer, "Some Popular Fallacies in Aesthetics." This challenged some ideas of Roger Fry and his disciple—so Buermeyer called him—Thomas Craven. In March, Craven wrote a caustic rebuttal. In April, Buermeyer replied. . . . This was more like it; this was the way Barnes liked it.

12

The Barnes Foundation

THE FOUNDATION INFORMALLY OPENED ITS DOORS IN THE spring of 1924. Its two cream-colored limestone buildings were set in a twelve-acre park, and its collection consisted of more than seven hundred paintings, including one hundred Renoirs, fifty Cézannes, twenty-two Picassos, twelve Matisses, many Daumiers, Gauguins, Van Goghs and other masters of the French school, together with one hundred works by American artists. In addition, it had a large number of sculptures stemming from widely diverse African Negro peoples which, according to Guillaume, the Foundation classified chronologically for the first time. These are only statistics. It was the generally high quality of the collection which made art lovers look forward with such lively expectations to seeing it.

Neither at the entrance to the grounds nor on the door of the museum was there a schedule of hours of admission.

The museum was not open to the public. This was Barnes's ultimate answer to the critics, the doctors and the rest of the people who had ridiculed his pictures at the Academy. If they had been so blind to the beauty of seventy-five of them, they did not deserve entry to the seven hundred. But was he not contradicting himself— once in rescinding a public statement of policy, and again in repudiating his own idea that the only way one could learn to like new art or new music was to keep exposing oneself to it? Well then, he contradicted himself. His hurt feelings overruled his understanding.

It has been said that, by putting his money into an educational institution, Barnes avoided paying heavy income and property taxes, and the implication is that he established the Foundation merely for that purpose. But the tax on a personal income of $1,000,000 was only $80,000 at the time, and if the property tax would also have run to five figures (Barnes's estimate was $7,500), he would still have had a considerable fortune at his disposal. The deed of gift which accompanied the charter provided the Foundation with a collection valued at $5,-000,000 and an endowment of $6,000,000, consisting of 900 shares of common stock of the A. C. Barnes Company, the buildings and the twelve-acre tract they stood on.

For several years thereafter Barnes contributed $450,000 to the endowment each year. If he had had to pay taxes, the collection might not have grown to the size it did, the scale of operations might have been reduced (the cost eventually reached some $200,000 annually), but one can hardly doubt that there would have been an equivalent institution. For Barnes was seriously concerned with the problem of art education: the Foundation was to become for him the focus of a new career, and one which made him a public figure. What the Foundation enabled him

to do was to enjoy and control a collection which had
become quasi public as if it were still his own.

He hand-picked the five trustees—himself, his wife, the
Mullen sisters and Captain Joseph L. Wilson. It was
Wilson's land, with its extensive arboretum, on which
the Foundation was built. He had sold out only after long
negotiations because he was getting old, and on condition
that the arboretum, which he had developed over forty-
five years, be maintained. As a bonus, Barnes made him
director of the arboretum and attorney and trustee of the
Foundation. When Wilson died soon after, he was replaced as trustee by Albert Nulty, the former family
chauffeur. (Having shown an interest in restoring the
antiques Barnes was beginning to pick up, he was given
a chance to learn the craft, even to study abroad.) None
of the trustees would think of opposing Barnes.

The by-laws which implemented the charter revealed
the extent of his authority. During his lifetime, he was
to have "the absolute power and discretion" to sell or
exchange works of art in the collection in order to improve it. His justification for by-passing the trustees was
"that he has created said collection and best understands
what may be necessary in the way of sale or exchange to
complete it, perfect it and render it more adequate."

Furthermore, upon his death no further addition was
to be made to the collection, and no picture was ever to
be loaned, sold or otherwise disposed of unless it had deteriorated to the point where it was no longer useful. During his lifetime, no picture was to be loaned.

Nothing more clearly reveals Barnes's use of the Foundation as his personal enterprise than a by-law which was
totally irrelevant to its affairs—a by-law which provided
that the Mullen sisters and Miss Geiger were to manage

the A. C. Barnes Company for five years after the death of himself and his wife!

This was surely the handiwork of Barnes, and not of Owen J. Roberts, as it must have been his own need which made the by-laws as rigorous as engineering specifications. They concerned themselves not only with such basic matters as the conditions of admission and the procedure for selecting future trustees, but also specified that there were to be not more than two gallery attendants and two watchmen for the arboretum at a maximum salary of $2,000 a year each, and one stenographer-clerk at not more than $2,500 a year; the hiring of cleaners and janitors was "sanctioned" for a gross expenditure of $6,000 a year.

As a good Philadelphian, Barnes also imposed his wish that if the collection were ever destroyed or if it should become impossible to administer it, the property and fund of the Foundation were to be applied "to an object as nearly within the scope herein indicated . . . in connection with an existing and organized institution in Philadelphia or suburbs."

By-law 31 provided that, until the gallery was constructed, the collection was to remain in the donor's residence, without his being obligated to insure it. Even after the gallery was built Barnes did not take any insurance on the collection, for the same reasons as stated in the by-law: that it was impracticable adequately to insure the collection, and that no insurance monies could repair or replace works damaged by fire or otherwise. In this he was following the practice of the Louvre.

Engineering specifications are not laws of nature—they are subject to modification as faults are discovered. But most of the changes in the by-laws of the Foundation were made to mete out reward and punishment. Having endowed the Foundation in perpetuity, Barnes meant to govern it in perpetuity. What his chances are, in this first decade of his eternity, will become apparent in time.

The by-law which immediately concerned the public was that laying down the conditions of admission. By-law 29 stipulated that during the lifetime of Barnes and his wife the art gallery was to be open to the public *on not more than two days of the week* (except during July, August and September, when it was closed), *and only by cards of admission.* Art students were to be admitted by special arrangement. These restrictions, the by-law explained, were imposed because the art gallery was founded "as an educational experiment under the principles of modern psychology as applied to education, and it is Donor's desire during his lifetime, and that of his wife, to perfect the plan so that it shall be operative for the spread of the principles of democracy and education after the death of Donor and his wife."

Even then the gallery was to be open to the public only *three* days a week, one of them Sunday, under regulations laid down by the board of trustees. But it was to be incumbent on them "to make such regulations as will ensure that it is the plain people, that is, men and women who gain their livelihood by daily toil in shops, factories, schools, stores and similar places, who shall have free access to the art gallery upon those days when the gallery is open to the public."

To make it quite clear that the purpose of his gift was "democratic and educational in the true meaning of those words" and that special privileges were forbidden, Barnes stipulated that at no time after his death "shall there be held in any building or buildings any society functions commonly designated receptions, tea parties, dinners, banquets, dances, musicales or similar affairs." Any citizen of the Commonwealth of Pennsylvania was authorized to present a petition for injunction to the courts if reputable legal counsel found that this stipulation had been violated, and the Foundation was to pay all the legal expenses.

In Paris, Guillaume celebrated the opening of the Foundation with a special number of *Les Arts à Paris.* Barnes was represented with an article, "Negro Art and America"; Buermeyer with a translation of his essay in *The Dial;* Mary Mullen with an excerpt from "An Approach to Painting." This was a brief illustrated essay, written in simple general terms, which was probably Barnes's trial balloon—a tentative statement on the elements of painting. The Foundation had published it in 1923. Guillaume himself soared to magniloquent heights:

Historiographers and philosophers whose mission it is to record and comment on the facts and events which leave their mark on an age; those who study the evolution of thought and the assaying of aesthetic judgment, will not know how to dwell long enough on the role which the Barnes Foundation plays in the world today. . . .

This generous judgment was premature. The collection was there; the plant was there; and a staff. Barnes had appointed as Associate Director of Education another former student of Dewey's, Thomas Munro, who was teaching philosophy and economics at Columbia. Munro had only a layman's knowledge of modern art, and was more versed, like Laurence Buermeyer, in aesthetics. To Barnes, their lack of a definite point of view in the plastic arts was a virtue rather than a handicap, for it made them all the more receptive to his own ideas. Before the Foundation opened, Barnes had sent Munro—and probably Buermeyer before him—on extensive trips abroad to expand his experience of art in the museums he had himself gone to as a tyro. Barnes himself was also to lecture, and he had graduated Miss Mary Mullen from the factory. As the third Associate Director of Education, she was to apply her experience with illiterate workmen to educated but aesthetically illiterate people.

But the Foundation did not yet have any prescribed course of instruction, nor had Barnes made any definite arrangements for the admission of students—he did not even know where they were coming from. Apparently he was trying to find out how people looked at pictures before expounding his own method. Feeling his way, he first welcomed groups of professional people—lawyers, bankers, professors—together with students and faculty from the nearby colleges: Bryn Mawr, Swarthmore, Haverford, the Tyler School of Art of Temple University. Buermeyer brought student groups from Princeton. On three days a week there were large numbers of young painters studying at the Academy, and their teachers, who were all practicing artists.

Barnes did not find the results satisfactory. As Mary Mullen reported in the *Journal of the Barnes Foundation* two years later: "We made no attempt at instruction, but spent our time in observing the behavior, including the remarks, of the professors and students." "We," according to the rumormongers, included Barnes, who put on workmen's clothes and mingled with the crowd to catch their remarks—a charge he dismissed as absurd. This was not part of Miss Mullen's report. She continues: "After about four months of this experience, it was clear to everybody, including the intelligent minority of the students, that nothing of educational value came of their repeated visits." In all of the visitors she observed "the same desire to daydream in our gallery." To Barnes's analytical mind, and to the echoing minds of all his disciples, to daydream before a Renoir was as horrifying as to spit at it.

Nevertheless, the Foundation was not giving up the attempt to redeem its lay visitors. "Our object," Miss Mullen went on, "is ultimately to offer to this class of people an integration of the values created by great thinkers and great artists, with life itself." If this sounds like pretentious nonsense, it is intended to be a capsule statement of the Dewey philosophy of education which Barnes was to apply to art education. Miss Mullen wrote what she did at Barnes's suggestion, perhaps at his dictation. The student of chemistry, the co-inventor of Argyrol, could speak of her article, based as it was on intensive eavesdropping, as "a scientific study."

Although Barnes still admitted casual visitors—e.g., Miss Grace Gemberling's class of girls from Oak Lane Country Day School, who could hardly be called informed art lovers—he next looked into the possibility of working with students in the School of Fine Arts of the University of Pennsylvania. This he found to be essentially a professional school for training architects. Such courses as it gave on design and the history of painting were envisaged in relation to architecture. This was historically sound: painters today look forward to a revitalized relationship with architecture, the mother art. However, the school did not provide any courses in the appreciation of art itself, and Barnes sought to fill this gap.

Presumably the university had left such courses to the many art schools in the city, but these too were vocational; they trained artists but took the understanding of art for granted. "Prospective teachers and artists also," Barnes wrote later, "suffer through the fact that nowhere in the city, or in the state of Pennsylvania, is the subject pre-

sented in its broadly cultural relations, in the light of
modern teaching methods, psychology and art criticism.
. . . The university seemed a logical place for presenting
art in this broad way."

By now Barnes had finally crystallized his own method
of analyzing paintings. The "plastic elements" he set forth
sharply modified those of *An Approach to Painting*.
(Strangely, the Foundation continued to publish Miss
Mullen's book, and still does.) Barnes offered to subsidize
a year's course on modern painting, one hour a week,
under Munro, who would illustrate—and validate—his
lectures by the pictures in the collection. The university
accepted his offer; the course was to begin with the fall
term of 1924, with students paying the usual tuition fee
to the university and receiving academic credit.

When the arrangement was announced, some time in
May, it was attacked by Charles Grafly, who, as a conservative sculptor, teaching at the Academy, did not
believe that the university should sponsor the indoctrina-
tion of youth with a favorable view of modern art. On
May 26 the *Evening Bulletin* printed a piece under the
headline

DR. BARNES' CHARGE
STUNS ART FACULTY

What had Barnes said? Merely that he had barred certain
members of the faculty of the Academy from his gallery
because they had come "habitually in a state of profound
alcoholic intoxication." The executive secretary of the
Academy, John Andrew Meyers, said, "It is impossible to
understand why Dr. Barnes is doing this." Nor would
John Frederick Lewis, president of the Academy, comment.

Barnes's statement can only be understood as a feverish

reply to Grafly's criticism. Recall his reference in the *Arts & Decoration* article to his "lifelong" artist friend. If that may be termed beneficent exaggeration, his attack on the Academy was malignant exaggeration. Like his statement on Glackens, this too must have had a kernel of truth—say *one* member of the Academy staff was high when he visited the Foundation, say even that he was dead drunk. Even though Grafly's criticism was strictly his own and not at all official, it was all the excuse Barnes needed to lash back at the Academy as if it were responsible for his attack—and for the hostile reaction to his pictures hung in its halls the year before!

Mad and libelous as Barnes's statement to the press seems, no one dared to sue him for libel or openly assert that he was mad. All Philadelphia was becoming afraid of him.

Perhaps echoes of the affair reached Paris. George Biddle, who was there at the time, writes me that whenever he mentioned the fact that he came from Philadelphia, the dealers "pricked up their ears and asked me if I knew Dr. Barnes. When I told them that I had known him quite intimately they became increasingly interested, but when I added that he had the reputation of being an eccentric madman, they seemed to lose their interest in further cultivating me."

On his trip to Paris that summer, Barnes approached Waldemar George to prepare a short history of European painting embodying his own now clarified analytical method. It is likely that Barnes wanted to farm out the job not because he lacked confidence in his own writing ability, but because he wanted to be free to develop a broader program for the Foundation. George refused his offer, he says, because he did not see eye to eye with

Barnes on the treatment of the subject he proposed. Nor was George willing to accept Barnes's invitation to discuss the matter with him and his staff in Merion. According to A. H. Shaw in *The New Yorker,* George (whom he did not mention by name) wanted too much money. In any event, Shaw said Barnes then hired an American writer on a salary basis, but the arrangement did not work out. The two men quarreled; Barnes fired the writer, who sued for breach of contract; and Barnes decided to write the book himself.

He worked on it intensively while its method was being applied in Munro's class of university students, and he is said to have finished it in six months—fast work by any standard, even if he was only trying for clear exposition, not literature. The text alone was a solid four hundred pages. If Barnes dictated on the spot the analyses of individual paintings which loom large in the book, the report is almost credible. Even if the book was done in a year, it was a feat.

Published in 1925 by the Foundation, *The Art in Painting* was dedicated to John Dewey, "whose conceptions of experience, of method, of education, inspired the work of which this book is a part." It was highly praised by diverse and discriminating critics. Joseph W. Krutch called it "a distinct and important contribution"; Alfred H. Barr, Jr., "an important book because it presents a systematic and confident statement of what is central in the 'modern' attitude toward painting"; Leo Stein, "something fresh and new and thoroughly worthwhile." Although Barr found it "as ponderous as a textbook" (and "the historical errors . . . too frequent to catalog . . . but they will only trouble the pedant"), Stein thought it was "very well written, comprehensive, systematic without pedantry."

Stein did raise a valid objection which Barnes answered

in the *Journal of the Barnes Foundation*, ending with an acute but cruel personal thrust: [Stein's] "is the criticism of one who, with no conception of the problems to be met, insists on ideal solutions that emerge from confused dreams. . . . It explains why the book on aesthetics which, fifteen years ago, Mr. Stein announced as forthcoming, has never materialized."

Stein was suffering from a deep-seated neurosis which prevented him from doing a concentrated piece of work. During his entire adult life he treated himself by his own method of psychoanalysis which finally, he thought, cured him. (This was the subject of a book he was working on at the time of his death.) Even if Barnes were not aware of his friend's affliction, it would have been heartless to point up his failure. This was the inarticulate Barnes of the past paying off the Stein who had always talked him down: Look, you glib word-spinner, *I* got a book out—where's yours? Actually, Stein's *ABC of Aesthetics* may have been well under way at the time, for it appeared in print two years later. Possibly Barnes's jibe goaded him to finish it. But the personal reference in Barnes's rebuttal was all the more ungenerous because, on the back cover of an earlier issue of the *Journal*, he had quoted Stein in praise of the book!

After this there were seven lean years of friendship: Barnes refused to talk to Stein, and possibly vice versa.

The high praise won by *The Art in Painting* confirmed Barnes in the belief that he had created a bible for the Foundation and for the world. As it became the source of instruction for his classes, he felt that he was justified in excluding the general public, for they would be in the way of students and teachers, who were free to consult any particular work in the collection any time. The policy that had sprung from the darkness of vengeance now had the support of reason.

While he was still writing his book, Barnes had tried to have his system adopted by the Philadelphia Board of Public Education; for to show the young how to look at paintings would be the most effective means of raising the art standards of the country. It entailed, however, a drastic revision of the curriculum. In the high school for girls, Barnes found, mechanical rules for color relations were taught, e.g., in dressmaking. In the drawing and water-color classes, students either copied other pictures or made pictures of their own to tell a story.

The cause of this obsolete system is partly mere inertia, partly the personality and opinions of Theodore M. Dillaway, Director of Art in the Public Schools. Mr. Dillaway came from Boston and brought with him the counterfeit thinking and threadbare conceptions of art which have never been regarded by educated people as anything but the unintelligent, ritualistic mummery attendant upon a total confusion of educational and art values. His public statements and his policies indicate a complete lack of understanding either of the first principles of art or the qualities which ought to belong to a man entrusted with control over public education.

Like Grafly, Dillaway had attacked the University of Pennsylvania for sanctioning Munro's forthcoming course; modern art was demoralizing to students and repulsive to all cultured persons.

Barnes described Dillaway's own method of teaching art. He would show pupils a color gamut—say, a solar spectrum, together with a set of pictures. He would then himself play the flute, asking them "to correlate the notes with the colors and the melodies with the pictures."

Many art teachers in the public school system, Barnes said, had asked to attend classes at the Foundation, but he had hesitated to accept them because his standards were irreconcilable with those of the system. He suggested that the teachers study both standards and make a choice. If they accepted his method and *taught it in their classes,* he would admit them to the Foundation. If they jeopardized their positions by going counter to the curriculum, he would call a town meeting and put it up to the people.

Teachers are not always made in a heroic mold and Dillaway indirectly came to their rescue. He took Barnes's slap in the face like a man, offering to let the Foundation give a course of lectures to the art teachers of the school system. Buermeyer gave the series, and nine months after Barnes had written his harsh criticism of Dillaway he thanked him "for his constant and hearty cooperation in making the course a success."

Barnes's exposé, "The Shame in the Public Schools of Philadelphia," had appeared in the first issue (April, 1925) of the *Journal of the Barnes Foundation,* which thus got off to a fighting start, as the Foundation itself was formally dedicated on March 19 by John Dewey "to the cause of education." It was "accepted" by President Josiah H. Penniman and Professor Edgar A. Singer, Jr., professor of philosophy, on behalf of the University of Pennsylvania; by Dr. John J. Coss, chairman of the department of philosophy, for Columbia University; by Leopold Stokowski, on behalf of the artists of America; by the Honorable John Faber Miller, the judge who issued the charter of the Foundation, for the county; and by the Honorable Fletcher W. Stites, state senator, "on behalf of the State and the Neighborhood."

In his speech, Dewey said: "I wish to express my conviction, my most profound conviction, that we are really celebrating here today one of the most significant steps taken in this country for freedom of pictorial or plastic art, for art in education, and also for what is genuine and forward-moving throughout the whole field of education."

Other speeches were made to the audience of several hundred persons by Munro, Stokowski, Singer, Barnes and Mrs. Barnes. Telling of the development of the arboretum, to which she was now wholly devoting herself, Mrs. Barnes was for the first time emerging from the dominating flesh and shadow of her husband. Barnes's subject was naturally the purpose of the Foundation, and he must have gone into considerable detail on his analytical method, for Stokowski afterward remarked to a friend in the audience that it seemed much too formidable, that it made of art a task rather than an enjoyment. (How bizarre that Barnes had named him—merely because he was a famous man he knew?—to represent the artists of America rather than someone in the plastic-art world.) Of course Stokowski was only a layman, but then Barnes was concerned with the education of laymen as well as specialists. The conductor was symbolic of the opposition he would have to overcome.

The first issue of the *Journal* was reassuring on this score. It reported that the three books published by the Foundation—*An Approach to Art* (1923); Buermeyer's *The Aesthetic Experience* (1924); and *The Art in Painting* (1925)—were "in use in thirty-five universities and colleges from Maine to California, and in the public school systems of six important cities." They were also used as text- and reference books by the Louvre and the Metropolitan Museum of Art. The claims have something of the quality of Barnes's euphorious letters. Proof that the claims were on the rosy side came with the May issue of the *Journal,* which raised to forty the number of collegiate institutions using the Foundations publications. The increase could not have been due to anything but library purchases.

The first issue of the *Journal* announced seminars, lectures, demonstrations and classes for nonprofessional people as well as for writers, painters, and teachers of art. To take care of the expected influx, Barnes appointed another teacher, Miss Sara Carles, sister of the artist. The Foundation also offered three summer courses to be held in the art galleries of Europe under the guidance of Munro, Buermeyer and Mary Mullen. Later on the *Journal* announced advanced courses for the same types of student as well as museum officials; the availability of lectures on "Present Tendencies in Art," "Primitive Negro Sculpture," and "Modern Methods in Art Instruction" for educational institutions, societies and art clubs; and a consultation service for colleges and galleries on courses of study in plastic art.

The most enthusiastic note in an early issue of the *Journal* was evoked by a report that Professor Singer's idea of correlating various university departments "has resulted in a new alliance between the resources of the university and of the Barnes Foundation for a study of aesthetics that is unequaled in the world." Buermeyer was to give one course in connection with the university course of Dr. Louis W. Flaccus; Munro was to give another series of lectures in the same field; and the Foundation was to award scholarships to those students who showed the greatest talent for research in aesthetics.

Like most overambitious prospectuses, the Foundation's was only partly realized. The summer course in Europe apparently proved popular enough to warrant repetition: it was offered for the third time, under Munro, for a fee of $100. But the most enthusiastic project, that of Buermeyer, Flaccus and Munro, came to nothing, for the experiment with the university students already begun was not proceeding as well as Barnes had hoped.

As some of the members of those first classes recall, instruction was quite informal. Barnes would make some introductory remarks and Munro would discuss one of the plastic elements—never more than one of them in a lecture. Barnes frequently interrupted to clarify a point or to make some relevant comment of his own. Sometimes he himself gave the lecture, always in his strictly analytical method. But the words were only an adjunct to the work of art, which was there to speak for itself entire while the lecturer commented on it piecemeal. This was Barnes's deliberate intention: his method of analysis was not a form of verbal remote control but a test to be applied in the presence of the painting. Both the method and the availability of the work under discussion were novel to students from the university, and those who had the capacity for it—apparently the minority—were stimulated.

As part of the instruction also, Barnes insisted on the students standing before a single painting long enough to soak it up rather than wandering from one to another in a casual marathon as people do in museums. And some of the twenty to thirty students who made up an average class—the Misses Mullen also attended, silently—found this sustained exposure more stimulating than the analyses.

Some time after the course started Barnes complained to the university authorities of the caliber of the students. They lacked the proper background of psychology, history, science and literature; they didn't know the meaning of such fundamental terms as "instinct" and "perception." If the officials thought his prerequisites for a course in art appreciation excessive, they nevertheless arranged with the department of philosophy to send Munro students who had also taken courses in psychology.

Barnes was not satisfied with this batch of students either. They "had also acquired bad habits of thinking. . . . They had learned definitions of 'unity,' 'variety,' 'the sublime,' etc., but they could not recognize concrete examples of these concepts when put before them." What they went in for was labeling facts and abstract argument.

Good students, bad students—not enough of either kind took advantage of the unique opportunity the Foundation offered them. Barnes therefore began to fill out the classes with any adults who seemed to him genuinely interested in art. One of these was Dr. Herman Schlaff, a dentist. Students were allowed to bring a friend on Sundays to listen to an informal talk and visit the gallery; later on there was to be music also on these occasions.

One day Schlaff telephoned his artist friend Julius Bloch and asked him to come along. Bloch, who was then teaching at the Academy and had tried to get into the gallery before, thought he was joking. But he wasn't; Bloch went with him; and there was no three-headed dog at the gate to turn him away.

That day Barnes was discoursing casually about artists, and in a derogatory way: he called most of them slobberers. Schlaff asked Bloch what he thought of the talk and the artist said he didn't care to say at the moment, since he was a guest. Barnes happened to come up behind them and Schlaff put it to him if his friend shouldn't answer the question. "Why not?" said Barnes in his gruff voice. Bloch said that he was afraid to. "I'm not that ferocious," said Barnes.

Bloch was present on another Sunday when Barnes lectured on one of Cézanne's greatest works, the version of *The Card Players* which was in his collection. At the

end he called for questions, but either nobody had any
or dared to ask. Munro put it to Bloch, who asked Barnes
to amplify his statement on line. Barnes talked for an
hour on that and afterward sought Bloch's opinion of the
talk.

The artist said that he shared Barnes's views on Cézanne.
"Where did you get your ideas about him?" "From experience." "Have you read my book?" "No." "You should."
Barnes had a copy of *The Art in Painting* brought and
handed it to Bloch. The price, he said, was six dollars,
and Bloch, though he needed the money for paints, paid
up like a gentleman.

Barnes asked him to come again the following Sunday,
and then invited him to join the regular Tuesday class
with the university students. At the end of the year Barnes
inquired if he had paid the $50 tuition fee (to the
university). "No, what fee?" "Well, if you won't say anything about it, I won't."

The regular students did not evoke his sense of humor.
Although he filled up the class with outsiders like Schlaff
and Bloch, he was still trying to increase the registration
of the university students. After considerable prodding by
Barnes, Munro's course was announced in the university
catalogs, but the response was still light. Barnes thought
that there should have been an "active follow-up" and that
there was none because the faculty was dead set against
new ideas. In the same sentence he complained, paradox-
ically, both of their "inertia" and their "open hostility"—
inertia in not urging the students to take Munro's course,
hostility in positively advising them to stay away from it.

In the early days of the course Munro suggested that a
committee be set up to arrange for better cooperation
between the faculty and the Foundation staff. The com-

mittee was formed but never met. Barnes invited its members to visit the Foundation as a group but they never came. Next he invited all the faculty advisers to discuss the work of the Foundation and only two or three attended. In the spring of 1926 Barnes extended the invitation to the entire faculty of the college, graduate and education departments, to consider a far-reaching plan of his. He did not realize that most people, including college teachers, were chiefly concerned with their own subjects, and that most college teachers, like other people, were only casually interested in art. He did not seem to have realized it even when only six persons accepted his invitation.

What Barnes proposed was to give the university— ultimately—control of the Foundation, with a subsidy to support it in perpetuity, and to provide instruction and scholarships. The offer, however, "was coupled with a frank review and criticism of the existing situation, including the organization of the School of Fine Arts." He would reorganize the school, with new courses which he would help work out and with a new head of department, though he did not insist on the immediate replacement of the incumbent. There was the plan: he asked for criticism, urged cooperation, "but absolutely nothing resulted."

He discussed it informally with a university trustee, wrote it out formally for the provost to lay before the board of trustees. This was in May. To his chagrin, to his mortification, months passed without even an acknowledgement. Finally one member of the faculty inquired about the matter, and the provost, together with the dean of the School of Fine Arts, sent what Barnes considered to be "perfunctory apologies." He couldn't accept them: was that the way to handle a project "involving millions of dollars and the entire future of the Foundation?" Even then there was no action: the whole affair was turned over for consideration to the dean, the very man who was the prime target of his criticism.

Barnes's patience was at an end. On November 27, 1926, in a letter summing up his vexations, he informed the university that he was suspending his arrangement with it. He was not, however, closing his doors to its students. Although they would now no longer receive credit, they could attend his classes tuition-free. Barnes must have come to his decision suddenly—and reluctantly, for on May 11 he had amended the by-laws of the Foundation to permit the university's students to visit the gallery on four days a week. There was a plaintive note in his letter: he had acted in good faith; he was now writing with the utmost sincerity. He honestly couldn't understand why it had not accepted his extremely generous offer: was there a university anywhere in the country, or in the world, with a collection of art remotely approaching his in quality? . . .

Priding himself on his knowledge of psychology, Barnes displayed a complete lack of knowledge of both himself and other people. He had complained of the faculty's failure to follow up the announcement of Munro's course. Do universities ever make a special effort to "sell" one course or another? His criticism of the School of Fine Arts may have had its merits, but does one publicly call for the ousting of a head of a university department? Finally, Barnes avowed in his letter that "no request of any kind was made by the Foundation for offices, favors or powers, and no attempt to usurp the power of university authorities was suggested or desired." He seemed to be unaware that he was proposing to leave them the full power to execute the policies he would dictate.

For the school year 1924-1925 Barnes had subsidized a

course in aesthetics given by Laurence Buermeyer at
Columbia University, without trying to exercise any sort
of control; and he had also transferred to the Extension
Division of Columbia another course in the same field
which Munro was originally to have given at the University of Pennsylvania. Of course he was not holding out
to Columbia the hope of inheriting the Foundation, but
that hope was also perilously remote for the University
of Pennsylvania—given the necessity of constantly pleasing a potential donor whose demands were exigent. It
looks as if Barnes had taken all Philadelphia for his
province but hesitated to assert himself in the regions
beyond.

This was in any case ruled out when Buermeyer left
the Foundation in 1925 to become assistant professor of
philosophy at New York University, and Munro resigned
the following year to assume a similar post with Rutgers
University. As a novice in modern art, Munro had at first
been willing to accept Barnes's point of view as all-suffi-
cient; after two years, as his knowledge and experience
broadened, he found it too restrictive. Possibly this held
true for his colleague also. In view of the common opinion
that Barnes sooner or later broke with everyone close to
him, it must be said flatly here, as it will be apparent later,
that he remained on friendly terms with both men, even
though their departure disrupted his program. It meant
the discontinuation, after five issues, of the *Journal,* to
which they were the chief contributors, as well as the end
of their classes. Dewey also left at this time, but it is not
at all certain that he resigned, for he was also on leave
from Columbia during the spring sessions of 1926 and
1928, and may have absented himself from the Foundation
temporarily to concentrate on his own work.

Turned down by the public school system after the one

course of lectures for art teachers, and himself rejecting the university, Barnes was receptive to the courtship of another institution, the Pennsylvania Museum of Art. On May 4, 1925, S. W. Woodhouse, Jr., acting director of the museum, had written him that he was chagrined to learn that Barnes had visited the museum with a group of students. "It would be my pleasure, should you be having another group at the Museum, to show you any courtesies or give any assistance that might be helpful to you. We were very glad that you should find the collections of the Museum useful to your educational purposes."

With cramped quarters and a low budget, the museum had played a passive role in the community. But the trustees were then planning to enlarge and activate it, and Barnes saw an opportunity to use it as a medium for his "educational purposes." In the fall they brought in as director Fiske Kimball, an architect by profession, who had been head of the department of fine arts at New York University. The appointment must have pleased Barnes, for he had received a letter in August from DeWitt H. Parker, professor of philosophy at the University of Michigan, which praised *The Art in Painting* in the highest terms and declared that "my friend Fiske Kimball . . . has been talking with me about your book, and shares my views regarding it." On the first of October Barnes invited the new director to call on him and see his collection.

Their meeting was entirely amicable. While he admired the paintings, Kimball may have been wondering how they could be useful to the museum. Meanwhile, the important thing was to keep Barnes interested in it, and to this end he told Barnes something of his plans. For one thing, the museum was preparing to give a series of public lectures on art—hardly a novel program but new for the museum. A few days later Barnes wrote him, proposing

Munro as one of the lecturers. After citing his experience in detail, Barnes said with charming candor that, unlike his own personality, Munro's was free of the "sharp edges which have cut into the art luminaries of this city," so that "he would be able to give the good of the Foundation minus its bad."

Though his offer was not accepted, Barnes apparently did not have any hard feelings about it. Seeking to retain his good will, Kimball wrote him on the fifteenth: "The October *Museum Bulletin* just out prompts me to hope that you will not hold me responsible for everything done here until trains of action which were started before I came have had time to run their course."

Encouraged by such subservience—if he needed any stimulus beyond his own drive—Barnes within a few months dispatched an emissary to Kimball to propose that the students of painting at the museum's art school be enrolled in a course at the Foundation. The fact that this offer was not accepted accounts for the tone of his letter to Kimball on October 27, 1926:

Repeated applications, similar to that which you made this morning, seem to indicate that you share a very prevalent idea that the Foundation is a place for more or less conspicuous Philadelphians to entertain their friends. When you assumed your present position more than a year ago, I told you that the Foundation would cooperate with you as an official in any move that could be intelligently interpreted as educational. [The statement of his recent plan and its rejection follows; and his letter continues.] Not a thing intelligent came of these proposals; what did happen was a series of requests to have your friends and acquaintances use the Foundation as a diversion. It is true that some other reason—that they were interested in art or in a particular artist—always attended the requests. . . . [If he were to grant them all] it would

make you or your institution a passport to the Foundation—
which is about the limit of exploitative absurdity. . . .

For casual visitors, whatever their alleged qualifications,
or under whatever local prestige they may be proposed, there
is absolutely nothing doing. I am writing you frankly so
that we shall be spared the nuisance of further 'phone calls,
pleadings and arguments.

Kimball must have honored this cease-and-desist order,
but he failed to catch the implication behind the fact that
the Barnes gallery was inaccessible. When he dropped
Barnes a note a month later requesting fifteen minutes of
his time to present a constructive suggestion, Barnes suspected another "exploitative absurdity" and Kimball
should have been forewarned when he received a reply
the very next day, which, though it was obviously dictated
by Barnes, was signed by N. E. Mullen. The note read:

I have charge of all matters of the kind referred to in your
letter of December 2nd. If you will send me a written statement of the essentials of your proposition, I can decide
whether Dr. Barnes would be interested, and will write you
accordingly.

Kimball was so much taken with the idea he had to
present that he accepted the slap in the face and, without
being aware of it, turned the other cheek. What was
happening was that the old Pennsylvania Museum of Art
was being gradually replaced by a new Philadelphia Museum of Art, a large, classical structure set on a cliff in
Fairmount Park. The first unit was scheduled to be opened
in the spring, and Kimball wanted to exhibit modern art
in it along with the art of other periods. This was a departure for the museum, and Kimball told Barnes that he had
won the museum authorities around to it. He gave a description of the proposed layout of the galleries, including

one on nineteenth century French art. In this, one long wall would be devoted to painters from Renoir onward. And now to his proposition:

I should like to give these modern masters the very finest representation possible. We could readily secure loans of certain fine pictures elsewhere, but I should prefer to recognize here the commanding position of the Barnes Collection in this field [How? By leaving the wall entirely for Barnes] to fill with outstanding examples of the work of this school. [If he had stopped there, Kimball would have been guilty merely of bad judgment, since he knew well enough by this time that Barnes did not wish to make his collection accessible to just anybody. But Kimball went on to suggest that this loan (if loan was what he had in mind)] would be merely the first step in a cooperation which could go much further as we secure additional gallery space as the floor specifically devoted to active educational work is finished and put in operation.

What did he think the Foundation was doing if not "active educational work"? And just how much of the collection was he hopeful of having transferred to the museum? Barnes told him off, through N. E. Mullen, the following day. Kimball's statements—that the French school of painting would, in the proposed gallery, "receive its due recognition as a culmination of European art," and that he would prefer to leave the modern wall to Barnes— "would make a horse laugh. They would be offensive to the intelligence if they were not so provincial and embedded in the matrix of the stereotyped blah which comes to us so often from performers who would like to annex us as a sideshow to their circuses. The setting makes the statements pure comedy."

It was a clumsy, a clumsily worded, blow, but it knocked Kimball down for the count.

Meanwhile, on February 23, 1926, Barnes had been made a Chevalier of the Legion of Honor "for the valuable services he rendered to the cause of French-American friendship in the field of art education and culture."

In the spring Barnes had invited the Guillaumes to Merion. One day he took them to hear the chorus of the Manual Training School for Negroes in Bordentown, N. J., "on the other side of that strange Indian river the Delaware," as Guillaume wrote later in *Les Arts à Paris*. The mixed chorus was directed by Frederick Work, who, with his nephew John Work, had collected many Negro folk songs whose deep feeling, reflected in his own intense, expressive face, he was able to evoke in the student singers. On this occasion only the Barneses, the Guillaumes, Buermeyer, the Mullen sisters, and Miss Laura Geiger (like the sisters, a graduate or about to graduate from the Argyrol factory) sat on the stage. The Bordentown chorus was to become the feature of an annual gala at the Foundation itself.

"In America," wrote Guillaume (using the pen name "Colin d'Arbois"), "a Packard is always warming up while one is working up a plan to go somewhere." However that may be, Barnes's Packard did take them to the firehouse, where Guillaume's effusive compliments and expressions of enchantment earned him an invitation to a ride on the firewagon. Seated between Fire Chief Nulty and Barnes, he was terrified as it sped like a bullet through streets and squares and "upgrades and downgrades are scaled, clung to. . . . In town, people stop to gape, their faces questioning; in dismay they try to guess where disaster will strike." When Guillaume asked Nulty to slow down, he stepped on the gas. . . . Back at the firehouse, the company named Guillaume honorary captain, leading him to dream (for literary purposes) of participating every year in the maneuvers of the big fire wagon.

On a Sunday morning Guillaume spoke on "The Discovery and Appreciation of Primitive Negro Sculpture." Probably he preceded Barnes, whose talk before three hundred "university professors, students, collectors and artists from all the cities of America" he reported: Barnes

stands erect, at ease; his look engages the audience as soon as he begins to speak. He goes directly into his subject—a subject he chose because it seemed to offer the most difficulties. His dialectics are suggestive, shrewd, compact, direct; he employs with facility the syllogism, the device of the dilemma. His speech is by turns gentle, irascible, musical, harsh. He takes pains not to become overtired—takes a rest, begins again. The faces before him express understanding, joy, enthusiasm.

Dr. Barnes has spoken like this [without notes] for thirty or forty minutes. He has finished, but he calls for questions again, for someone to propose a controversial theme. After some seconds' hesitation, a member of the audience rises and ventures a query which has been weighing on his mind. Dr. Barnes replies, himself develops the question, studies it, clarifies it, folds and unfolds it, turns it over, twists it, toys with it, gives a satisfying answer to the questioner, to the audience, which, the time having come, regretfully leaves the hall.

In Paris, where the idea of art is almost always allied to that of entertainment [Guillaume wrote in his magazine] one can scarcely understand, unless one makes a special effort to do so, all that there is of the solemn, the serious, the great, the essentially important in such a program as that of the Barnes Foundation. One must have been there, have lived this studious life in the presence of the supreme works of the masters, in the constant, fervent evocation of *la plus juste tradition,* of the most authentic past, analyzing with lucidity

the true relations of the great aesthetic phenomena, extracting the precise formal quality of the material in hand, cal-
culating the imponderable, the impalpable, the indefinable
values—one must have seen to understand the immense incomparable work which goes on there, under the impulsion of
one man, in throwing a greater light on the means of appreciating the things of art. [Discount the perfervid rhetoric in
what measure one will, the concluding sentence of the passage
may be taken at face value.] The works which one has the
happy stupefaction to find here are of such an order and
number that one may boldly assert that if such a museum
existed in France it would better represent French art than the
Louvre and the Luxembourg combined.

Guillaume's account of his visit was illustrated by a
picture of himself on a beautiful horse, with a similarly
mounted colored rider retreating into the shadow of his
own skin. The caption had an anthropological ring: *"Paul
Guillaume Chez les Noirs de New-Jersey."* There was
also a snapshot of Barnes (with Buermeyer), in which he
looked quite different from the hard businessman (*typus
americanus*) of a decade previously: here he was more the
cultured banker or even the cultured scientist (*typus
germanicus*).

Oddly enough, nowhere in Guillaume's articles was there
any mention of his wife's impressions of the visit. It is
possible that Mme. Guillaume wanted to remain in the
background of what she regarded as strictly a business relationship. But since she had consented to participate as
deeply in its social aspect as a voyage to America entailed,
one must perforce suspect that she may have been somewhat less delighted, less enchanted, less bedazzled, less
overwhelmed, than her husband.

13

Few Are Chosen

THE FACT THAT THE COLLECTION WAS NOT IN FRANCE BUT at home made it all the more important for the American public. For in the middle 1920's the Barnes gallery was the only place in the country where one could see, under one roof, so great a range of modern art. Even in New York, the nation's art capital, one had to look at exhibitions in many galleries for its equivalent in range, let alone quality. The Museum of Modern Art, with its great retrospective exhibitions, did not open until 1929. Hence the tremendous demand for admission to the Barnes collection. It was a "must" for art lovers: See Merion and die.

But admission remained restricted. As the collection grew year after year, the number of the disappointed—bewildered and resentful—grew with it. They wondered whether you needed a connection to get in or whether it was enough to write, or was it perhaps necessary to call in person? Did you have a better chance of being admitted if you lived near Merion or in Chicopee Falls or New York? If you called in person, would you have a better chance if you were well- or shabbily dressed, if you were clean- or unshaven, fairily perfumed or proletarian sweaty? Writing, did you have to hit on some grouchomarxian "secret word" like "folderol"? Calling, did you have to pronounce a magic formula like "Open Argyrol"? The answer to every question of this kind, reasonable or silly, was yes and no.

Did you have to live near the Foundation to get in? A man out for a Sunday morning stroll met up with his famous neighbor walking his dogs. In an exchange of small-talk Barnes was so amiable that the man was emboldened to say that he had heard of the fine collection and would like to see it. Barnes's manner stiffened. "I never admit curiosity-seekers to my gallery," he said. That was the usual reply to mere neighbors. "Well then," retorted this one, "you can go to hell. I was only trying to be polite." Barnes at once backed down: "I will be very glad to have you come in any time you want to."

Another story is told which may be literally, as it is symbolically true, of a man who, wanting to see the paintings, pretended to be very much interested in the arboretum. Mrs. Barnes invited him to tea, and while he was there Barnes walked in. Casually he asked the visitor whether he would like to look at the pictures, and he said, "Oh, do you have pictures here, too?"

Did you need a connection to get in? It helped friends of his lawyer; it did not help former students, such as Mrs. Dorothy Norman and Mrs. Sarah B. Weinberg. Shortly after the Foundation was dedicated, Barnes met at an art lecture two of his protégés from the Polish-American project—Frances Bradshaw and Brand Blanshard, who were now man and wife and teaching at Swarthmore. Mrs. Blanshard's field was aesthetics and Barnes invited her to bring her class. In the course of several years he allowed her to bring to the gallery friends from England. Once, Mrs. Blanshard did not even make an appointment. Barnes himself opened the door and gave them the run of the gallery for a morning. The next time Mrs. Blanshard was more discreet: she wrote for permission to come and Barnes granted it. After that he refused her a couple of times and finally sent her the same "rejection slip" which went out to unknown applicants.

Actually this was the statement of the Foundation's policy: "The Barnes Foundation is not a public gallery. It is an educational institution with a program for systematic work, organized into classes which are held every day, and conducted by a staff of experienced teachers. Admission to the gallery is restricted to students enrolled in the classes."

This form had been worked out early, when art students in particular tried hard to see the collection. A considerable contingent from the Art Students League in New York went down to Merion and insisted on it so strenuously that on January 23, 1926, Munro requested the League to make it known that "the Foundation was not a public gallery. . . . If you as an institution are interested in cooperating with us to the extent of having one or more classes study regularly at our gallery, that could be arranged." Munro wrote a similar letter to the Academy in Philadelphia itself. Neither organization replied.

The artist Ben Shahn journeyed down to Philadelphia one morning in hopes of seeing the collection. Having heard that the doors of the Foundation opened with difficulty, he artfully thought of using influence as lubrication. In all artfulness, in all innocence, he decided to try to get a letter of introduction to Barnes, and from whom? From someone you would naturally expect to have the closest ties with him. In New York, the young artist would not have dared walk into the Metropolitan Museum of Art and ask to see the director. Not even in his home town would he have been bold enough to drop in on the head of the Brooklyn Museum. But in Philadelphia, in the provinces, he could be venturesome. He went to the Pennsylvania Museum of Art, asked for the director, saw the acting director, Dr. Samuel W. Woodhouse, Jr.—only to be told that Woodhouse himself had been unable to get into the Barnes gallery and did not know anybody who had had better luck.

Shahn thinks he tried another museum (the Academy's?) and a couple of art dealers, with the same negative result. What next? To go to the Foundation itself, he sensed, would be the end of his quest. Instead, he went straight out to the Argyrol factory.

It was a bright idea, but he was not the first to conceive it. The year before, when the Carnegie Institute of Pittsburgh had been planning an exhibition of French paintings, Homer Saint-Gaudens, director of the Institute, had requested some loans from the Foundation. Barnes didn't take the trouble to write him a nasty letter—he just didn't answer. On the chance that it might be an oversight rather than an affront, Saint-Gaudens thought that a personal appeal would bring quicker results. It did. Saint-Gaudens went to the Argyrol plant, and sent in his card. Barnes came out front, still reading it. He didn't say anything as banal as "What can I do for you?" All he said was: "You mind your business and I'll mind mine," and turned around and went back to his business.

Shahn fared better. Barnes received him and was favorably impressed by the personable, serious-looking young man. "Have you read my book?" he asked. Although he was fairly well read in the literature of art, Shahn didn't even know that Barnes had written a book. But he felt equal to any question which might be put to him and he said yes, he had. Fortunately for him, Barnes did not ask him what he thought of *The Art in Painting;* the points he raised, Shahn was able to answer intelligently. Barnes ordered his car and chauffeur and sent Shahn out to Merion in style.

When he arrived, Barnes was already there to meet him! And he accompanied Shahn on a tour of the galleries for more than two hours. On the steps of the museum the artist thanked him and vaguely hinted at the possibility of a return engagement. Barnes said, "Are you rich?" Unable to weigh the significance of the question, Shahn stumbled into a middle course. "Moderately," he replied. He was well fed, and, if he was wearing that day the becoming warm brown tweeds he favored at the time, and he probably was—it was his one good suit—his answer might have seemed plausible. At least, it satisfied Barnes, for he told Shahn that if he would come on a certain train on Thursdays, there would be a car at the station to meet him. Shahn could always raise the fare to Philadephia for so delightful a cause and he enjoyed a series of visits.

There came a time when, too confident of his welcome, he overplayed his hand: he brought along a friend, uninvited. Though Barnes didn't like it, he admitted them both. But the friend was not content to enjoy his privilege —he was rash enough to tell Barnes that his collection was not really "modern," that he had stopped short of the newer movements. Barnes told him, and his friend Shahn, too, to get the hell out.

Few people living at a distance had the leisure to drop around on the chance of being admitted. Most applied by

letter, and the clever ones tried to figure out whether it
would be more effective to be impersonal or flattering, art-
ful or artless, self-confident or humble. Actually, Barnes
liked a good straightforward letter, preferably with a
touch of humor. But there were hundreds of them. Unable
to choose from among them, Barnes was governed to a
certain extent by categories. Art dealers were definitely
not wanted, because by definition they were not art lovers
but salesmen, and Barnes didn't like to be "sold"—except
by dealers of his own choosing.

Art critics? Their chances were worse. Ever since the
unfavorable reviews of the Academy exhibition, Barnes
seemed to hold all critics guilty by association. Ten years
later he could write to Carl Van Vechten that he was welcome to come out on a certain Sunday, "providing that
you are unaccompanied by art critics or newspaper writers:
these, after our dogs are finished with them, we bury in the
manure pit."

His bark was worse than his dogs' bite, for the ban was
far from absolute. In 1925 Barnes met the twenty-five-year-
old James Johnson Sweeney aboard ship, bound for Siena
to study literature. A few years later, turning to art, he
became a frequent visitor to Merion and was welcomed
even after he became an art critic.

Museum officials? Motoring through Merion, a member
of the Hispanic Society of America staff stopped at the
Foundation and asked to see a certain El Greco. Why did
she want to see it? Because she liked El Greco. At this
moment, it was good enough for a pass. Yet Lloyd Good-
rich, of the Whitney Museum of American Art, could
not gain admittance on several tries and finally gave up.
Alfred H. Barr, Jr., of the Museum of Modern Art got in
twice while he was a student at Princeton in the group
visits arranged by Buermeyer, but after his review of *The*

Art in Painting (Barr thinks) he became *persona non grata* and for his next visit had to join a group of Maine schoolteachers under an assumed name.

If dealers and critics were especially disfavored, actors—great actors—had readiest access to the gallery. Barnes was not interested in them as mere celebrities but as artists. They were in the class of people he invited who were famous for cause: Albert Einstein, Thomas Mann, William C. Bullitt, Roger Fry. . . . Playing in Philadelphia, Katherine Cornell requested admission for herself and an English friend. Barnes replied that he would be delighted to see them both; and he graciously showed them around himself. Miss Cornell was a frequent visitor after that, always warmly received. The first time Eva Le Galliene came to Merion (she, too, was performing in Philadelphia), she was allowed to bring several members of her company with her. Barnes was not at home, but he was there when she called a second time and was extremely cordial. Later, Charles Laughton came as a visitor and stayed to become a friend. Barnes repeatedly asked Carl Van Vechten to bring down Ethel Waters and Marian Anderson, but neither was sufficiently interested in painting to respond.

Of all those who sought admission, Barnes treated art collectors most brutally. Perhaps it was because they were rich by inheritance; partly, perhaps, because they were rivals. Miss Lillie Bliss, a serious collector, a founder and vice president of the Museum of Modern Art, who bequeathed it the nucleus of its permanent collection, was granted permission to come to Merion—at eight in the morning. Although the time seemed bizarre, Miss Bliss did not question it. She went to Philadelphia the night before in order to be punctual for her early class. When she arrived at the heavenly gates, behold, they were closed.

No one was there to receive her, not even to hand her a rejection slip, an explanation, nothing: the intention was to humiliate her utterly.

Walter P. Chrysler, Jr., of the automobile family, had a large and more advanced collection than Barnes in the early 1920's. Knowing how incalculable the master of Merion was, he humbled himself to write:

We have so many mutual interests in connection with modern art which are as deeply rooted with me as they are with you that I feel confident you will not think me too presumptuous in writing you to ask if it might be possible for a close friend of mine and myself to take advantage of your hospitality in seeking your permission to view the magnificent group of pictures you have collected in the Barnes Foundation.

The painfully painstaking letter prompted Barnes to answer, in the name of a fictitious secretary, Peter Kelly:

It is impossible at this time to show to Doctor Barnes your letter . . . because he gave strict orders that he is not to be disturbed during his present efforts to break the world's record for goldfish swallowing. However, since I take it from . . . your letter that you are very important and also a punctilious observer of the social amenities, I shall assume the responsibility of breaking a universal rule and enclose a statement of the regulations concerning admission to the gallery of the Barnes Foundation. The rule I break is that the card is sent only to those who enclose a stamped envelope for reply.

The last statement was literally true. A secretary of Barnes's some years later—but it was apparently already his practice at this time—wrote that if he was in good humor he allowed her to send the card, the rejection slip, if the applicant had enclosed a stamp without the envelope. (Mind you, he stood by over these petty operations; and he seemed to think that the average person was a professional writer, familiar with the standard magazine requirement.) "If the request were enticing enough to suggest a savage reply, he paid for his own stamp and envelope. The more prominent the applicant and the more assured of gaining admission, the faster the application hit the trash."

Barnes did not treat every rich art collector as he did Miss Bliss and Chrysler. To Sam A. Lewisohn he merely sent a standard rejection slip, and later, at the request of George Biddle, he relented. From time to time, he opened the door to other collectors.

Barnes vented his sardonic, at times sadistic, humor on other applicants. No doubt many of his letters were called "vile" by the rejected, out of resentment. Thus, he is said to have denied admission to the wife of a prominent local publisher, declaring that she was not only an ignorant woman but a whore, and that he had given orders to have her thrown out if she appeared on his property. But he is also said to have sent a vile letter to Henry Luce, publisher of *Life,* and Luce denies that it was vile.

Some four years after Barnes had complained that there were too many Jews on *The Dial,* he wrote to Mrs. Helen B. Jastrow, widow of Morris Jastrow, who had been a professor of Hebrew and librarian at the University of Pennsylvania:

I showed your letter to the Secretary [of the Foundation] and she said: 'File it in our records with the communications that represent a fusion of effrontery and the rampant emotion which results when phantasy-building is balked. Tell Mrs. Jastrow that the facts remain as stated in my letter of March 9th, and suggest to her that the movies are better adapted than our gallery as entertainment for herself and her friends.

Tell her, also, that her exultation in having once obtained admission to our gallery by trickery is consistent with her psychological ensemble as revealed by her letters. Her sense of the ethical significance of English seems to be defective— so write her in Yiddish.'

But since my knowledge of that language is inadequate to render the nuances of the Secretary's meaning, I shall have to content myself with giving you the message in English.

The letter was signed, "Rachel Cohen, Third Assistant Filing Clerk."

Barnes's slurs on Jews were too infrequent to spring from anything worse than the residue of an anti-Semitism which prevailed in his early environment and was not perhaps absent from the climate of his mature years. There is no record that he ever went or wanted to go beyond an expletive or irony.

Whatever may have been in the letter of March 9, the charge of trickery has the familiar sound of Barnes's kind of exaggeration. Not that he was never tricked. A student at Swarthmore three times applied for admission and three times was turned down. Then, not long after, an "illiterate young steelworker" from Pittsburgh put together enough words to compose a letter and he received permission by return mail to come to Merion. So, not dressed in his best clothes and trying to look like a son of toil, young James A. Michener (Swarthmore '29, *summa cum laude*) went down there and, without remorse for his deceit, thoroughly enjoyed himself.

There was one person who stood up to Barnes, confronting him in person with his protest. This was the artist Abraham Walkowitz. An inveterate gallery-goer, he had applied several times for admission to Merion, without success. One day he went to the exhibition of his friend Glackens at the Kraushaar Galleries and Barnes was there.

When Glackens introduced them to each other, Walkowitz
at once began to reproach Barnes for keeping his treasures
to himself. Horrified, Glackens made shushing sounds and
gestures in an effort to ward off a Barnesian explosion. But
Walkowitz was not a man to be shushed and he was not a
man of few words. He told Barnes that he should open
up his gallery to the public, that he should give artists,
especially, access to his masterpieces, that he should lend
his pictures to exhibitions . . . all the things that everybody would have told Barnes if they were not afraid of
him. Walkowitz was not afraid of him and Barnes, hearing out the little fellow he could have licked with one
hand tied behind his back, did not explode. Did he
respect in the artist the eternal child whose innocent eyes
see the emperor naked? Barnes invited Walkowitz to
Merion, and the artist went there several times without
making an appointment in advance, and was always
cordially received.

Once admitted, visitors usually had the run of the
gallery to themselves for two hours. There was no mob
at the door, no jamming of the rooms, no need to stand
on tiptoe to peer over someone's shoulder to get a look
at some particular work, as happens at a special event in
a public gallery. There is no need to dwell on the fact
that a visit to the Barnes collection was a special event:
everyone agreed that it was incomparable. This attempt to
give the visitor an idea of its scope and an opportunity to
linger over at least some favorite works was the good side
of Barnes's too personal guardianship. If he was present
himself, he was never perfunctory in showing the collection, never less than enthusiastic, and always eager for
true appreciation from any visitor, famous or not. One
thank-you letter pleased him so enormously that *he* sent
the writer a gift—a case of Argyrol.

Mention has been made of Mrs. Blanshard's statement that, in the days when the collection was still in the Barnes home, he would hide behind the draperies to overhear the comments of visitors. In the new gallery, more than one person has asserted, he no longer hid behind the arras (possibly to be stabbed—or punched in the nose—by an angry Hamlet), but planted microphones. Although Barnes denied the charge, there was, more than once, a remarkably short interval between a visitor's critical remark and the time he was asked to leave. Barnes's presence could be as effective as a microphone in censoring people's critical views. Out of common tact, the curator of a great museum refrained from giving his opinion that the old masters in the collection were much inferior in quality to the new.

Fear of expulsion kept another visitor from discussing the work of John Marin after Barnes indicated his dislike of it. How much greater the restraint when the pictures owned by his host—by the Barnes Foundation—were in question. Guiding a group of Bryn Mawr students, the head of the art department made some critical remark about one picture. They were all asked to leave.

"No psychologist will deny," Barnes wrote in the 1920's, "that, to enjoy most deeply the things we like, we must share them with others. This truth shows itself best among us in the enjoyment of the great spiritual forces which have always constituted the most important part of the life of humanity."

A scant half-dozen years before the Foundation was chartered, Barnes had described himself as a king happy among his treasures. Enthroned in the Foundation, he was a more powerful king but a troubled one, because he could no longer share them as he did then. Half a dozen years after the Foundation opened, Barnes said he had tried giving up one day a week to visitors to satisfy the requests for admission. Actually, a by-law of the Foundation provides that two days be set aside for the public. Apparently he counted Sunday as a public day, when he allowed his students to bring friends. But the point is academic, for all seven days of the week during the school year would have been insufficient to accommodate the applicants. If they were to be admitted only a few at a time, they would be in the way of the students. A class ran for three hours, so that when the Foundation was on full schedule there was only one two-hour interval each day when visitors could be alone.

The simplest way out would have been to keep the gallery open during the three summer months, when there were no sessions. All that was required was sufficient custodial care. But Barnes was unwilling to let the gallery go unsupervised by himself or his associates. He could not even allow a secretary formally to handle the requests for admission.

In poking fun at a stuffed shirt or a pretender who sought admission, Barnes was only indulging in clean legal fun. It may be said that when he used brass knuckles on other applicants—with all the advantages of height, weight and reach on his side—he was satisfying a sadistic streak in his nature or compensating for a sense of insufficiency, in addition to defending his policy. All those ways of saying no, with humorous or cruel variations, and with an occasional yes thrown in by chance or in reason, made a zestful game, catlike in its suspense before the pounce and the surprise and ambiguity of withdrawal. But largely, in abusing those who reminded him of the difficulty of his position by seeking admittance, he was, as we shall see, trying to relieve his conscience. Bedevilled as he was, did he ever think what would happen to his pre-

cious classes when, in future years, the public was to be
allowed in three days a week? If he did, he must have
been as resigned to it as he would be when the time came.

The Foundation's related policy of not lending pictures
to other museums for special exhibitions also had its unpleasant repercussions. If one of the Renoirs, say, were
taken out of the gallery temporarily, the students would
have been deprived of indispensable study material. So
Barnes thought or liked to think, for after his first ad-
ventures in collecting for collecting's sake, he was ostensibly buying more pictures, especially of the masters, only
because they illustrated some phase not evident in the
pictures he already had. If Barnes were not a millionaire,
he might have found a dozen Renoirs sufficient demonstration of his career. With all his wealth, and his gift for
rationalization, he persuaded himself that he needed—
eventually—two hundred Renoirs, not simply because he
loved Renoir or because he wanted to own more of his
masterpieces than anybody else, but because each one
illustrated something or other. Nonetheless, this policy,
too, gave him pangs of conscience.

In 1926, so soon after the Foundation opened, his
conscience may not have been overburdened. If he was
aware of the ill will building up against him, he carried
on—his triumphs helped him carry on—as if he were not.
More disinterested viewers than Guillaume gave the collection "rave notices," and in the summer, six months
after the French government had given him the ribbon
of the Legion of Honor, Barnes won another and more
deeply satisfying award from John Dewey. In a memorial
piece in *Commentary*, Dewey's friend Sidney Hook, head
of the philosophy department of New York University,
was to write of him that "he was a man of no pride—no

pride of dress, literary style, social origins, or intellectual achievement. He was prepared to learn from anyone."

In his sixty-seventh year and world famous, Dewey accompanied Barnes on a trip to the museums of Madrid, Vienna and Paris, listening to him like a schoolboy, taking notes, still trying to acquire a feeling for the individual work of art. (True, he fell asleep at the Prado when Barnes was talking about Raphael, but he excused himself on the ground that he had read Barnes's low opinion of the Italian master and did not have to hear it over again; and may not a schoolboy occasionally nod?) If the reversal of their roles of master and disciple did not make Barnes Dewey's equal, it at least partly counterweighed the intellectual imbalance between them.

In August, 1926, Barnes was in Port Manech, where he had spent so many summers and dollars that he was named—or was soon to be named—an honorary citizen. This time he was honored by being allowed to march at the head of the Assumption procession. In the winter he took Glackens away from his family in Paris to Basel, to look at some pictures. The following spring, unable to persuade his old friend to join him, he moved on himself from Paris to Berlin to attend a sale, with some city in Belgium as his next stop. The collection was growing, still for the benefit of a few.

14

Understanding Art

What really demands rationality, what makes it a good and
indispensable thing and gives it all its authority, is . . . our
need of it . . . in the pleasure of comprehension.
—SANTAYANA: *The Sense of Beauty*

Everyone wants to understand art. Why not try to understand
the song of birds? Why does one love the night, flowers, everything around one, without trying to understand them? But
where art is concerned people must understand.
—PICASSO

ANYONE WITH A MILLION DOLLARS TO SPEND, SOME FEELING
for art, and the sense to seek the advice of more experienced art lovers, can assemble a first-rate collection.
Even with half a million. . . . To create an intellectual
tool which would be enduringly useful was an achievement
of a different order. To Barnes it was even more important
than his work in chemistry, for he did not make Argyrol

either in the necessity of creative play or with intent to benefit mankind, but simply to make money. One could now say to make money which would allow him to indulge in disinterested creation. The development of his approach to art was a labor of love, prompted by inner necessity. Directly or indirectly, its propagation became a continuous part of his life and indeed often determined its course.

His system is fully set forth in *The Art in Painting;* the books he wrote in collaboration with Miss Violette de Mazia on the French Primitives (1931), Matisse (1933), Renoir (1935) and Cézanne (1939) merely applied the method it expounded. What Barnes set out to find was a method of judging paintings as objectively as possible, which "reduces to a minimum the role of merely personal and arbitrary preference" (in its lowest form: I don't know anything about art, but I know what I like. With a method of measuring the intrinsic values of a painting available, what you ignorantly liked would not mean a damn, any more than if you preferred codfish roe to caviar.) He therefore analyzed paintings into their basic elements, on the assumption that it was the way artists handled these elements which determined how good or bad a painting was. Barnes found that there were three basic elements in all paintings of whatever time or place: color (associated with light), line and space.

These he carefully defined in great detail, as a brief summary of his exposition of color may indicate. This element, he points out, may be used structurally or superficially. When an object seems to be actually made of the color it is painted, when a gray rock looks convincingly gray all the way through, color has been applied structurally. But if it remains on the surface, if the rock gives us the impression of merely wearing a *coat* of gray, which

could easily be wiped off, the artist has used color superficially. To achieve variety, richness and harmony of
color, it is not necessary to use a variety of colors. A great
colorist like Rembrandt obtained his rich golden effects
from subtle gradations of a single hue. Raphael's color
was either dull or overbrilliant; Leonardo's, relatively
barren. Renoir's color was "juicy"; Poussin's, "dry."
Finally, Barnes considers color in its relation to light and
design.

When the basic elements—"plastic means," Barnes
called them—are composed in an expressive design, they
achieve plastic unity or (again in his term) "plastic form."
That is to say, it is the balanced use of all the plastic means
which makes a good painting. "When the integration of
the plastic means is successfully executed, the picture
achieves reality; when it is one-sided or mechanical, conviction is lost and the painting becomes academic and
unreal." Thus Barnes rated Leonardo lower than traditional critics do because of his excessive dependence on
light as his plastic means; and he shook Botticelli's pedestal
because of his overemphasis of linear rhythm. If an artist
expresses grief by painting a figure in a striking posture
which breaks out of the design to call attention to itself,
or by the use of a glaring color which does not harmonize
with the neighboring ones, or by an emphasis of light, a
spotlight, which nullifies the rest of the drama, he defeats
his purpose. "Any deficiency in the ability to achieve
plastic embodiment results in a loss of human values in
subject matter: examples of this are found in Delacroix,
Böcklin and Millet." The same point is made in the discussion of art and mysticism. "Painters of that type [Arthur
Davies, Böcklin, etc.] are but feeble purveyors of the
mysterious and transcendental because they lack the prop-

erly plastic force which would make of their poetry a substantial reality [i.e., as art]."

When he had condemned minor American art critics in "How to Judge a Painting," Barnes himself did not know what "intrinsic quality" was. Now that he was certain that he had the key to it, he focused his attack on a major critic, Bernard Berenson.

Mr. Berenson's work [he wrote] deals not with the objective facts [i.e., the plastic means] that enter into an appreciation of art values, but with a form of antiquarianism made up of historical, social and sentimental interests entirely adventitious to plastic art. It would be unworthy of serious attention except for the regrettable influence his writings have had in filling our universities with bad teaching in art and our public galleries with bad Italian paintings. . . . The instruction offered at such institutions is a mixture of spurious sentiment and historical data, elaborated into a system that has no relevancy to either the plastic values in painting or the principles of scientific education. . . .

This was hardly just to Berenson, who had also attempted to analyze the formal elements of painting. Barnes may have in part been paying him off for having failed to appreciate his paintings on his visit to Merion. In a later edition of *The Art in Painting* Barnes eliminated most of his strictures on Berenson because, he said, it was no longer necessary since the battle was won; possibly also because, with his satisfaction to sustain him, he could allow his personal resentment to wane. But if he was unjust to Berenson himself in 1925, his criticism did apply to many of Berenson's disciples. What he condemned so vehemently was the sort of thing Frank Jewett Mather, Jr., wrote of the familiar Giorgione *Pastoral Concert* in his *A History of Italian Painting:*

A courtly lover has struck a chord on the lute, and gazes intently, perhaps sadly, at a shepherd sitting close to him. A rustic, nude nymph whose back only is seen takes the pipe from her lips to listen. A proud beauty turns toward a fountain, light draperies slip away from her superb form, and with a graceful gesture of idleness she pours back into the fountain a trickling jet from a crystal pitcher while she bends to note the ripple and catch the pleasant idle sound. This strange scene takes place on the edge of a vale that winds down to a glittering sea, affording a path to a shepherd and his flock. The meaning? Modern criticism is loath to look beyond contrasts of nude and clothed forms, swing of treetops and of sky, subtle interplay of light and shade. My own reading is merely based on the contrast between rustic and urban lovers, and an intuition that the courtier in peering so wistfully at the shepherd is merely seeing himself in a former guise. In lassitude, perhaps in satiety, beside a courtly mistress who is absent from him in spirit, there rises the vision of earlier, simpler love and of a devoted shepherdess who once piped for him in the shade. The vision rises as his listless hand sweeps the lute strings in a chord unmarked by the far lovelier mistress at the fountain. The golden age of love, like Arcady itself, is ever in the past.

This genial yarn could be expanded indefinitely. The author might have added, for instance, that the lute player in the picture was probably performing a transcription from an organ composition by Adrian Willaert, who was perhaps at this moment filling St. Mark's Cathedral with heavenly harmonies, the while enchanted crowds listened on the Piazza, feeding—or forgetting to feed—the pigeons. . . . Such storytelling, Barnes rightly insisted, was utterly irrelevant to an essential understanding of the picture. Long before him, Pater had pointed out that such paintings "belong to a sort of poetry which tells itself without an articulated story."

Barnes's analysis of the same picture may be taken as an example of the modern criticism Mather refers to:

This picture is surely one of the greatest achievements in the history of painting. The composition cannot be analyzed adequately from the standpoint of a central mass with balancing right and left masses as chief compositional intention, yet the arrangement of objects would lend itself to a composition of that kind. The painting is held together by the rhythmic use of line, light, color, mass, space, bathed in a charming all-pervasive glow. The use of color structurally is perfect. The light seems natural rather than over-accentuated, yet it forms patterns similar to those which are the main theme of Bellini's *Allegory of Purgatory*.

On the right the background functions as a balancing mass to the green mound and trees at the left; it is a picture in itself; it is a group in relation to the central group, to the standing nude, to the group of trees, to the castle in the middle distance, and to the pattern formed by the long streak of light in the clouds. This little group of men and animals approaches a study in chiaroscuro and has much of the feeling of a Rembrandt.

Nothing in this picture is overdone. There is no preoccupation with light design, such as might be charged against Bellini's *Allegory of Purgatory,* nor is there anything academic in the color, composition or any use of the plastic means. It has infinite variety in all these respects, yet the composite effect is simple. There seems to be no element that can be criticized plastically at the expense of any other element.

Hence its charm, Arcadian quality, power, splendor, majesty, deep peace and mystic effect, deep but satisfying, are justifiable because the painting has sufficiently objective reference to which the mystical emotion can be rationally attached. Every spot on which the eye rests gives satisfaction and carries the eye to other spots equally restful and satisfying.

Barnes's account purports to be superior to Mather's in that he points out the aesthetic elements in the picture

and relates his feelings for it to those elements: *they are*
the picture. Anyone looking at it can verify him or at
least follow him a fair distance. Mather's is only one of a
hundred stories which can be read into the *Pastoral Concert:* it gives the person inexperienced in art no clue as
to its real meaning—its aesthetic meaning. The Barnes
analysis provides a guide for the person whom a story
would only mislead.

Barnes's interpretation of the *Pastoral Concert* was one
of his most successful analyses. Yet it revealed the basic
flaw in his method: it was not, *in fundamentals,* objective.
He said that the structural use of color is "perfect," that
the picture has "charm, Arcadian quality, power, splendor.
. . ." In the Barnes-de Mazia book on the French Primitives the paintings are often characterized as "gentle" and
"delicate." These terms occur quite as frequently as
"color," "light," and "space": apparently they were as
important to the authors as the plastic means.

This was the criticism Leo Stein made in his review of
The Art in Painting. When he declared that an objective method should forego subjective judgments altogether,
Barnes answered that such "sublime aloofness" could "only
result in a bald statement of facts, destitute of any aesthetic
significance whatever. 'Here is a patch of red, here is a
patch of blue': this is a coldly impersonal statement about
color, and its critical status is that of the information in a
timetable or list of stock quotations."

To pursue his own analogy, without pretending that it
is exact, we may say that what the method gives, insofar
as it is objective, is precisely the information of a timetable. This is not to be belittled; it is useful information;
but it tells us nothing of the quality of the service: the
same timetable serves Pullman and coach, first, second
and third class, alike. A really objective analysis will sound

very much the same whether the picture which is its subject is first-, second-, or third-rate; it tells nothing of its quality, its individuality. If an objective analysis could speak for itself, Barnes would not have had to say: "This picture is surely one of the greatest achievements in the history of painting."

There is a question, too, if preference will always remain, as Barnes recognized, whether it will not remain *dominant*. Not only can an objective analysis not make another observer feel that a painting is good or bad—it cannot even persuade him of the degree of value of an artist's plastic means. What is sensitive drawing to one man is eccentricity to another. What is free composition to one man is mad to another, and he means loony. Barnes finds the color harmonies of Matisse original and subtle: many people do; but Mather said that Matisse's paintings were "garish" and that he had never achieved "a notable work in color." To call this a fantastic underestimate of Matisse is beside the point, which is that Barnes's analysis cannot budge Mather. To him, Matisse was "fundamentally . . . a fine draughtsman gone wrong."

Further, there are important areas where objective analysis is either ineffective or superfluous. There are passages in a painting (as in a poem), and they are often the most expressive, which the artist takes in his stride as the result of his certainty of vision and skill in his medium. In such passages the plastic means are so subtly fused that analysis cannot separate them: it can do little more than assert their quality. Such a fusion, such an intangible unity, is characteristic of the greatest paintings as a whole. Either they are simple formally or, if they are complex, they are organized with such sweeping certainty that they are instantly comprehensible to the viewer if the idiom is not too strange.

The *Pastoral Concert* is certainly complex, yet, as Barnes said, its "composite effect is simple." That is why even the untutored are impressed by it; and a man of Mather's experience must have taken its aesthetic quality for granted in his *feeling* for it, no matter how silly the story he read into it. When Barnes succeeded after many years in buying Renoir's *The Henriot Family,* he wrote to Carl Van Vechten that "it is a peach of a picture." Of course this was the informality of a letter, but a two-page objective analysis would not have conveyed his *response* as pointedly as the hackneyed slang expression.

Barnes achieved something in his analysis of the Giorgione painting because it lends itself to analysis. In applying his method to another masterpiece, Rembrandt's portrait of his wife Hendrickje, in the Louvre, he met with disaster:

Every area in this painting is a source of wonder and mystery: we *feel* the wonder and mystery—we only see the objective fact that calls them up in a way we cannot explain. . . . And yet no flesh ever showed more clearly its origin in the supernatural in which we all believe in our mystical moments. In all this, in the unreal-real hair, face, nose, eyes, mouth, is that pervasive, indefinable addition which ties our mystic, religious nature to this world by a definite, specific, visible objective fact which is in front of our eyes, in the painting. The expression of the mouth is not sentiment, it is the feeling of the person herself and the same feeling that we have in looking at it. It is mysterious, noble, sublime, all merged into a religious experience, without reference to or use of adventitious aids like storytelling or the use of religious episodes. Rembrandt paints in terms of the broadest universal human values.

Here is no inventory of plastic means, but something close to slush. Though Barnes clings with pathetic obstinacy to his "objective fact," he has in reality scrapped his analytical method.

What Barnes overlooked is that one's reaction to a painting usually *precedes* analysis, and that if one does not like it at first viewing, he will seldom like it after analysis. Further study may better acquaint him with its merits, but study will not change too much his emotional response—his deepest judgment. It took so discerning a critic as Henry McBride years to "see" the work of Henri Rousseau. He could parse the style easily enough in the beginning, but it was only as its spirit gradually dawned on him that he could solve, without aesthetic algebra, Rousseau's personal equation. In Barnes's aesthetics the personal equation was not even mentioned. Yet he himself had the same experience with Rousseau as McBride. He would have passed him by as of no account if Picasso had not urged him to look and look again. (*Time* magazine was to say, with a fine disregard for time, that "he found a $40,000 Henri Rousseau in a jewelry shop, paid $10 for it.")

Actually, there was a built-in a priori judgment in Barnes's system. He said that plastic unity or form is achieved when the plastic means are composed in an expressive design. This means nothing more than that if a picture *looks* unified, it has unity, thus presupposing that one first experiences the expressive design. His concept therefore is the equivalent of the equation $1 = 1$.

The dissection of great paintings, no matter how skillful or delicate the surgeon, will never give the clue as to why they stir us. The demonstration that the first movement of Beethoven's *Fifth Symphony* is built up on variations of a four-note motif will not reveal why the music is so poignant at first hearing. If you do not feel it so when the music is played, the demonstration is only pedantic.

When Barnes first heard a Stravinsky composition, played by the Philadelphia Symphony, it gave him sleepless nights. An analysis of the instrumentation or harmony might have been sedative, but it would not have hastened the day when he was able to denounce Stokowski for playing conservative programs! Only further hearing— further experience—made him accept the Russian composer and allowed him to look beyond him.

Barnes taught that art is universal, that we can understand the paintings of every place and age because they are based on the same plastic means: all great art is great in its handling of the plastic means. But in his determination to exclude description, social factors, biography, and the like from criticism, he in effect made each work of art an isolated creation, taking it outside the framework of society and history. Yet we do not enjoy the cave drawings in France and Spain simply as the fine drawings they are: they move us the more deeply just because they are the work of prehistoric men. To Barnes, this would be adventitious fact, in the same category as Mather's storytelling. He would not admit aesthetic impurities in his system. As a chemist, he should have known that certain reactions do not take place unless some impurity is present.

Logically, Barnes should have accepted, should have welcomed, a wholly abstract art in which there is no apparent subject but the plastic means. In his book, he quoted, without disapproval, an attempt by Buermeyer to reconcile abstract and realistic art, but in the end he declared that at best abstract art could only be a lower order of creation—mere decoration. It remained for a disciple, James Johnson Sweeney, to accept the implications of the Barnes method, in his recognition of abstract art as the characteristic idiom of present-day painting.

Unwittingly, Barnes made the sharpest criticism of his system himself. Having convinced himself that he had the key to aesthetic truth, he had the courage to apply it as very few critics would—by telling a working artist where he was wrong. And it was no ordinary artist, but a man of the stature of Soutine. When Barnes pointed out the faults of form and color in certain of his pictures, Soutine was so impressed that he reworked them. As a result, Barnes admitted, "The form was now perfect, but in making it so he had taken the guts out of the pictures."

Probably John Sloan had not heard this story when he wrote in his *Gist of Art* (1939): "Today he [Barnes] knows more about art than any artist needs to know."

Inevitably, the value of any analytical approach to art is limited because art is essentially an experience, for the viewer as well as the creator. When Barnes wrote that "Corot has never revealed to me a composition as satisfying to a critical analysis as is the composition in a painting by . . . Thomas Benton," he seemed to imply that a picture exists *for the sake of being analyzed*. It was his experience of the greater Corot which made him reverse his initial judgment of the two artists. To love Titian and not to understand Cézanne, Barnes said, is to practice self-deception, yet he himself did not understand or love Cézanne at first sight.

Before the turn of the century, George Santayana had written in *The Sense of Beauty,* a book Barnes held in reverence: "Verbal judgments are often useful instruments of thought, but it is not by them that worth can ultimately be determined. Values spring from the immediate and inexplicable reaction of vital impulse, and from the irrational part of our nature . . ." This is experience. (It was only after this passage that Santayana continued on to the sentence in the first epigraph to this chapter.) Great art yields a profound experience; mediocre (not minor) art, an experience equivalent to eating rewarmed hash.

True, art lends itself, like the primal experiences of life, to analysis; and if the scope of that analysis is confined, it may serve to clarify values. The mind acts as a check on a wholly nonrational approach to art, which would lead to obscurantism, as it does on a headlong experience of life, which would lead to chaos. But art cannot be "understood" by pure logic alone—by "scientific" analysis alone—any more than personal relations can. Art criticism is to the actual experience of art what reading about love is to the experience of love. It is an elementary guide to the perplexed, in a field where there are no advanced textbooks. Nor do Barnes's fill that gap. Insofar as they pretend to, his method fails. But perhaps an elementary guide is all that is needed. Then, as a corrective to the sentimental, anecdotal approach, as a check on emotional response alone, as an assertion of the primacy of the aesthetic elements in a work of art, his method has its important place.

If Barnes had acknowledged the limitations of his method, he need not have cut off the public from the collection. He could even have been a little indulgent to that "daydreaming in our gallery" which Miss Mullen-Barnes utterly condemned. Long before Freud, Dostoevski wrote: "Poor people have dreams: it is a provision of nature." Suppose that a certain number of visitors—even most of them—daydreamed, in the most empty sense of the word, could they not be tolerated for the saving remnant? And the look interpreted as daydreaming could have been a look of wonder, which is no crime against aesthetics. Indeed, wonder without analysis is a truer appreciation of art than analysis without wonder.

If there was anything more horrifying than daydreaming to Barnes and his disciples, it was rhapsodizing. A visitor who exclaimed before a painting, "Isn't it marvelous!" exposed himself to expulsion. While such exclamations may be foolish, they may also be the equivalent of applause after music. This, too, is not a reaction after analysis but a spontaneous response which may or may not include analysis but in either case transcends it.

In the propagation and defense of his method, in his zeal for the doctrine of reason, Barnes sometimes went to irrational lengths. Since he was convinced it was the one true approach to art, he felt justified in his violence. But this was in reality the expression of his character, not of his mind.

Taking advantage of various criticisms and second thoughts, Barnes prepared a new edition of *The Art in Painting* in 1928. Having learned that the distribution of books is a business which cannot be carried on effectively from the back room of an art gallery, he turned over the plates to Harcourt, Brace & Co. According to Donald Brace, they got along most amicably in the course of its production. If Barnes was not modest in his opinion of his book, he was not overbearing either, even though no less a critic that Ezra Pound had recently written that it was "by far the most intelligent book on painting that has ever appeared in America."

Barnes thought that his method was original. Though this has been denied, it has not been shown that he borrowed substantially from other writers. Obviously, "plastic form" is a modification of Clive Bell's "significant form." (Verbally at least, it is a more rigorous concept, suggesting an integral relation with the plastic elements of painting.) Even in later editions of his *Art,* Clive Bell did not expand his original statement that significant form was achieved by a proper combination of lines and colors. Barnes amplified its meaning and exposition. If his plastic elements were in a measure implicit in Pater, Bell, Fry and others, it was in rendering them explicit and in defining them with a great degree of precision that he achieved originality.

15

The House on Spruce Street

IT WAS IN THE SAME YEAR THAT THE SECOND EDITION OF
Barnes's book appeared that Shaw wrote in *The New
Yorker* piece previously quoted: "Ironically enough, the
courses at the Foundation are now [three years after it was
dedicated] almost back to the point where they started,
as seminars in Dr. Barnes's factory." For the lectures given
by Barnes and his two lady assistants "the audience usually
consists of his employees and a few of their friends." If
the Foundation was in the doldrums, Barnes himself was
far from becalmed. In March, for instance, he had had
to beg off an appointment with Glackens in New York
on a certain Thursday because in the afternoon he was
to give his class a talk on the Italian Primitives at the
Johnson Collection, in the evening he was to speak at a
Negro church, and the next morning he had to conduct
another class at the Foundation. And he proposed a

stag party for two at the Spaghetti House on Mulberry Street one day the following week, when he was to give a talk on the radio.

The two classes do not sound like a meeting of employees and a few friends, and by the time Shaw's article was printed, on September 22, regular classes were surely resumed. After losing Buermeyer and Munro, Barnes thought of a new source for teachers. Instead of going back to Dewey for more of his graduate students, who might depart as quickly as their predecessors, he looked nearer home, to students in his own classes, who, lacking qualifications for academic posts, would consider it a privilege to remain with the Foundation indefinitely.

It could have been a happy accident that he made his first choice from the ranks, and considered afterward what a good thing it was. The French-born Miss Violette de Mazia had studied painting in London before she came to this country. Enrolling at the Foundation in 1925, she was a keenly interested student with an assiduous notebook. In two years she made such a good impression on Barnes that he appointed her instructor in the fall term of 1927. At the same time he sponsored her literary debut —an article in *Les Arts à Paris* on the older art in his collection, which already included works by Giorgione, Tintoretto, Rubens, Veronese, Canaletto, Watteau, Lorrain, Wolf Huber, Corneille de Lyon and Clouet.

Unlike other disciples, Miss de Mazia did not become a mere echo of the master. She was cleverer than that, making his approach to art so much her own that she was able to speak, and before long to write, with all his authority while retaining a semblance of independence. People who saw them together much of the time said that they were a perfect complement to each other:

Barnes was the rigorous brain, she the leavening sensibility. And she became a dedicated person. The four remaining books done at the Foundation were a collaboration between Barnes and her, and she is said to have done all the writing, though one may suppose that he dictated a good many analyses. His—their—second book was on a subject she suggested, in a field of which he had been quite ignorant: "The French Primitives and Their Forms."

Except as a source of income, the Argyrol factory had long ceased to interest him. Like other profitable businesses, his was sought by allied companies, and in 1928 he finally sold out to Zonite Products Corporation for either four or five million dollars. It was a stroke of luck that he disposed of the company when it was enjoying peak volume, just as the antibiotics, which cut into its sales drastically, were about to come on the market.

According to one source, Barnes was abroad when Owen Roberts closed the deal, but there is a good story to say that he was on hand when the check came through. Several other men besides his lawyer were present and they went out to lunch together. But not to celebrate, not at Barnes's expense. It was strictly Dutch treat. The check was turned over to the Foundation.

Perhaps that gave it the impetus for taking on two more teachers for the fall term of 1928: Herbert Jennings and Miss Laura V. Geiger, who was, like Miss Mary Mullen, a graduate of the Argyrol plant. She conducted a class in composition for teachers and advanced students; Jennings, a class for painters and another for teachers. There was a Tuesday class, under Miss Mullen, for people who were interested in pictures as a part of general culture. Barnes himself had a class on the relation between music and painting every day including Sunday until, as he said later, he had "a little nervous breakdown" and had to give it up.

Prerequisites for attending the Foundation classes were no longer a knowledge of psychology, science, history and literature, but simply intelligence and a sincere interest in art, a combination which would presumably enable their possessor to understand an analytic approach to art. There was nothing as formal as a written examination, hardly even an oral examination, merely an interview; sometimes no more than a casual conversation in the gallery was enough for Barnes to make up his mind. He could be fooled, to the extent that many students, especially those who were aspiring artists—and their number multiplied at the Foundation—were interested primarily in the works of art and cared little for the course of study. Even so, the informal selection of students was more effective for Barnes's purpose than a formal examination would have been since he was not interested in their acquired stock of knowledge, preferring a *tabula rasa* on which he could inscribe his own ideas fresh. With all the new staff, however, the number of students by the end of 1929 was averaging only fifty to seventy-five a year.

While Barnes did not envisage an ever-expanding student body, he may have been put out that all his resources did not attract more students. Perhaps it was this, and the accumulation of strains from his various conflicts and the rejection of people who wanted to see the collection, which brought on his little nervous breakdown.

It was only a passing weakness, however: he was still full of fight. In the course of their studies for "The French Primitives and Their Forms," Barnes and Miss de Mazia had taken a group of students to the John G. Johnson Collection, which was then operated as a separate gallery. The curator, Henri Marceau, put himself out to help them, setting up whatever works they were interested in for their convenience. Barnes returned the courtesy, inviting Marceau to his collection. Knowing that an invitation to Merion was not automatically an invitation for two, Marceau asked permission to bring his wife, and Barnes granted that, too. On the day the Marceaus made their visit, they not only saw the collection but also heard an excellent recital of chamber music. Having thoroughly enjoyed themselves, they thanked Barnes warmly and he invited them to come again. The second visit was as pleasant as the first and Marceau felt that he had made a friend.

When he became curator of paintings at the Pennsylvania Museum of Art soon after, he thought it was time to put an end to the strained relationship between Barnes and the museum staff. He had been given to understand that Barnes was a monster, but he had seen the man plain and knew better. The trouble was that the others had not known how to handle him. Marceau took the first opportunity that offered to demonstrate his superior tact.

In the December, 1929, issue of the museum's *Bulletin* he published an article entitled "The Art of El Greco in Philadelphia," and he hoped to follow it up with an exhibition of the works in question. Naturally, his friend Barnes's pictures would be included in the show. All that he had to do was to ask for them politely.

On December 18, 1929, Barnes replied:

You ask me to deprive an educational project of pictures which are indispensable to that plan, in order to further what would be essentially a grotesque parody on art and education. The only purpose your proposed El Greco exhibition would serve would be to entertain an uninformed public and continue to discredit the intelligence of Philadelphia by the pretentious parade of "society" people and *fonctionnaires*. That prediction is assured of realization by your own recent article on El Greco in which you eulogize two pictures which every well-informed person knows are fakes. . . . The exhibition would be as offensive to a cultured intelligence as was a recent lecture by one of your staff, which I heard at the Museum, and which consisted of a recital of the article on the painter as published in the *Encyclopaedia Britannica*.

Exit Marceau by a knockout in the first round.

And what of Barnes's charges? That a member of the museum's staff should follow the practice of high school boys in writing compositions does not seem likely. If, however, he had made a quotation or two, an overlong quotation or two, from the encyclopedia article, which *was* written by an authority, Barnes could, with poetic license, call it the whole article. If Barnes did not name the El Grecos he considered to be fakes, there were two fairly weak pictures in the group discussed by Marceau which he may have had in mind. Now, a generation later, scholars consider one of them to be probably a studio work but not a fake, and they are divided in their opinion of the second, with the majority believing it to be authentic.

Barnes often used Miss de Mazia to deliver a message from her sponsor. When Jules Pascin came to Merion again, he had to listen to her lecture before dinner. He was bored to the bone, as he would have been by any lecture on art. At the end Barnes said, "Isn't that the way artists think, M. Pascin?" Sheepishly, the artist nodded. How the hell did he know how he or any artist thought! —he just painted.

They dined on terrapin, canvasback ducks, sherry, white wine and burgundy [wrote George Biddle in his autobiography, *An American Artist's Story*, with whom Pascin was staying on this trip]. The table was cleared and the champagne served. Then Pascin, whose inner being had been mellowed, noticed that servants had trooped into the room and were standing at attention in grateful silence. The learned aesthetician and collector was formally addressing them: "Tonight," he said, "we have with us an artist who, in Berlin, in Tokio, in Paris, is equally famous for the sensitivity of his composition. M. Pascin, a great *dessinateur* of all time, will now honor us with a few words."

Pascin rose slowly to his feet and started once or twice to speak. The sweat poured down his brow, and the faces about him melted away. It was the first and only speech of his career.

He was awakened by the droning voice of the doctor: "And, Sam, I know that you are interested in having heard M. Pascin, knowing and admiring as you do his water colors."

"Yas suh, yas suh, Dr. Barnes, ah luv dat skich uv Mister Pascin dat hangs in de hallway between de Picasso and de Matisse!"

This was Barnes showing off illustrious visitors. Pascin's —or Biddle's—conclusion of the story, however, if meant to be funny, shows him in a better light: that he took his educational experiment with his employees seriously and that it was, with one humble servant, successful.

Barnes was in Paris in the summer of 1930 when the restless ever-traveling Pascin, having no place else to go at the age of forty-five, committed suicide. Along with a great number of friends and perhaps even some of the many who had sponged on Pascin, Barnes attended the funeral. After the rabbi had performed the ritual service over the unbeliever, the critic André Salmon began to speak, but his voice failed and the whole gathering of sophisticates broke into sobs.

A couple of weeks later Barnes received a clipping of a Sunday feature article about Pascin in the Cleveland *News*. Astonished at what he must have considered a provincial newspaper taking note of Pascin's death, Barnes wrote Milton Fox, the author of the piece, an appreciative note, informing him that he was trying to raise funds for a monument to the artist. If the project went through, would Fox print a notice of it in the *News*? The writer promised that he would, and he was rewarded, though the monument did not materialize, with permission to visit the gallery. (Barnes asked him to become a student at the Foundation, but Fox, who had long been associated with the school of the Cleveland Museum of Art, was interested only in an instructorship.)

That same year Barnes erected a memorial for his father, who died at the age of eighty-six. According to the inscription on it, John J. Barnes served in the Union army for the duration of the war rather than his actual six months. Was it the father in his lifetime who exaggerated his period of service, or the son after his death? Barnes must have at least known that the battle of Cold Harbor took place nearly a year before the war was over.

Only five years after the Foundation opened, there was not, despite the small student body, enough room in the administration building for the office and research staff. Instead of adding a wing or erecting another building, Barnes looked for off-campus quarters. Either he was unable to find a suitable place in Merion, or he thought a three-story brick building at 4525 Spruce Street in Philadelphia proper a better buy, and he bought it for $50,000. While he went off with John Dewey on a trip to the

University of California (which, he said later, offered him a professorship), the city imposed school and property taxes on it. Barnes appealed for exemption and when his claim was disallowed he took the case to court.

The burden of his contention was that the building was essentially a part of the Foundation even though it was physically separated from the main buildings, and since the Foundation was exempt from taxes as an educational institution there was no reason why the annex should not be. This was the crux of the case and the best the tax people could do was to assert that it was a new building, with hardwood floors and elegant furnishings, and did not look like a place of business. Actually, Barnes testified, the building was twenty-seven years old and renovated. The allegedly "elegant furnishings" cost $200 all told, and came straight from the Argyrol factory, where they had seen ten years' service.

Of course it was a place of business; it was the Foundation's administrative and publications office, occupied by the Misses Mullen, Miss Geiger, Miss de Mazia and a half-dozen clerical workers. He himself had a private office there, with an "electric cabinet" to give himself heat treatments twice a week (the court transcript says twice a year) "for the rest of my life because of some internal disturbance" (a kidney condition). The defense did not suggest that a medical installation made the place a home rather than an office. Barnes's testimony at this point trailed off in frivolities, e.g.: Question: Was any business for profit carried out on the premises? Answer: No, not unless the janitor was running a crap game or something like that.

Barnes was represented by a new attorney, for Owen Roberts had entered on a new career. He had been named special counsel by President Calvin Coolidge to prosecute those suspected of participation in the Teapot Dome frauds, and "in a tireless and tenacious investigation," as *The New York Times* called it, he had succeeded in obtaining evidence which sent Albert Fall, for one, to jail. When the next vacancy occurred in the Supreme Court in 1930, President Herbert Hoover appointed Roberts to fill it. Though Barnes was sorry to lose him as his attorney, he was proud to retain him (and to proclaim him) as his friend. Barnes had bought a farm near the Roberts home and had often dropped in informally. (Some time after this—apparently because of a Barnesian tiff with the university, of which Roberts was also a graduate—Roberts was cool to him for a while; he did not invite Barnes to the wedding of his daughter.)

Barnes's new lawyer was Robert T. McCracken, of Montgomery, McCracken, Walker & Rhoads. (Characteristically, Barnes would have nothing to do with any of the other partners, concentrating on one man who satisfied him.) McCracken saw the issue simple and clear, but his client saw fit to make the case a production number. Not only did Barnes himself testify at extraordinary length —he had everyone in any way associated with the Foundation on the witness stand. John Dewey testified that he was in Philadelphia that day to get Barnes's advice on a course on the theory of art he was to give at Harvard in the spring. Dewey also said that he was familiar with the work being done in Merion for some fifteen years, and that four universities recognized the work of the Foundation. [He must have meant Columbia (i.e., himself), New York University (Buermeyer), Rutgers (Munro), and the University of Pennsylvania (formerly); but Munro and Buermeyer were again teaching philosophy, not art.] Buermeyer was there to tell of his past connection with the Foundation and his present position. The whole staff was introduced, one at a time, as if to show that there was a staff.

Mrs. Barnes made an excellent witness, telling of her studies in Kew Gardens, the English gardens in Munich, the Palm Garden in Frankfort on the Main, and giving an elaborate account of the arboretum. It had had a few hundred varieties of trees in Wilson's time; she herself had planted several hundred new varieties of trees and shrubs. Experimental work had been done on two hundred varieties of wild flowers, of which one hundred and thirty-eight did not survive transplantation. The lilac plantings were unequaled in this part of the country; the collection of pteridophyte ferns was unique. In half a dozen years the Foundation had spent, for a greenhouse, new trees and shrubs, and gardeners, the sum of $176,835.35. The arboretum was doing for the United States what the experimental Alpine garden at the University of Berne in Switzerland was doing for that region.

Robert Wheelright and Frank A. Schrepfer, respectively chairman and assistant professor of the department of landscape architecture of the University of Pennsylvania, testified that it would be detrimental to the remarkable arboretum Mrs. Barnes had described if a new building were added to the grounds.

The Court of Common Pleas ruled in favor of the Foundation; the tax board appealed the case to the Superior Court and then to the Supreme Court, where it was heard twice—first before four judges and again before the full court of six. They upheld the ruling of the court of first instance by a vote of four to two. All this rigmarole took three years.

Why had Barnes gone to so much trouble to avoid paying a tax of $756? Obviously it wasn't the money. Right at the start he had offered to donate that sum to any

charity the attorney for the Board of Education, T. F.
Jenkins, would name. Since Jenkins declined to be diverted, Barnes offered the money to the police pension
fund. If not the money, was it the principle of the thing?
No, not even that. Was he seeking personal publicity?
That could have been his motive in part, for he had a
field day in court, or so he thought, hardly aware of the
odiousness of some of his statements as he spread himself
on the record with a loosened tongue unchecked by a
liberal, perhaps a personally curious, judge.

He told about his ancestry, his schooling, his early
interest in art, his special training in Heidelberg, "his"
invention of Argyrol. He told about his psychological
and humanitarian approach to his employees and of his
experiences with Johnny the prizefighter, Theodore the
artist, and Jake the sadist. He gave financial details of the
books published by the Foundation; e.g., the first edition
of *The Art in Painting* cost $4,705 and brought in $4,320;
the revisions cost $2,102 and royalties on the second
edition thus far were $1,164; and he dilated on the new
book on the French Primitives he was doing with Miss
de Mazia, whom he did not mention.

This work had required three years of research and had
cost at least $50,000. "It is like science—not something
you can write out of your head. This is pioneer work.
Universities usually do not attempt it. No private individual, unless he has a lot of money, can do it. That
will become part of the working educational capital of
America—not only of America, but of the world." And
he gave an account of how the material for the book was
gathered. Since this was not a prepared speech, it is loose,
but in a sense that makes it more graphic than a para-
phrase would be.

I take a couple stenographers with me, and I go to the
Louvre or the Prado [in an aside to Jenkins, who had praised
the Prado]: I don't think it is as good as the Barnes Foundation—I take the stenographers with me and I get in front
of a picture and I dictate, and when that stenographer falls
over we get another one. She is right on tap there to take it.
And then we correlate that [the court transcript reads *color-
ate*]—in the afternoon we correlate that and we go back the
next day to see if it is right. The next year we go back to the
same path. We do that only in the summer. In that summer
we work up the material and see how it lines up, and the next
summer we go back. And in the meantime, on reflection and
observation, we work out our material. It is ramified and we
have to go on a good many tracks. And then the second time
we try to corroborate it. We go back again to work over it,
and this year I thought the book was all done, and in the third
season we went over there and found a lot of new material,
and I came back from Europe with 500 typewritten pages of
material which is germane to our new subject, and it has to
be incorporated into the book.

It took six separate trips to Europe to collect the material. The past summer (1929) he had five assistants with
him. He worked, and they worked, incessantly; he came
back sixteen pounds underweight, and one of his assistants (Miss de Mazia, his collaborator?) lost twenty pounds.

Barnes told of the enthusiasm of those he invited to see
his collection. He quoted a letter of R. Sturgis Ingersoll,
a young attorney of a socially prominent Philadelphia
family, that "Sunday afternoon was a glorious experience,"
and that "*The Art in Painting* comes so close to being
the only intelligent book on the subject that it should
have a wide and useful scope. Your contribution to life
here is immense."

He had three hundred similar letters, he said, of which

he quoted one more written by Clarence Ayres, of the
department of economics, New York University. Mrs.
Ayres was deeply interested in art, and "after a few hours
of intense, excited concentration, her brain was reeling
and sun specks were floating before her eyes." Her husband
practically had to carry her out. . . . Barnes's "superbly
competent use of great resources is, in my opinion, quite
as rare as the artistic achievements which you have so
uniquely gathered."

Above all, Barnes told—boasted—of the influence of
the Barnes Foundation. He mentioned the posts held by
three illustrious former students, counting Buermeyer as
one of them. He cited the institutions which used the
books of the Foundation and sent teachers to it for training. He pointed to "fifty or a hundred letters" in evidence
from teachers who acknowledged their debt to the Foundation. For an institution only five years old the record was
impressive despite the exaggerations and Barnes's spread-
eagle manner of presenting it.

But in that presentation he had gone beyond mere
publicity for himself. It was true that at one point he
declared that he was contesting the case because he
wanted to know why the city was bothering him: his
theory was that it was a symptom of Philadelphia's pro-
verbial sleeping sickness, i.e., that it did not wish to be
disturbed by an innovator like himself. But at another
point he said that he didn't care whether he lost the suit.
He had to come to court to tell how his work was being
recognized all over the world or he would not be doing
his duty—his duty to the Foundation.

His tongue became so loose that he allowed himself to
say: "It [the Foundation class] is no place for the rabble."
Sorry!—a professing democrat's slip of the tongue. "I
have nothing to say against the rabble, only that it is a

rabble. I come from the ranks [not the rabble] myself."
Most people were not interested in pictures; for them an
art gallery was only a place for killing time and being
entertained. (By that criterion, all classes of society were
rabble.) All of a sudden he thought it would be better
to get together with the authorities in this tax matter. "I
do not want to fight any more. I am sick of crusading."

The encounter at the Academy, the exchange of shots
with the public school officials, the two skirmishes with
the Pennsylvania Museum, and the battle with the University of Pennsylvania, have got him down. What then?
Did he expect the infidel to surrender Jerusalem at his
first challenge? This was an impatient crusader.

Looser and looser wagged his tongue. According to
the legal instrument accompanying the charter, his con-
veyance of property to the Foundation was irrevocable.
But there was a joker of a clause. "If, at any period during
the lifetime of the Donor, the Board of Trustees decide
that the experiment [with his system of art education]
is a failure, they may, by appropriate resolution, dispose
of the paintings, by gift or otherwise, to any individual,
institution, museum school or college, specified by the
Board of Trustees."

This seems to mean that if and when Barnes was dissatisfied with the results of the Foundation's program, he
could have the collection handed back to himself. In
court, Barnes made the threat explicit. After telling of
his contributions to the Foundaion, he said, "There's a
string on that. If the people do not behave around here,
I pull that string back and it all drops in my lap." But
he quickly added, "I don't expect to pull it unless they
hit me too hard." Perceiving his folly, McCracken interjected that his client was only joking. Pennsylvania law
forbade such a reversion of a foundation's resources. If

the Barnes Foundation were to be dissolved, the courts would dispose of the collection to a charitable organization as nearly similar to itself as possible.

In keeping with the extraordinary candor of his testimony, Barnes said at one point: "My collection of pictures got beyond me." He simply did not know what to do with the people "who wanted to come to see it from all over the world." This did not sound like the same man who wrote exultant letters of rejection. Not long after, Barnes said to Carl Van Vechten, "After my death, I'll have the pictures burned"—like those Hindus whose widows were cremated alive on their husbands' pyres. What could have induced in him so hideous a thought—which he must have known he would never execute—if not the burden of a collection which had got beyond him; not indifference to future generations but a sense of guilt to his own?

If Barnes was seeking publicity for the Foundation through the tax case, it had to come chiefly through the reports in the press. But he hated the press. After the first hearings, the editor of the Philadelphia *Record,* thinking that an article on the Foundation would be timely, gave one of his best reporters the assignment. He wrote a respectful letter requesting an interview and an opportunity to visit the school. Ignoring him, Barnes directed his reply to the publisher, charging the newspaper with venality and calling the reporter "only a piano player in a whorehouse."

16

Pertaining to Matisse, Mostly

IN 1930, AFTER HIS FIRST VICTORY IN THE TAX CASE, BARNES was on his way to a more significant triumph. That year Matisse had been asked to serve on the jury of the Carnegie International Exhibition in Pittsburgh, where he had won first prize in 1927. Barnes of course invited him to Merion: he had great plans for the artist. So eager was he to make his proposition that he is said to have suggested to Matisse that he forget about his assignment in Pittsburgh and come straight on to Merion. Matisse failed to take the hint, but when the jury had finished their work Saint-Gaudens took them on a little tour which included two days in Washington and one in Philadelphia. Matisse's colleagues on the jury were Karl Sterrer and Glyn Philpot, and to act as French, German and English interpreter among them, Saint-Gaudens engaged Dr. John F. L.

Raschen, head of the modern languages department at
the University of Pittsburgh.

Matisse had an appointment with Barnes for ten o'clock,
while the rest of the party were at the Pennsylvania
Museum. They were all to have luncheon in Merion with
Mrs. John Braun, wife of the president of the Philadelphia
Art Alliance. Since Matisse did not speak English and
Saint-Gaudens was not sure of Barnes's French, he had
Raschen accompany the artist to the Foundation. Barnes
met them at the door and told Raschen to take a walk
while he was busy with Matisse; let him return at noon
to pick up the artist.

There were then some forty Matisses in the collection.
Many of them Barnes had bought from the greatest single
collector of Matisse, the Danish merchant Christian T.
Lund. Barnes surely wanted to show them to the artist in
their new setting, and the artist would certainly have been
interested in seeing them. But the first thing Barnes said
when he greeted Matisse was that he had been waiting for
him a long time, because he must do the murals in the
great hall.

Although the artist's gift for decorative design lent itself admirably to mural work, he hesitated to accept the
commission. He had many other projects in hand, and
the mural presented a difficult problem. The space allotted
for it was high up on one wall—three lunettes above tall
French windows—in a room already dominated by several
large and important paintings. The artist would have to
decide whether to create a picture to compete with them
—to hold its own against them—or a complementary sort
of decoration. The mere size of the mural—$11\frac{1}{2} \times 42$
feet—was formidable.

While he was considering so knotty a problem, Matisse
probably did not hear the doorbell ring at noon. En-

grossed in "selling" him the commission, perhaps Barnes did not hear it either, though it rang again and again. Perhaps he had forgotten about Raschen. Perhaps he had meant to say, instead of, "Come back at noon," something like "Get lost!"

But Raschen had been entrusted with the person of the artist, to deliver him in time for lunch at Mrs. Braun's. He would not fail his duty. Nobody answered the bell. He tried the door. It was closed. Raschen tried the back door of the gallery. It too was closed. He looked up for an open window; he looked down—and saw a coal hole! Off with the cover and down the hole went Raschen and through darkness to light. The not absent-minded professor came up in the sacrosanct gallery, listened for voices, found the room where the master had been detained, took his arm and hurried him out to a waiting taxi without saying a word to Barnes.

As for the mural, Matisse said he would give his decision when he returned to this country, which he expected to do before long.

While the lawsuit was pending, Barnes made a belated call on Alfred Stieglitz at his new gallery, An American Place. It was an austere place on the seventeenth floor of an office building at Madison Avenue and 53rd Street overlooking the city to the north. Stieglitz no longed went forth to do battle with the Philistines—they had to meet him on his chosen ground where, among the Marins, O'Keeffes and Doves, he armored himself in invincible monologue. A hundred times a day Stieglitz would assert that he was not a dealer, that he did not sell pictures for a commission—did not sell pictures at all. Oh, if someone was interested he could arrange an exchange of canvas and cash (all of it going to the artist). Primarily he was a defender of the faith in art. As such, he was too proud (and too shrewd) ever to have approached Barnes, hat and Marin in hand. For that very reason Barnes may have delayed making the first move. But An American Place was the talk of the art world and Barnes was still the explorer.

Barnes was big and powerful; Stieglitz was a smaller man, who gave one the impression of being big and powerful. They came out of their corners, heavyweights circling each other warily. They were not sizing each other up for weight and reach: these were colossal egoists, apprehensive of the other's mental punch. Each had his achievements for reinforcement, but Barnes was febrile where Stieglitz was poised. Himself a gifted artist, in photography, Stieglitz may have allowed himself to think of Barnes largely as a man of money, a mere buyer of art—who had not the insight to buy Marin, O'Keeffe or Dove! And Barnes may have felt inferior to Stieglitz, as a man who had exhibited Matisse, Rousseau and Cézanne before he himself had ever heard of them, a man who, as defender of the faith in art, was honored above the guardian of a closed collection.

There was a peculiarly appropriate witness to the encounter: Mrs. Dorothy Norman, who had been in one of the University of Pennsylvania classes at the Foundation and was now one of Stieglitz's supporters. She says that the two men soon got over their mutual mistrust and came to like each other. She herself won Barnes's favor. Since her student days she had been denied re-entry into the gallery. Now it became accessible to her and even to her friends.

Probably on that first visit Barnes bought two O'Keeffes for $2,400, but he soon returned them. Later on he was interested in other pictures of hers, and particularly in the *Canadian Barn* which is now in the Metropolitan

Museum of Art: Barnes was unwilling to pay the price Stieglitz put on it.

Earlier that year Barnes had told a visitor in Merion that he did not care for Marin's work, whose water colors "pertaining to" Maine and the sea demand of the viewer more of intuitive perception than intellectual analysis. All that Barnes could find to say of Stieglitz's protégés in the last edition of *The Art in Painting* was this: "The work of John Marin (1870-), Georgia O'Keeffe (1887-), the three Pinto brothers . . . , Luigi Settanni (1908-) and a few other painters is entitled to respect because it represents personal visions embodied in individual plastic forms."

A bracketing of Marin, already considered a master by most of Barnes's peers in criticism, with four of his own protégés, none of whom had yet made his reputation (nor has still), was damning with faint praise. As with O'Keeffe, it could have been price which prevented Barnes from buying Marin later on. No one knew better than Stieglitz that any good painting is without price. But as a tough-minded idealist he felt that as long as works of art are market commodities he had perforce to put a high valuation on the products of the artists whose interests he safeguarded. Stieglitz was heard to say in his gallery: "People have asked me the price of a Marin. I don't know. What should the price be? It depends. Is $10,000 too much for a fine Marin? I don't think so. That's what they ask for a Matisse and I think a fine Marin is worth as much as a Matisse." If Stieglitz talked to Barnes in that vein, there is no doubt of the response.

Matisse was back in Merion in January, and with an affirmative answer. He did not work up the mural on a relatively small scale, to be blown up to full size—he hired an abandoned movie studio in Nice to set up the 42-foot canvas, and completed it the following year. When it was to be installed, it was found that the painting was some thirty inches too short—he had been given the wrong dimensions! After the enormous amount of work he had put into it, he was faced with the task of doing it all over again. Moreover, being the artist he was, he could not bring himself to rework the design somewhat, to fill out the additional space, but had to create an entirely new design. He began the second mural in the fall and finished it in April, 1933. The following month he was in Merion again to supervise the installation.

As the point of departure for the work, Matisse used the canvas called *The Dance* (1909-1910) bought by the Russian collector Shchukin, but he changed it radically as he proceeded, so that the mural in Merion is an entirely different design on the same theme. In his monumental book *Matisse: His Art and His Public* (1951), Alfred H. Barr, Jr., observes: "The powerful, varied, even paradoxical effect of *The Dance* of 1933 is amusingly though unconsciously demonstrated in the enthusiastic reactions of both Matisse and Barnes just after the mural was installed." On his return home, so exhausted that he had to rest for several months, Matisse told the writer Dorothy Dudley that the mural had a different meaning on the wall than it had had in his studio.

There in the Barnes Foundation it became a rigid thing, heavy as stone, and one that seemed to have been spontaneously created at the same time as the building. . . . From the floor of the gallery one will feel it rather than see it, as it gives the sense of sky above the green conveyed by the windows [i.e., the view outside]. . . . It is a room for paintings: to treat my decoration like another picture would be out of place. My aim has been to translate paint into architecture, to make of the fresco the equivalent of stone or cement.

Barnes said of it, Matisse reported: "One would like to call the place a cathedral now. Your painting is like the rose window of a cathedral." And Matisse added, as he held out photographs of the mural as seen from below: "When one looks at it from this angle, one would say, too, it is like a song that mounts to the vaulted roof." (No analysis of the plastic means here!)

Barr's own opinion, based on photographs, for he was not allowed to see the mural, was that the Shchukin picture "gives a sense of dynamic spontaneity; the later compositions, of perfect control and resolution." Others call it "rather dry and overstudied." Whatever the final judgment on the mural may be, if there is such a thing, it was a triumph for Barnes to have the first and, as it turned out, the only mural by Matisse in this country.[1] (For his part in installing it, Nulty got a sketch from the artist.)

Greatly as Barnes admired Matisse, he could not help trying to dominate him. Around noon one day the artist started to leave. "Where are you going?" said Barnes. "To a luncheon engagement," said Matisse. "Oh no, you stay right here—you're having lunch with me!" Matisse said he hadn't heard about it, and left.

About a month after Matisse had accepted the commission, Barnes received a telegraphic request for a consultation on a certain painting by Matisse. The telegram came from the same R. Sturgis Ingersoll, whose letter in

[1] The first version of the Matisse mural was shown at the Paris Exposition of 1937, after which Matisse gave it to the Musée de l'Art Moderne de la Ville de Paris.

praise of the Foundation Barnes had placed in evidence at the tax-case hearings.

Having become a member of the board of governors of the Pennsylvania Museum of Art, Ingersoll was on the lookout for paintings to build up its modern collection. At the Valentine (Dudensing) Gallery in New York, *The Three Sisters*, a triptych painted by Matisse in 1916-1917, impressed him. It was a rather difficult transitional work and he felt he should consult an authority before recommending its purchase by the museum.

Forgetting his rows with Kimball and Marceau, Barnes agreed to meet Ingersoll at an early date. On seeing a photograph of the painting, Barnes said that Matisse had been trying to get him to buy it for years, but that he did not think much of it. Although Ingersoll held to his own high opinion of it, the discussion was entirely amicable. Barnes said that he was pleased to find a progressive art lover associated with the museum and agreed to Ingersoll's request to look again at the painting itself.

A few days later Ingersoll dropped into the Valentine Gallery. Dudensing asked him if he had seen Barnes, who had just left. "Barnes has bought the Matisse for you. If you don't want it for the museum, he'll buy it for himself." Ingersoll got in touch with friends of the museum. When he had collected the required sum he telephoned Barnes, only to be told that it was too late. "The painting is now on a truck bound for Merion."

The episode has been given so far as Ingersoll recalls it. Barnes's version, as reflected in two letters, was quite different. On February 21 he wrote Ingersoll that he had seen the painting that day. "*I like it as much as when I last saw it several years ago* [italics mine] and I think you will not find another Matisse of that quality anywhere.

In fact I like it so much that if you do not buy it I shall get it for our collection within the next few days."

The next day Barnes wrote Ingersoll again that he considered the picture "one of the finest Matisses" he had ever seen and that the price was exceptionally low. Dudensing had offered it to him for $15,000 and "went up in the air" when he learned that the picture was for the museum, for he had quoted Ingersoll a price of $20,000. He agreed, however, to accept $15,000 from Barnes "for the prestige of having the picture in our collection." In effect, Barnes said, he was giving the museum his option to purchase.

Three days later he bought the painting. What happened, according to Barnes, was that he had obtained a few days' grace for the museum on the twenty-first and that he had telephoned Dudensing on the twenty-fifth requesting him to give Ingersoll another week to raise the money. Dudensing refused. He was buying a villa in France and had to have his money the next day or he would dispose of the painting to another client. Barnes sent him a check immediately. In response to a protest by Ingersoll, Barnes wrote him the following day that "the situation called for cash and quick action and you lost because you offered the substitutes of hope and delay. I met the situation and the picture is already hanging where Matisse said it should hang. It's going to stay there and money would not buy it."

If it is impossible to reconcile Barnes's purported statement to Ingersoll that he did not care for *The Three Sisters* and his written opinion a few days later that he liked it as much as when he had last seen it, what are we to make of his visiting the Valentine Gallery *just then*? If he had praised the painting when Ingersoll showed him the photographic reminder of it, what need was there for

him to look at the original? His favorable opinion was all
that Ingersoll wanted. If he had given it, there would
have been no need for him to see the dealer on Ingersoll's
behalf. Of course he could have made the visit out of
pure curiosity, but it seems plausible that he should have
gone there—just then—at Ingersoll's request since it is
implicit in Barnes's own letters that the museum was to
have the first chance to buy it. It is less important to re-
solve the contradictory evidence than to fix Barnes's intention. That is crucial. If he really meant to do the
museum a good turn, what difference whether it took two
days or two months to raise the money? If the dealer had to
have it immediately, couldn't Barnes have laid out the
money while Ingersoll was making his appeal? Indeed,
why couldn't he have given the painting to the museum
to encourage its progressive tendencies?

It is possible that, seeing the picture afresh after a lapse
of years, he found that he liked it, and the fact that there
was competition for it improved his appetite. But the
fact that the museum had an option on it? That went by
the board when Matisse said that it should hang in such
and such a place. How did Matisse come to say that? In
the absence of a positive answer, the technique of a certain
realtor-philanthropist in selling a parcel of land to some
religious or other nonprofit-making institution comes to
mind. On the morning of the day the group's building
committee was going to ask his price, he would say to his
wife: "Make me an offer of so and so much for this piece
of property. The wife would comply. With the utmost
candor he would then tell the prospective buyer, "Only
this morning I had an offer for $100,000 more. . . ."
Barnes might have said to Matisse, Wouldn't you hang
The Three Sisters on this wall? What else could he reply

but *mais oui*. And there you are: "The picture is already hanging where Matisse said it should hang." Who was he to disobey Matisse?

Ingersoll thought of suing but decided not to. As his version of the affair got around, and Barnes heard of it— once, twice—*he* was prepared to sue. But he also decided against it. Instead, he stored up his resentment and kept further count. . . .

The Matisse mural must have aroused a great deal of discussion in the University of Pennsylvania's School of Fine Arts, since it envisaged painting, as Matisse himself did, as a part of architecture. Even if few of the members of the faculty saw the mural or liked it, they became aware once more of Barnes's status and a new dean, George S. Koyle, tried to renew the relationship his predecessor could not sustain. Early in 1933, just as if nothing had happened between Barnes and the University, Koyle approached him with ideas to improve the School of Fine Arts, and on March 10 Barnes replied civilly, as if nothing had happened. He favored a series of experiments to find the best men for the program in hand.

As professor of music he proposed the thirty-year-old composer Nicholas Nabakoff, who would teach one day a week and be paid by the Barnes Foundation. To teach the appreciation of art, he suggested Dr. Julius Held, a German refugee who had been an assistant of Max Fried-lander at the Kaiser Friedrich Museum in Berlin. He was not so sure of Held, however, for he said nothing about subsidizing him. But he sent a newspaper clipping about Nabakoff, mentioning, too, that a symphony of Nabakoff's was soon to be played by the New York Philharmonic Orchestra. Diaghilev and the Ballet Russe in

1928 had produced his ballet-oratorio, *Ode, or Meditations at Night on the Majesty of God as Revealed by the Aurora Borealis*.

The following year Pierre Monteux in Paris and Serge Koussevitsky in Boston had performed his *Lyric Symphony*. Barnes was therefore in good company when he was impressed by Nabakoff's music, influenced though it was by Stravinsky and Prokofiev, as he may well have been impressed by the fact that the youthful Nabakoff was a friend of both of these major composers. He had met them in his parents' home, where the musical world of St. Petersburg foregathered, and had seen much of them later in Paris. And Barnes probably enjoyed Nabakoff's exuberance as much as his talent. Now he was offering to share this spirited and gifted young man with the university.

Koyle replied tactfully that, although the music department lacked certain educational courses, it was strong in others. Appointments to that department had therefore to be made cautiously: he would have to study further the exact niche Nabakoff could fill. They could try him out for a year anyway. But there was no school of fine arts anywhere such as Barnes envisaged, so that what he would like to see was a Barnes professorship established in the appreciation of the fine arts, the appointment to be approved by Barnes, the course to be given in conjunction with the collection. The course was also to include English, foreign languages, history, music, physical and social science, including anthropology, philosophy, psychology. . . .

Doesn't this sound strangely familiar? It was in fact the very plan, unintentionally burlesqued, which Barnes and the university had already attempted to carry out.

Barnes's response was swift and tough. He knew what

Koyle was after, he said, but even so he was amazed at his "crust" in asking him to tie himself up to "the intellectual, educational and aesthetic sewer" which the Fine Arts Department had been and still was.

The principal offense of your letter is in asking me to be the sucker you were looking for when, in honest response to the face value of your request, I suggested a tentative practical working plan to relieve the death and desolation at the very core of your department. . . .

[As for the music department: its teaching of the appreciation of music was] lousy. For me to ask Mr. Nabakoff, a scholar and creator of the first magnitude, to take a subordinate position in that department would be an insult about on [a] par with spitting in his face. And as for trying to buck up your decrepit departments of painting and drawing with our material and our educational program, the very suggestion is enough to make a horse laugh.

This letter concludes my efforts to make our resources available to the University of Pennsylvania. In fact, steps have already been taken to make sure that, after my death, the University will have no finger in our pie.

Nabakoff's lectures were confined to the Foundation. Barnes was pleased to invite the composer's friends Archibald and Ada MacLeish for a weekend, and Mrs. MacLeish sang some of his songs. Friendly as his relationship with Barnes was, Nabakoff stayed at the Foundation only a single year.

All the time *The Three Sisters* hung in the place where Matisse said it should hang, reminding Barnes of Ingersoll, reminding him to keep count. At the count of six, he hauled off. That is to say, he wrote an open letter to Ingersoll (with carbon copies for the press and his own private mailing list), enclosing a copy of a letter from

Valentine Dudensing which confirmed Barnes's version of
their transaction, as if that were the whole truth.

Since the truth must be defended and the best form of
defense is attack, Barnes went at Ingersoll with brass
knuckles. He had refrained from suing Ingersoll before

because I know that in economic, intellectual and aesthetic
capital you are what is termed 'a poor fish.' Before you sent
me the telegram . . . asking for my help to keep up your bluff
in public as an art connoisseur, I was already familiar with
your reputation in Paris as a boob to whom the dealers could
sell any worthless picture so long as it bore the name of a
well-known artist—a reputation amply corroborated in Philadelphia by the junk you exhibit in public as your collection
of modern art. I knew also of your activities among the
groups of tea-tasters, morons and social parasites to whom you
purvey piffle in the form of lectures on modern art. For the
past three years I have known you as the alleged circulator
of a libel; in short, as a person who has neither the basis of
fact to face an issue in Court or the guts to settle a grudge
with his fists.

I have you listed with some of the other notorious bluffs of
the Pennsylvania Museum of Art for analysis when the time
comes to tell the public just what that institution and its leaders mean in relation to intelligent conceptions of art education
and public welfare.

If Barnes had such a low opinion of Ingersoll, why had
he bothered to discuss *The Three Sisters* with him? Did
Ingersoll lack the basis of fact to bring the issue to court?
Well then, why didn't Barnes sue him for libel? But it is
futile to try to evaluate every charge in his letter. We have
seen the pattern of his fury before; we shall see it again.
Usually there was somewhere in fact a point of departure
for it, but the more outraged (or guilty) he was, the more
he fantasticated the fact out of sight. As for Ingersoll set-

tling the issue with fists, there was the tough guy from The Neck talking. At the age of sixty-two, exposed every day to the spiritual influence of great art, he could still compose a difference by an invitation to "come on outside." Of course it had become merely a manner of speaking by now, yet one sometimes feels as if he half-expected to hear an announcer proclaiming, "In this corner, 'Battling Al' Barnes of South Philadelphia. . . ."

Meanwhile, in 1933, Barnes and de Mazia's book *The Art of Henri Matisse* had appeared under the imprint of Scribner's. "A volume of over 450 pages," Barr writes of it, "it presents a detailed examination of Matisse's 'plastic means' and formal analyses of particular paintings more thorough and objective than any ever bestowed upon a living painter before or since. The insistently empirical method results at times in some repetition and tedium, but there are many discerning and even eloquent passages." It is especially noteworthy that Barnes did not go overboard in his praise of Matisse and took pains to note his limitations.

Barnes had another gratifying response to his book, and a more personal one. In his *ABC of Aesthetics* Leo Stein wrote that he had come to Cézanne with great enthusiasm, but that his interest in him had died out. "He is for me more completely the squeezed lemon than any other artist of anything like equal importance." When Milton Fox was a visitor at the Foundation in 1930, Barnes said to him that *Stein* was "a dried lemon." A year or two later, Stein saw Barnes in a Paris art gallery and took the initiative in breaking their long silence. Barnes responded: they had a pleasant conversation.

Now Barnes made a conciliatory gesture, and it was a grand one: he dedicated the Matisse book to Stein, in acknowledgment of his casual suggestion many years be-

fore that a study of Matisse was needed. But it must have
been more than that. It was also atonement for his injustice
to Stein and a reflection of his desire to make up with
a man who had written so good a book on aesthetics.

This time Stein's "review," in a letter to Barnes, was
more uniformly pleasing than his review of *The Art in
Painting;* he made no basic reservations. "The style is
more elastic and agreeable"; the treatment of the artist
was "very fair." Stein regretted only the absence of illustrations in color, which would have made the analyses of
the pictures in question more useful. "But the book was
very satisfactory, and I am quite content to stand godfather
to its remote beginnings." Stein took Miss de Mazia for
granted as collaborator, never considering that she may
have been responsible for the improvement in style: he
was recultivating Barnes's friendship.

17

"To Albert C. Barnes in Gratitude"

STEIN DID NOT HAVE BOOKS DEDICATED TO HIM EVERY DAY; Barnes did not often receive unqualified praise from so discerning a critic: they were friends again. Unwittingly, Barnes immediately put a strain on their renewed relationship when he sent Stein, along with the Matisse book (as well as the one on the French Primitives—just in case Stein had missed it) a copy of John Dewey's new book, *Art as Experience.*

This had a far broader frame of reference than any of Barnes's works, which cultivate one field. But where Dewey deals specifically with the values of painting he follows his master slavishly, except perhaps in this one passage: "I do not think it can be denied that an element of reverie, of approach to a state of dream, enters into the creation of a work of art, nor that the experience of the work when it is intense often throws one into a similar state." If Barnes approved of this, he must have made some private distinction between *reverie* and the *daydreaming* he deplored.

To Leo Stein the book was "50 per cent bore and 40 per cent tedium . . . twaddle (perfectly honest, reliable twaddle at that) and oh! so dull." It reminded him of the anecdote of the Italian political prisoner who was given the choice of reading Guicciardini's *History of Italy* or submitting to the headsman; after plowing through one volume, he called for the headsman. "I woke up with an inspiration this morning. I shall tell Barnes that Dewey's book is sound though not very lively (sound without fury)."

Stein wrote thus frankly to an old friend with whom he was on easier terms than he was with Barnes. When he said to her that "Barnes and me has become the greatest chums that ever was," the arch self-consciousness of his expression qualified its truth. He could not in fact be equally frank with Barnes, but wrote him (as he informed the same friend a few weeks later) "a very tactful letter. I said that I had always been interested in aesthetics, therefore although Dewey's book was both comprehensive and sound it was inevitably all familiar to me, and therefore not very entertaining [*sic*], since Dewey was important rather for what he said than for the way in which he said it."

Quite a fancy piece of footwork for a man who wrote: "Honesty is something one can really live by if one can somehow also get the necessary food and shelter"—which he had. Quite a wabbly-based friendship when one of the parties writes about it so self-consciously and archly. Maybe it was less important for Stein to be honest to Barnes about Dewey's writing than his own. Even with that dubious justification, Stein was not the forthright fellow who had reviewed *The Art in Painting*.

In a memorial piece on Dewey in *Commentary* eighteen years later, Professor Sidney Hook wrote:

Yet critics were not wrong about his character even though they did less than justice to his philosophy. Dewey's goodness was so genuine, constant, and sustained, even under provocation, that I sometimes found it somewhat oppressive. I confess I used to keep a specially sharp lookout for anything mean or petty in word and action so that I could grasp him by the small side, so to speak, by which we reduce men of greatness to our own dimension and make it possible to live easily with them. It was almost with relief that I discovered a serious shortcoming in him. That was his indulgent friendship for Albert C. Barnes. . . .

At different times I would challenge Dewey on why he put up with Barnes. Dewey would explain Barnes as a man with an inferiority complex—he had originally been a pugilist—and claimed that since he was the only person who could talk back to Barnes and exercise any restraint on him, it wouldn't improve Barnes to break off with him. In addition, he confessed that he found his company interesting, especially when he talked about pictures, and that he owed him an intellectual debt. I could not see, however, that Dewey achieved much with Barnes. Every time Barnes got into a scrape as a result of browbeating, insulting, or cheating someone, he tried to drag Dewey into it. He was exploiting Dewey and Dewey didn't seem to care.

And the intellectual debt? Hook does not give it further consideration. Although, as he informs me, he himself was never treated by Barnes other than respectfully, he hated him so much on presumably objective grounds that he makes the wildest kind of statements ("he had originally been a pugilist") and abandons the analytical astuteness which distinguishes his other writings. The debt Dewey owed to Barnes—and for what kind of debt would he be more grateful than an intellectual debt?—he handsomely acknowledged in the dedication and preface to *Art as Experience*. And it was these Barnes meant Stein to read, rather than the rest of the book.

"To Albert C. Barnes in gratitude," runs the dedication, which the preface explains:

> My greatest indebtedness is to Dr. A. C. Barnes. The chapters have been gone over one by one with him, and yet what I owe to his comments and suggestions on this account is but a small measure of my debt. I have had the benefit of conversations with him through a period of years, many of which occurred in the presence of the unrivalled collection of pictures he has assembled. The influence of these conversations, together with that of his books, has been a chief factor in shaping my own thinking about the philosophy of aesthetics. Whatever is sound in this volume is due more than I can say to the great educational work carried on in the Barnes Foundation. That work is of a pioneer quality comparable to the best that has been done in any field during the present generation, that of science not excepted. I should be glad to think of this volume as one phase of the widespread influence the Foundation is exercising.

Dewey dared to rate Barnes's work with that of the most original men of science—Bohr, Planck and Einstein; and Barnes's work was based on Dewey's thinking: is this not the equation of the perfect circle of friendship?

It is true, as Hook says, that Barnes often used Dewey as a front, and he did not always grant Dewey's requests. Barnes was not the only one who read *Art as Experience* in manuscript; Dewey's colleague at Columbia, the art historian Meyer Schapiro, had reviewed several chapters. Afterward, when Dewey asked what he could do for him, Schapiro said that he would like to see the Barnes collection again. He had only been to Merion once before, through a mutual friend of his and Munro's. But Dewey could not get him a card of admission now—Barnes sent him a disagreeable letter instead. From Dewey's apologetic explanation, Schapiro gathered that Barnes was angry with him because, in a long study of Matisse, he had said it was "regrettable" that some of the artist's work in Moscow and in the Barnes Foundation were absent from the great Matisse retrospective held at the Museum of Modern Art in 1931.

"I can hardly believe," Schapiro wrote the author, "that this one phrase in the article accounts for Barnes's refusal." Moscow may not have been greatly troubled by that phrase, but Barnes was, for it wounded both his pride and his conscience. Pride, because he could not tolerate questioning—all the more so since he was as uneasy in mind at depriving other museums of an occasional loan as he was of restricting admission to the gallery: this was the prick of conscience. His no-loan policy was not directed particularly against American institutions—none of the Foundation's examples were to be loaned to the important Cézanne memorial exhibition in Paris, where he was himself honored and where many pictures from other American collections were shown. Barnes violated this policy twice, for the Glackens and for the Prendergast memorial exhibitions. Questioning it was grounds enough for barring even a friend of Dewey's.[1]

---

[1] Aside from the few exceptions noted, the Barnes Foundation did not, and does not now, even permit photographs of its pictures to be reproduced. Hence their absence from these pages.

18

Some Favored Students, and the WPA

IN THE SPRING OF 1934, A GROUP OF STUDENTS WERE GATH-
ered about Barnes, listening to him discourse on his
favorite subject: the quality of his collection. None,
neither the flatterers nor the sincere among them, disagreed
or even had a mental reservation: it *was* the greatest collection they had ever seen. Barnes startled them by re-
marking, "But these paintings are nothing. You have to
go to Europe to see real paintings."

One of the group, Abraham Chanin, eagerly picked up
the lead. "But we can't go to Europe," he said.

"Why not?"

"We haven't got any money."

"What's money? I'll take care of that." Turning to
eighteen-year-old Ann Eshner, he said, "Will your mama
let you go?"

Her mama did, and three other girls' and eight boys' mamas did, and the party of twelve soon after boarded the *S.S. Statendam,* to begin a four and a half months' exciting voyage of discovery through the museums of Holland, Belgium, Germany, France, Italy, Spain and England. One of the group, Michael Ellis, had recently returned from a long stay abroad on his own, but he had not been in all these countries and Barnes insisted that he go right back to see the art treasures he had missed.

Barnes named one of the party nominal supervisor and paired them off to economize on hotel bills. He supplied all the ship and train tickets they required and gave each of them $100 a month for living expenses. On the *Statendam* they had tourist-class accommodations, luxury enough for these young people, all but one of whom came from poor families. They found even the deck chairs a novel delight, and every meal a near-banquet. Toward the end of the voyage, Miss de Mazia, traveling on the same ship first class, invited them all to a lavish dinner party.

Many a student in Europe was living on very much less than $100 a month, rather on the penurious scale Barnes himself had lived during his student years abroad. When his protégés spent enough time in a place to stay at a pension instead of a hotel, they managed to save money. Most of them bought a reserve stock of artists' supplies, which were so much cheaper than at home. Miss Eshner confessed to having spent her surplus on beautiful trinkets—no, treasures—which she still cherishes. No doubt she spoke for most of her companions when she said, "For the first time in my young and miserable life, I had plenty of everything." Their windfall came to about $1,000 apiece—the same sum which the Pennsylvania Academy of the Fine Arts awarded as traveling fellowships to its brightest graduates.

Barnes met the group at least once, in Madrid, where he took them all to a bullfight.

Although this trip received some mention in the press, most of Barnes's bounties were not publicized. He sent some of the group abroad one or more times, as well as other individuals. The Pinto brothers—Angelo, Salvatore and Biagio—in whose talents Barnes had great faith, are said to have painted several years in Morocco under his patronage. At home he was giving out-of-town students at the Foundation $100 a month for living expenses.

Barnes also encouraged students who had talent in other fields than painting. One of these was a pretty Negro girl from California who had a good natural voice. Barnes helped her to have it trained while she was in Merion, and eventually she gave a public recital. Her performance was so bad that Barnes remarked to a student, "I could cry." To ease the disappointment of the girl, he encouraged her to write. Thinking that it would stimulate her imagination, he arranged a tour of the South for her. Subjected to segregation and discriminations which she had never known before, the poor girl found the experience harrowing.

Though he favored her in part because she was a Negro, Barnes did not hesitate to say to her once, in an amiable way, "All Negroes steal." Her gentle reproach came swiftly: "Only in small amounts, Dr. Barnes."

On another occasion he was crude enough to ask her, in public, whether she was a virgin. She was shocked. Afterward Barnes "explained" to the group: "Frenchmen come over, first thing they want is a colored girl." (Barnes could be ribald with visitors, too. He showed a genteel woman a figure painting, perhaps by Gauguin, in which the female genitals were explicitly drawn. When the visitor said she didn't like the picture, he said, "You mean you don't like this part of it"—which he shaped with his fingers.)

His ribaldry could pass over into action. Though he indulged in the conventional misbehaviors outside the Foundation, he seldom abused his powers within it. If he occasionally backed a pretty girl into a corner, many a woman would gladly have given him the right of the first— or fiftieth—night to enjoy the privileges of the Foundation or the pleasures of his purse. No doubt some did, but to others he had to lay siege like other men and, like them, take the rebuffs with the yieldings.

Barnes did not limit his subsidies to students of the Foundation. He helped a young Negro organist, Kenneth Goodman, pursue his studies; he financed a young doctor, De Haven Hinkson, in his research work in Vienna and Paris. Barnes learned of Hinkson in an odd way. A Negro employee of his had died at the Neurological Institute of the University of Pennsylvania. It had been a difficult case, and Dr. Hinkson succeeded in diagnosing it at a late stage. Some time later the widow of this man became insane, pulling a knife on the doctor when he came to attend her. After Hinkson had applied for a fellowship of the Guggenheim Foundation without success, its Pennsylvania representative told Barnes about him and Barnes gave him a stipend sufficient to support him and his wife for a year. Through an introduction from Barnes, he had the opportunity to work with Dr. Gasset, a senior professor of medicine at the Sorbonne.

Dr. Hinkson believes that Barnes helped him, and also others, simply as an individual, not as a Negro. Whether or not that is so, what is true is that there was never any great number of Negro students at the Foundation and Barnes did not contribute freely to *any Negro* cause. He turned down, for example, an appeal for funds from the

Association for the Study of Negro Life and History because he felt it was a one-man organization.

His gifts for study abroad gave Barnes particular pleasure. As he ran into his protégés—Dr. Hinkson in Paris, the twelve in Madrid, one of his teachers in Brittany—he must have been proud that all these young people were broadening their experience thanks to him. On a terrace in a Paris café, he saw Michael Ellis and joined him. Barnes ordered Napoleon brandies and showed the young man how to drink it properly. That, too, was educational.

Mrs. Barnes's attitude had also changed since the time she turned away a former fox-hunting companion of her husband's seeking a contribution to a community fund. At least, Ira Glackens speaks of her as a woman "of strong humanitarian and charitable impulses," though the particular example he cites because his mother figured in it is hardly impressive. One day in July Mrs. Glackens found Mrs. Barnes addressing Christmas cards to members of a leper colony off the coast of Africa because, she explained, "The lepers think they are forgotten." The tough-minded Mrs. Glackens said, "And they are dead right."

Unfortunately for Barnes's reputation, the kindness, generosity and charm in his private relations, to which many of his students and associates attest, were seldom manifest in his public relations. In the winter of 1934-1935 there was need for good will and good deeds nearer home. Independent as he was financially, Barnes did not allow himself to ignore the depression. He was one of the very few men of wealth in his area to support President Roosevelt and the New Deal. It was not only the recollection of his own poverty which made him sympathetic but also the plight of the artists of the city.

In 1933, for the first time in American history, the Federal government established a relief program which recognized the specific need of artists as such: the Works Progress Administration provided them with a weekly subsistence wage of some $23 in return for their paintings, sculpture, craft work. In Philadelphia as elsewhere, the administrators of the program faced the difficult problem of deciding who was eligible for the jobs available, and of applying regulations over which they had no control. Inevitably, as they had to meet the protests of the justly dissatisfied as well as of malcontents, they had their own competence called into question. Since some of his own students were involved, Barnes also raised his voice: he was only too glad of the chance to strike back at the supervisor of the art project, against whom he had a personal grudge, and at Kimball, who was, *ex officio,* on the advisory committee of the project.

In Philadelphia as elsewhere, the artists were particularly irked by the requirement that they work in their studios from 9 to 12 and from 1 to 4 from Monday to Friday, and report to the project office on Saturday morning between 10 and noon. On February 11, one of Barnes's students, Fortunato Amato, apprised him of these conditions because they prevented him from attending his Monday afternoon class. Barnes replied that he had had the same complaint from other students, "who say they have been browbeaten and intimidated into choosing between two of the necessities of the artist's life—bread for his body and a study of masterpieces as a nutriment for his spirit. The conditions imposed upon you are obviously either the result of a fundamental error in the plan of relief, or a by-product of the fact that a person who imposed them was expelled from the classes of the Barnes Foundation because of charges of incompetence and misconduct"—a reference to Miss Mary Curran, supervisor of the project. Barnes advised Amato to make up the two hours of the Foundation class for the project at another time, but in a succeeding letter, he would not allow him to make up his class at another time:

If you had the guts of all the others who have been put in a similar predicament, you would continue to devote the two hours a week to the class, thereby defying the dictator to put you off the relief roll. If they do dismiss you, the mere exercise of your legal rights as a citizen would result in a very positive direct action that would be of incalculable benefit to the reputation of the city.

In prompt response to a request for an explanation, he said: "You could call a mass meeting and precipitate a question of public welfare that would bring to your support not only the best legal talent but a host of outstanding artists and educators. I know of at least a dozen persons of distinction who would volunteer to speak at such a meeting. . . ." (He would not, however, grant Amato the leave of absence he requested "because a break in the continuity of the course destroys its central and most important feature.") The artist chose not to fight the authorities single-handed until reinforcements arrived with speeches.

Barnes had meanwhile written to Robert L. Johnson, head of the State's Emergency Relief Board:

Governor Earle's expressed fear of bread riots prompts me to report an incident which indicates that Philadelphia is likely to be the scene of the kind of disorder the Governor warned against last night [February 17].

A group of artists, badly nourished and poorly dressed, called at my office yesterday and asked my advice as to the advisability of their throwing bricks through the windows of Mr. Fiske Kimball, Miss Mary Curran, and your local administrator, Mr. William H. Connell, the trio who, they claimed, are responsible for the situation revealed by the enclosed photograph clipped from last Saturday's *Evening Ledger* [showing the picketing of the project office]. The artists, obviously facing despair, claim that Miss Curran, who awards the relief jobs, had dismissed their appeal in a highhanded manner and had refused to accept from them a written statement of their case. The artists told me that when they carried the matter to the two men above mentioned, all they obtained was a demonstration of specious buck-passing, which leaves no doubt that *de facto* Miss Curran controls the situation.

The persons who called on me have the reputation of being peaceful citizens and competent artists who do not believe in Communism. Under normal circumstances their commission of illegal acts such as they proposed would be unthinkable. But they are driven to desperation by dire need which is exaggerated by the incompetence and injustice which they claim they can prove exists in the local . . . situation. I advised them to throw no bricks, but to lay before you in person their grievances and pray [in the legal sense] for relief.

Last week, when I saw the local trouble developing, I wrote letters to Mr. Kimball and Miss Curran and also sent to Mr. Connell copies of letters illustrative of one phase of the situation. Not any of these letters were acknowledged, the conditions have grown worse, your local office is picketed daily, and the idea of brick throwing has been seriously proposed.

The complaints have reached me because of my position as President of an educational institution with about one hundred and fifty (150) students, most of them poor artists, only three of which [sic] are on the relief roll. I am charged by Miss Curran with having instigated the attack on her incompetence and inhumanity by the Federation of Art Workers. I have had no more to do with that organization or their attack than President Roosevelt has had. If Miss Curran can substantiate her charge in Court, I shall relieve you of a part of your burden by providing the necessities of life to every needy artist in Philadelphia. I shall deal with Miss Curran's libel in my own way after the sky is cleared of the present adventitious clouds.

Just to play the game straight, I am sending a copy of this letter to Mr. Kimball and Miss Curran, which means that I open the way to a public inquiry into their activities and mine. I have not given a copy to the newspapers. I want to help you solve the problem, not add to its difficulty.

After conferring with Kimball, who discounted the demands and the role of the Federation of Art Workers, praised Miss Curran and disparaged Barnes, Johnson turned Barnes's letter over to his assistant, Frank Schmitt. On March 15 Schmitt wrote him a long, frank, straightforward letter explaining the limited powers of the state and local administrators of the project (this was plain fact) and justifying one or two premises which were open to question. Barnes replied:

I am glad to have your letter . . . because it shows that the ignorance and stupidity which characterize the local . . . officials are modeled on your own. It is, nevertheless, an insult to me, a man who averted a crisis of social disorder brought about by your local officials, to be inflicted with such a farrago of nonsense, irrelevancies, hot air and issue-dodging. . . . It is a smoke-screen that would not pass the intelligence of a sophomore; it says, in effect, "Oh go away and let me sleep."

From the megalomania of his second sentence, he descended to triviality when, in challenging Schmitt "to either a public debate or a Court inquiry," he offered *to bet him five to one* "that the first effect of a disinterested investigation would be to crystallize the organized public indignation which manifested itself in the picketing of your local office . . . with a social force that would sweep into the discard the politicians who are now trifling with basic human needs."

Bewildered, Schmitt turned, like his chief before him, to Kimball, seeking advice on how "to stop this constant flow of abuse from such an irresponsible individual."

Kimball replied:

He [Barnes] has been trying to get under my skin for years, and is now trying to get under yours. Personally, I don't do anything about it, because he seems to hope that I will do something about it, and because it seems to annoy him more that I don't. The chief objections to going after him are that he would like nothing better, and that he would devote himself twenty-four hours a day to the fight, whereas you and I have something else and something better to do." [If Schmitt did want to go after him, Kimball suggested that he might look into Barnes's importation of some paintings under exhibition bonds which he did not exhibit.]

P.S. One friend of mine, whom Barnes has been baiting, says there is no use going into a pissing contest with a skunk.

The exchange of blows ended with no decision; the project went on its uneasy way with continual unrest among the artists and sporadic overt protests over the years. In February 1938, for example, the Artists' Union members and Barnes Foundation students picketed an exhibition of WPA art arranged by Miss Curran and Kimball, and Barnes, speaking at the People's Forum, told reporters to join the line. The general level of the work was, according to Miss Grafly, writing in the *Record,* higher than that of the regular exhibitions in the city. The complaint of the dissidents was that the project held only ten shows a year, whereas the New York project held thirty-six: this was only one sign, Barnes said, of the fascistic way in which the local project was being operated. To which Kimball retorted, "That's a lot of rubbish."

Barnes published his criticism in a pamphlet called *A Disgrace to Philadelphia,* and these and other charges were

repeated in another leaflet called *Philadelphia's Shame*.
To give his criticism of the museum a broader base than
his own personal animus, Barnes had organized a small
group into the Friends of Art and Education, of which
John Dewey was honorary president, Barnes president,
the artist Robert Gwathmey vice-president, the writer
Henry Hart secretary, Dr. Hinkson treasurer, and Leonard
J. Schwartz attorney. After producing three or four pam-
phlets the Friends quietly expired.

It was Hart, then employed by Barnes, who signed *Philadelphia's Shame,* but was not the style familiar? "Miss
Curran is not only profoundly ignorant of what constitutes
a work of art but is so mentally handicapped that she is
incapable of obtaining the experience that would enable
her either to form an intelligent opinion of art values, or
to direct any project participated in by normal human
beings. . . ."

Miss Constance Pendleton, head of the art department
of Kensington High School, wrote Dewey to ask if he
was really acquainted with the situation alleged in *Philadelphia's Shame* or whether he had put his name to it
merely as honorary president of the sponsoring group. Miss
Curran, she wrote him, was "courteous, cordial and not
only willing but anxious to cooperate with the school in
way possible. . . . She was always most emphatic in her
desire to protect the artist in his right to his own method
of expression, and also to provide him with the maximum
amount of publicity [when his work was assigned to the
school or exhibited in public] that the means at her disposal would permit."

Anyone in Miss Curran's position, Miss Pendleton went
on, could never appoint all the artists who applied for
jobs on the project; those who were not taken on were
naturally dissatisfied. All the charges against Miss Curran

had been investigated by the proper Federal authorities and she had been exonerated.

From Key West, Florida, Dewey replied that he believed the charges in the pamphlet were fully justified, and that the investigation was a perfunctory whitewash. Kimball was no doubt correct in his assertion that Dewey had not himself checked both sides of the story: he was merely echoing Barnes.

Despite his involvement in so many controversies, Barnes had been honored, in the spring of 1936, with an invitation from Central High School to deliver the Barnwell address on April 23. This was one of a series of annual lectures "by notable leaders in education, letters, science and allied fields" subsidized by a legacy of a former student and teacher of the school, James G. Barnwell. Barnes chose as his subject, "The Art of the American Negro." He had often spoken on this topic at the Foundation, and, as at Merion, he had the Bordentown chorus illustrate his address.

Besides praising the Negro spirituals, Barnes did not flinch from considering the position of the Negro in this country. He had gone over the ground many times, but one of his messages he felt was worth repeating endlessly to new audiences: "If we learn the lesson that . . . [what is needed] to give interest and color to our prosaic civilization is precisely the poetry and drama which the Negro actually lives every day, it is incredible that we should not form a working alliance with him for the development of a richer life, to which he will contribute his full part."

Barnes went on to explain the meaning of the term "artist." For him there were artists in every walk of life. In common usage an artist is one to whom the most interesting features of a fire, say, are "certain relationships of

colors, shapes and movement" which "stimulate him to
express his emotion by means of a painting." But Ross
Davis, head of the city's fire department, was also an artist
in the way he stimulated and directed his men in putting
out a fire. George Ferrier, a battalion chief, was articulate
about his experience, and that made him "an artist of
the first rank." It was

a short and logical step to extend this artistry of the firemen
to that of the greatest painters, sculptors and musicians of all
times. . . .

The greatest artist Philadelphia has produced is Connie
Mack, leader of the Athletics Baseball Team. Let me attempt
to reconcile this apparently wild assertion with the facts of
the case. Connie Mack would not accept a recruit who would
not rather play baseball than do anything else in the world.
He gets team-work out of men concerned primarily with their
own excellence. When Connie Mack is successful, his team
has the attributes which all aestheticians agree are the indispensable requisites of great art—unity, variety, individuality, and the production of aesthetic pleasure in others. . . .
Connie Mack gives honest aesthetic pleasure to more people
than anybody I know of in a lifetime spent in Philadelphia.

Was that not a great deal for the president of the Barnes
Foundation to concede?

Barnes came by his elaborate discussion of fires and
firemen through his childhood experiences and through
his long association with the Narberth Fire Company.
Down the years he attended its monthly meetings regularly.
He was still the regular feller Joel Rubincam recalled,
horsing around with the rest of them. They tell of Barnes
driving up to the service station across the way from the
firehouse and asking the attendant if they couldn't use a
good mechanic. The man said he thought they could.
"Well, there's a man in the back seat needs a job." The

attendant looked in and there was a fat man sprawled at his ease; looked again, and so it was: Charles Laughton.

That was Doc Barnes for you, always out for a laugh, and even in fun thinking of helping out a guy. A regular feller all the way, a real democrat. One night there was a meeting of the board of directors. An important matter was on the agenda, and of course Barnes was there. As they talked about their equipment, Barnes proposed that they buy a new fire truck. One man thought they didn't need a new one yet; another said it would be too costly. . . . It was a wonderful demonstration of democracy in action, a town meeting in miniature. Men of little means and of moderate means, men of lowly occupation and professionals, talking it out, arguing it out, with a millionaire, a man of many professions.

Barnes hinted that he would make a liberal contribution to the new piece of equipment. This was not a political promise, an empty vote-getting gesture. No one doubted that he would send in a sizable check if the measured passed. With all arguments pro and con presented once and again and maybe two or three more times, the proposition came to a vote. The majority said no. Barnes got up and walked out. After a quarter-century of association with the fire company, he never went back.

19

Tapestries, Plagiarism, and Cézanne

IN SPITE OF HIS ROWS WITH KIMBALL, MARCEAU, INGERSOLL
and Kimball again, Barnes made a handsome gesture of
good will to the museum while he was still sporadically
attacking the art project officials. During the depression
in France, which paralleled our own, the famous tapestry
mills of Aubusson and Beauvais, owned by the French
government, had come to a standstill. To get the unem-
ployed weavers back to work, Mme. Marie Cuttoli, wife
of the senator, conceived the idea of having the plants
turn from traditional designs to the designs of contemporary masters, for which she saw a good market. After a
strenuous campaign, she had men and machines translating
Picasso, Matisse, Rouault, Dufy, Lurçat and Leger into
tapestry. The results were excellent aesthetically, and when
they found ready buyers as well, the Bignou Galleries
arranged for an exhibition in New York in April, 1936.

(Etienne Bignou became Barnes's favorite dealer after the premature death of Paul Guillaume in 1934 while undergoing an operation by their mutual friend Dr. Gasset. From that exhibition, the first held outside of France, Barnes bought a Picasso and two Rouault tapestries.

He also delivered a talk on the new work over the NBC network on May 8, not without a commercial for the Barnes Foundation. He began with a reference to recent newspaper reports that he had refused to sell for $6,000 a painting by Picasso which he had bought in Paris some twenty-five years previously for $10 and that he had likewise refused an offer of $50,000 for a Renoir he had bought at the same time for $800. The story was true, Barnes said, but it was significant as a demonstration that original masters are but slowly recognized by their contemporaries; for the offers had come from Paris art dealers commissioned to buy the Picasso for the Luxembourg Museum and the Renoir for the Louvre. This led him to consider the relationship of other artists to their time, a topic suggesting the scientific method of studying art developed at the Barnes Foundation which could, presumably, lead to a more certain recognition of talent. One of the basic postulates of that method was the continuity of the tradition of painting: the tapestries were another link in the chain.

Barnes sent a copy of his talk to John S. Jenks, a member of the board of governors of the museum. Some time later he suggested that the tapestries would make a good show; Jenks agreed; and Barnes indicated that he would cover such expenses as the museum was unable to meet since this would be a big event for the city.

Before the negotiations had gone this far, Barnes had suffered another unpleasant experience at the museum. On October 8 he complained to Kimball that on the previous afternoon one of the attendants "who uses various names to suit his dishonest purposes" had created a disturbance in order to interfere with his study of the German paintings then on view; and he had been "aided and abetted by other individuals employed in the gallery."

Who was this man of many aliases? A gangster? A safecracker? A passer of bad checks? A confidence man? No, he was just an artist named Josef Presser working on the WPA project at the museum. Presser had once written a highfalutin stilted letter of application for admission to the Foundation's classes, was turned down, and tried again. On September 1, 1936, he wrote that his instructor in Los Angeles, a Monsieur Hugette Nuthin, a former student of Matisse, had suggested that he communicate with Barnes concerning admission to his classes. He—Piero Dela, as he signed himself—had read *The Art in Painting* and Barnes's books on Matisse and Renoir, and said they were "of the utmost benefit" to him. Nelle E. Mullen replied, asking him to call at the gallery on October 6 at 1 P.M. to see if it would be possible to place him.

On October 6 Presser called at the appointed time. . . . Later that day a letter was sent him, addressed to "Mr. Piero Della (Francesca)." "We liked the humor of your letter of September 1st so much that we invited you to come to the gallery today. When we recognized your identity, we told you that you could come to the Monday class because we were sure you have not the guts to repeat the masquerade." The letter was signed "Hugette Razzed by the Secy."

What was Presser's offense at the museum? Had he baited Barnes for not allowing him to study at the Foundation? Before, Barnes had admitted enjoying the humor of the letter, which was largely in the pseudonym. Now he heavy-handedly referred to it as if it had been used for illegal or immoral purposes.

Barnes concluded his letter to Kimball with a triple threat, of which the first will suffice: if there were "any suggestion of a repetition" of the disorder on his next visit to the museum, he would make a public issue of it. On the same day he wrote to Jenks since Kimball, as he said, had ignored all his communications: "For more than two years I have been trying my damnedest to keep my public mouth shut about a number of bad things at the . . . Museum. Some of them were born of petty spite and jealousy but, since I have let them go, the offenders have blundered to the extent that I would be disloyal to everything I stand for, if I don't blow the lid off."

Before the day was over, a "practical idea" occurred to him and he wrote Jenks again. His idea was to assemble all the employees of the museum, including those from the project, who were present in the rooms of the German exhibition on the afternoon of October 7 between 2 and 4 P.M. (it began to sound like a murder trial)—to assemble all those employees at 10 o'clock Monday morning, and he would present the evidence, behind closed doors, on which his letter to Kimball was based. "Upon that evidence, and other documentary data, I shall ask the Trustees of the Museum to take the necessary action to clean up the moral sewer that has been running through the Museum for a considerable time. . . ."

A practical idea? Only for a man who was the exact center of the universe.

Perhaps Kimball took Barnes's approach to Jenks on the tapestry exhibition as a sign of the abatement of his hostility to the museum generally; perhaps he even looked to some beneficent sequel. At any rate, this time he did not ignore Barnes's letter. Investigating the charge the same day, he apparently found it justified. He learned, too, that Presser had already been fired once from the project for decorating a barroom during the project's working hours. Kimball dismissed him, and apologized to Barnes for the annoyance the artist had caused him.

Now the tapestry show could go on. . . . It turned out, however, that the French government had bought the best examples and that what was left was inadequate for the proposed exhibition. Barnes assured Jenks that if it got to the United States at all next year, "I'll do my best to give you first crack at it."

As consolation, meanwhile, he invited Henry P. Mc-Ilhenny, who was to have had charge of the exhibition, to come out to Merion with a friend, Evan Randolph. There were to be Negro spirituals "and if I'm not too lazy I'll have something to say about the relation between what the Negroes sing and what our painters put into their pictures." This was a formula Barnes often used, and he seems never to have been too lazy to make his favorite demonstrations of the analogies between art and music.

In the Matisse book there is a provocative chapter on the painter and Stravinsky. Barnes compares the bright palette of Matisse to the orchestral color of the composer, their common use of primitive and exotic themes, and their common emphasis on decoration: neither rarely or ever "attempts a rendering of the major human values." In a study of Cézanne published not long after, Barnes analyzed a characteristic landscape. The succession of planes receding to the pyramidal Mt.Ste. Victoire in the distance he found comparable to the interrelated and piled-up rhythms in a Bach fugue, "but the components are even more complex and varied."

In January Barnes was able to write Jenks from Paris

that he had arranged the tapestry exhibition for the fall: he was working out the details. . . . After all these preliminaries, the exhibition never took place.

On the day after Barnes had enjoyed the honor of delivering the Barnwell address at Central High School, he was brought low by an exhibition which opened at the museum called "Forms in Art." Ignoring differences of time and place of origin, E. M. Benson, who arranged the show, classified all paintings in four categories: naturalistic (realistic, in the ordinary sense); impressionistic (in a broad sense); fantastic; and calligraphic. The object of the exhibition was to demonstrate that all great art had the same basic qualities, as expressed in one of the four categories, or forms.

A few days after the exhibition opened Barnes wrote J. Stogdell Stokes, president of the museum, charging that it was a plagiarism of his own approach to art, and cited "thirty-four specific proofs" from his books to prove it. The next day he wrote again to say that he had received many letters in support of his protest. In response to a request by Stokes, Barnes wrote him again the following day, promising not to take any action until Stokes proposed a solution. Since Stokes mentioned that Benson had studied with Dewey, Barnes sent the philosopher a copy of the exhibition catalog and of their correspondence. Apparently Stokes's solution was to have Benson explain his position directly to Barnes, as he did on May 1:

I fear that you have been rather hasty in your judgment. When your book [*The*] *Art in Painting* appeared, I read it respectfully, enjoyed and was stimulated by it. But I also have read Faure, Woelfflin, Ozenfant, Kurt Witt, Fritz Burger and many others—all of whom, in their own way, arrived at analogous conclusions, each through his own experience. These writers, including yourself, have undoubtedly left their mark on the development of my ideas, but nothing could have or would have come of it, if fresh personal experience with art and life over a period of many years had not confirmed a point of view. [He had published many articles in which his approach in *Forms in Art* could be traced from its embryo.] We may be walking towards a similar goal, but we are traveling different roads. Mine is one I have painfully blazed for myself.

I have tried for years, unsuccessfully, to see your unique collection. I regret that I have thus not been able to see your approach actually put in practice on your walls.

It was my hope that you would be among the first to come to my support and I regret that you resent, rather than welcome, any similarity in our aims.

Benson got no comfort from Dewey either, who asserted that he had borrowed the central idea of *The Art in Painting* and corrupted it. "That Mr. Benson should be thus confused personally," Barnes quoted from Dewey's "report," "is not a matter of great importance. That a great public Institution should lend itself to propagating the confusion is serious. . . ." The Arists' Union also protested the plagiarism in terms and tone strangely familiar.

This was not the end of the matter. But the immediate consequence was that on May 18 Barnes wrote McIlhenny:

I think it is only fair to give you ample notice that I intend to tell the French officials that I cancel my request to have the modern tapestry show in Philadelphia next fall. The reason for this decision is recent factual corroboration of my previous statement that the Pennsylvania Museum of Art is a house of artistic and intellectual prostitution. . . .

Some time later Barnes pursued his quarry in *The Progressive Decay of the Pennsylvania Museum of Art,* a pamphlet signed by Harry Fuiman, an earnest young research lawyer who was, and is, deeply interested in

Barnes's educational work. Fuiman avows that he wrote the pamphlet voluntarily, refusing Barnes's offer of compensation. It demonstrates how strong Barnes's influence was when, in terms and tone, Fuiman sounded just like— Henry Hart!

Fuiman declared that he had read all of Benson's articles as well as the books he cited as the germinal sources of his ideas for the "Forms in Art" exhibition. He had not merely read them, but, as Barnes was wont to do, "minutely studied [them] from all relevant viewpoints—aesthetic, literary, educational, civic, moral and legal—and each aspect carefully documented. . . . As a result of this research it can be stated, without qualification, that no article or series of articles published by Mr. Benson prior to March 1938, contains even a suggestion of the ideas and principles which he is accused of plagiarizing. . . ."

Benson may have been mistaken in saying that he had written of the universality of art, but it does not necessarily mean that he was unfamiliar with the idea. If Fuiman (and Barnes?) really plowed through the black forest of Burger, the flowery acres of Faure, and the rest, it was the research of a mole. For Benson said that he had read these authors *and many others,* of whom Clive Bell was surely one. It was Bell's *Art* which had given Barnes his own aesthetic start in life, and in that book it is stated that to those who are aware of significant form "what does it matter that the forms that move them were created in Paris the day before yesterday or in Babylon fifty centuries ago?"

Benson was in error if he implied that his four categories were anything more than descriptive, since they do not touch on the *qualities* common to great art. If he was guilty of anything, it was not of plagiarism, or of corrupting Barnes's analytical system, but of ignoring it.

In the fall, Thomas Munro, who had become curator of

education at the Cleveland Museum of Art, canceled a lecture he was scheduled to give at the Pennsylvania Museum
of Art in December. "Information has just reached me,"
he wrote Benson, of some trouble between your Museum
and the Barnes Foundation, in regard to the 'Forms in Art
Exhibition,' last spring. I have been further informed that
my lecture might be made an occasion for some public
controversy in this connection. Ordinarily, I do not mind
taking part in controversial situations. But my associations
in Philadelphia have been such that I would much prefer
not to take part in this one."

Barnes vs. Kimball, Barnes vs. Marceau, Barnes vs.
Jenks, Barnes vs. Kimball, Barnes vs. Benson, Barnes vs.
Kimball. . . . And still he did not break off relations with
"the house of artistic and intellectual prostitution." Where
else could he go? It was the only "brothel" in which he
could make the madame listen to him or, failing in that,
make tremble. In his first letter to Stokes concerning the
Benson exhibition, he had cited as evidence of his good
intentions toward the museum the fact that he had refused
to talk or to publish his comments on that "offense to
morals and education." He had accorded Kimball "un-
believable charity and forebearance in view of what I
could have done with the record of facts in my files." More
than art and education were in question: "I have a big
stake in the good name of the city which my ancestors laid
out"—without, apparently, the helping hand of a Welsh
or Price.

So then, a year after the Benson affair, Barnes made a
good-will offering to the museum—not *The Three Sisters*
(that would have been too much like a fairy tale), not a
work of "fine art" at all, but a good, sound thread winder,
for the Pennsylvania German room. It was a minor gift,
valued at perhaps $300, which the museum might have

declined from another donor for lack of space. Accepting it after some hesitation, Stokes asked Barnes if he would sell him a certain metal plate and acknowledged that the kraut cutter which he himself had donated was there "due to your kind suggestion." That lubricating chore done, Stokes briskly advised Kimball that his letter to Barnes would suffice for the museum's thanks and acknowledgment. "I do not want to give him too many opportunities to reply."

That summer of 1937 Barnes was invited to speak at a great memorial exhibition of Cézanne's work held at the Musée de l'Orangerie under the auspices of the French government, which also advanced him, on July 22, to the rank of officer in the Legion of Honor. Back home he was not receiving equivalent honors, in part perhaps because he seized so much attention himself, and no one was acclaiming him for the authority he was on Cézanne. Otherwise his next row with the museum need not have taken place.

It was in November that he read in the newspapers of the museum's purchase of Cézanne's *The Bathers* from the Pellerin collection in Paris: "Hailed as the greatest masterpiece by one of the greatest painters of all times, the museum stated that 'a smaller picture, a second version, is in the collection of the Barnes Foundation at Merion.'"

Possibly the museum's publicity people did not intend the statement to be an invidious comparison, but not only a hypersensitive Barnes read it so. He must have felt, and rightly, that to the general public a smaller picture was a less important picture, especially since nothing was said of *its* quality. A proper comparison of any two paintings is difficult and beyond the purview of a newspaper release; it was indiscreet, if nothing worse, to refer to his "version" at all. For five days running Barnes asked Stokes to have the museum issue a corrective statement, and when it did not, he gave out a statement of his own. This he had enclosed, in his first letter to Stokes, warning him that he would make it public if the museum did not give him satisfaction.

The two pictures, it said, "have practically nothing in common: they differ in drawing, color, kind and quality of pigment, technique, space composition and modeling. . . ." The museum's painting had the effect of a water color, while his own recalled "the feeling of the frieze in the Parthenon." It was a completed painting; the museum's was "of the nature of a sketch." That was why it had not found a purchaser in ten years "in a market avid for Cézanne's work." The former owner had once offered it to him for $80,000; later an art dealer had suggested to him that an offer of $50,000 would be accepted. But he had let it go. He admitted, nevertheless, that "much could be said in favor of the picture" as one "in which Cézanne worked out numerous experiments . . . which proved useful to him in achieving his mature, fully expressive form." But to compare it with the Barnes picture on the basis of similar subject matter only created confusion.

In a later leaflet of the Friends of Art and Education, however, in which he made a more detailed analysis of the museum's picture, he omitted what could be said in its favor, leaving the reader with the feeling that it was "an unfulfilled promise." According to an official statement by "the French government," he said, Cézanne had "abandoned the work unfinished." And he called Joseph E. Widener, the art collector who had been the museum's intermediary in making the purchase, an ignoramus; the purchase itself was a waste of public funds. Comparing it with his own picture, the museum officials had only themselves to blame "for the resulting world-wide scandal."

How strange, then, was Barnes's encounter with a fellow Philadelphian and artist-collector, Earl Horter, in Paris two years previously. Barnes had seized him by the lapels and exclaimed, "Horter, there's only one Cézanne to see in Paris—*The Bathers* in the Pellerin collection."

On December 3, The *Evening Bulletin* published a letter which took issue with the statement that *The Bathers* was incomplete. The writer, who signed himself "Syndic," pointed out that Cézanne's paint had a thin, dry appearance in his later work. This was not weakness, however, but "the synthesis and profound summing up of all his experience, a synthesis developed ultimately into the shorthand technique of his water colors." Syndic congratulated the museum for buying "this superb canvas."

In a letter which recapitulated all his grievances against the museum, Barnes said:

A final word of caution to the Museum officials and their friends is that I shall not tolerate the repetition of any such cowardly, unsigned vilifications as those of the supposedly unknown "Syndic." . . . I shall match all such dirt by the public spilling of more potent dirt, and validate it by corroborative testimony: for example, Tyson's admission that he was half-drunk when he talked to the reporter about the Museum's Cézanne *Bathers;* that the reason so many respectable women consider your pot-bellied friend . . . the most disgusting man in the city is that—these women claim—his lecherous looks and manners make personable women feel as if they were being stripped naked in public.[1] Ingersoll has had a sample of my wares in matching dirt throwing.

[1] Carroll S. Tyson, a wealthy painter and collector, was a member of the board of governors of the museum for twenty years. Barnes's charges against him are hardly to be taken at their face value. At a loan exhibition of French masters at the museum, Barnes pointed to one owned by Tyson and said, "Carroll, I could have bought that picture for a song." Said Tyson: "Why didn't you?"

Even Barnes could hardly have dared call Syndic's difference of opinion as to the merit of the picture *vilifications* and *dirt*. What he was referring to was Syndic's opinion of *The Art in Painting* as "a masterpiece of dull and pedestrian writing." A harsh opinion, but is it a *vilification?* Barnes assumed that Syndic was either a member of the museum staff or a person known to them: hence the museum was responsible for his statements. Barnes found room in the lower left-hand corner of his long, single-spaced letter for a postscript: "I never fight with concealed weapons; hence a copy of this letter has been mailed to four separate persons." They also no doubt received a copy of the broadside mentioned earlier, *A Disgrace to Philadelphia*. This was his answer, he told Stokes, "to the calumnies referred to in my letter of December 8, 1937, denied as of official source in your letter of December 9, reasserted as backed up by legal evidence in my letter of December 10, and still being circulated."

Some weeks after the controversy began, Frank Crowninshield, editor of *Vanity Fair,* was to speak at the museum of the University of Pennsylvania. A collector of modern art himself, Crowninshield had reproduced in his magazine a portfolio of modern paintings in full color. Barnes must have approved of his job, for he gave Crowninshield permission to visit the gallery on the day of his lecture, though he usually turned away wrathfully anyone who presumed to take in his pictures in passing.

The appointment was for some time between seven and eight in the morning. When the editor appeared, a silent attendant admitted him, then retired to a desk in the corner. Crowninshield had the gallery to himself for a couple of hours, and when he was leaving asked the attendant to convey his profound gratitude to Dr. Barnes

for his great experience. The story goes that as Crowninshield looked over his audience at the lecture he espied
the "attendant" of the morning, who was none other than
—who else?

The fact is that Crowninshield's letter of thanks to
Barnes on December 5 gave no sign of their having met.
"I was amused," he wrote, "to find at the luncheon which
they gave me at the [university] Museum, that no one was
talking of anything but the Cézanne incident, and all of
them talking of the picture in terms of dollars per figure,
rather than in terms of art, as if Cézanne had painted with
the idea of selling pictures *by the figure*, rather than by
the spiritual content of the canvas. The main point—
quality of content—had apparently escaped them."

Crowninshield and Barnes, who found his letter deeply
touching, were being supercilious. Authors who are seriously interested in literature may small-talk about royalties
among themselves; museum people may take the aesthetic
quality of a work for granted when they talk about money
values; and Barnes himself made quite a to-do of the
museum's allegedly overpaying for *The Bathers*, as he had
previously reproached it for paying $36,000 for a Cézanne
which he said it could have had for $24,000.

Barnes blandly applied Crowninshield's criticism of the
personnel of the *university museum* to that of the *Pennsylvania Museum of Art*. His letter, Barnes said, rendered
"a genuine public service in putting a spotlight on the
core of the city's throbbing boil, which, sound public
opinion [i.e., the Friends of Art and Education] says, needs
the kind of lancing I gave it."

And still he did not relent. On January 23, 1936, an
anti-Fascist mural painted by Rachel Kapustin was un-
veiled at the New Theatre. Although it is said to have

been more admirable in its intention than in painting quality, Barnes was there, partly because in this case he was more concerned with the intention, partly because he admired the theater's director, Lem Ward, and partly because it gave him another chance to attack the Kimball museum as "fascistic."

20

Parallel Events

FOR ALL OF BARNES'S APPARENT CONCENTRATION ON THE museum (in 1938 renamed the Philadelphia Museum of Art), he was doing many other things in the 1930's. He was still actively collecting. In the first year or two of the decade he made the acquaintance of a young Russian art dealer, Vitale Bloch, in Berlin. Besides having a good time in his company, he bought from Bloch an angel by the anonymous fifteenth-century Florentine painter known as Maestro del Bambino Vispo. In the year that he began to be concerned with the lot of the artists on the Federal art project, Barnes was happy to pay $50,000 for Renoir's *Portrait of Mlle. Jeanne Durand-Ruel as a Young Girl,* one of the most exquisite paintings of childhood in the world. He also obtained possession of another important Renoir he had been pursuing for years: *The Henriot Family.*

In 1936 Barnes got rid of the irritation of the Benson exhibition by a grand splurge on his summer trip to Europe, spending half a million dollars on additions to the collection. In Switzerland he bought Cézannes—*The Drinker* and *The Woodchopper,* and he picked up in various places four more works of Matisse, Manet's *Le Linge,* two Raoul Dufys, an Egyptian sculpture from about 1800 B.C., and two Greek sculptures dating from 700-500 B.C. Though few were chosen to see the collection, Barnes did not keep his purchases a secret from the press. At least one Philadelphia newspaper reproduced a new Manet, *Le Linge.*

When he returned home in September he told the press that Paul Valéry, the distinguished poet and essayist, would lecture at the Foundation that winter if his health permitted. Apparently it did not (nor did Valéry come to Merion before his death in 1945), but another famous man made his appearance: the sixty-nine-year-old Ambroise Vollard, the "discoverer" of Cézanne and Renoir. Persuaded by Bignou, Barnes took this occasion to end his long-standing hostility to the New York art critics. Their chief fault was that they were in the same profession as the Philadelphia art critics who had derided the Academy show. Inviting the New Yorkers as a group was less an act of good will than of public relations. In one stroke Barnes would gain the good will of the most important newspaper critics in the country and do honor, through their presence, to Vollard. As much as Barnes's purchases, this invitation to the critics was a measure of Bignou's influence over him.

In the gathering were Henry McBride of the *Sun;* Edward Alden Jewell of *The Times;* Carlyle Burrows of the *Herald-Tribune;* Malcolm Vaughan of the *Journal-American;* Alfred M. Frankfurter of *Art-News;* and Margaret Breuning of the *Evening Post,* who thought, perhaps mistakenly, that she was invited only as the wife of the drama critic John Anderson, whom Barnes admired.

One critic missing was Emily Genauer, then with the *World-Telegram*. Some years previously, when she was covering an exhibition at the Pennsylvania Academy, she decided at the last moment to try to look in on the Barnes collection on the same day. She telephoned Barnes to ask for permission. It was not as simple as all that. One did not walk into a telephone booth, look through the directory for "Albert C. Barnes," and call him. His name was not listed in the directory; neither was the Barnes Foundation. Few persons were privileged to have the unlisted numbers, and one of them was Bignou, not only because he was a friend, but also because he might at any moment have hot word of some masterpiece up for sale. As a friend of Miss Genauer, Bignou let her have the number. She telephoned Barnes and he curtly said no, she couldn't come that day. But he fixed a future date, at ten o'clock of a Saturday or Sunday morning.

Miss Genauer was there at the appointed time. She had driven down with her husband, but she did not dare ask him to come along: the invitation was definitely for one. The door opened to her ring; she was admitted. But only to the anteroom. The attendant handed her the Foundation's formal statement of policy on admissions, and when she had finished reading it she was at once escorted to the door: reinforcing the courtesy of the attendant were two huge and fierce-looking dogs (so Miss Genauer recalls them; in her fear, she forgot her journalistic duty to note what breed of dogs they were). On the reverse side of the Foundation's statement was a special message for the critic. It said, in effect: Keep this as a souvenir of your visit, payment for violating the privacy of my employer by using his unlisted phone.

Possibly Barnes did not know that she had obtained the number from Bignou, but perhaps it would not have made any difference. What made him so vengeful was Miss Genauer's intention of throwing in a visit to Merion *incidental to* seeing an exhibition at the *Academy*—the place where his own great exhibition had been insulted and himself humiliated. Merion should be a place of pilgrimage.

When Barnes came to invite the critics as a group, he did not include her. Bignou was disturbed about it and persuaded Barnes to change his mind. Too proud to ask her directly, Barnes had Bignou invite her in his name. But Miss Genauer was in turn too proud to accept an invitation at secondhand.

McBride wrote many years later in *Art News:* "We were a rather gay party going down, almost filling a Pullman." At the North Philadelphia station "a flock of motors" were on hand to take them to Merion. They were warmly welcomed; Mrs. Barnes "made a particular point of seeking me out and being particularly kind." McBride did not mention that Barnes himself gave a talk before introducing Vollard. According to Burrows, it was a rather bristling talk, in which Barnes called the critics sentimentalists and rebuked them for being unreceptive to modern art. (This was certainly not true of the majority of them: Barnes was still attacking the Philadelphia critics of 1923.) He also told his audience what a great privilege it was to be admitted to the museum.

Vollard's address, which students of the Foundation had been invited to hear, was a concise but comprehensive appreciation of French art in general and the quality of the Barnes collection in particular; McBride called it "very rugged and invincibly bourgeois like himself." Bignou translated the talk; the students left; and Barnes served his guests a Scotch whisky which they all seem to remember at least as vividly as the collection. Thus Miss Breuning: "Our host, being a chemist, measured out the highballs as carefully as in a laboratory operation, and balancing the relation of water, ice and whisky so admirably that the highballs were memorable." (The whisky is said to have been the product of a small "captive" distillery—Barnes bought its entire output.) So stimulated, the critics were allowed to wander through the galleries on their own.

"By the time the dinner hour arrived," McBride's account continues, "we had all made sufficient discoveries to put us in a holiday mood and the table-talk was animated in the extreme." McBride did not say whether he was able to hear Vollard, who was entertaining those seated near him, in his Madagascar-flavored French, with a series of ribald stories. "The dinner itself [others called it a buffet supper] was admirable in every way, good food, more of that fabulous whisky (of which the Doctor was said to have an unlimited supply) and the sense borne in upon all of us that we were participating in a really exceptional occasion. If there had been the faintest touch of eccentricity anywhere in this entertainment I failed to notice it."

Three years previously the Knoedler Gallery in New York had exhibited paintings from the Vollard collection. Having, for example, bought Cézannes before the turn of the century (when nobody wanted them) for from two to twenty dollars apiece, he had more than enough canvases to satisfy current demand. . . . In the foreword to the catalog, Barnes wrote:

So many exciting stories about Ambroise Vollard have gained world-wide circulation, and so few persons even in art circles have known him personally, that he appears more as a

legendary character than as a man of flesh and blood of
our own time. Almost invariably the tales illustrate the
penetrating insight, the wise judgment, the independence of
thought and action out of which the normal imagination
tends to create a superman belonging rather to the world
of myth than to the real one. The group of pictures exhibited now to the public for the first time furnishes tangible
evidence that the most thrilling stories about Vollard's
qualities of mind and spirit are not legends but historical
facts.

Soon after his visit to the Foundation with the critics,
Vollard returned the compliment. Speaking over station
WINS on November 9, he said: "You have all probably
noticed that on your return from a foreign country only
a few outstanding experiences remain in your memory.
The great experience of this very short trip to America
has been my visit to the Barnes Foundation. With the
authority which my age permits me to assume, I assure
you that there does not exist and will never exist in the
world another collection of masterpieces of the two greatest
artists of the nineteenth century, Cézanne and Renoir,
comparable to the one assembled by Dr. Barnes."

In January of 1937 Barnes came back from a three
weeks' trip abroad "with a wealth of new things."

Later that year Vitale Bloch was in Merion to show
Barnes a panel by Hieronymus Bosch which was a small
replica of *The Temptation of St. Anthony* of the famous
triptych in Lisbon. He was young and timid; it was his
first visit to the United States; he had only a very limited
knowledge of English; and he was anxious about the
reception he would receive. There was a lecture going on
when Bloch arrived at the Foundation and he sat it out.
When it was over, Barnes announced to the class: "Here

is Mr. Vitale Bloch from Europe, who will give us a talk on Bosch."

The picture was put on an easel, and the bewildered young man, in his faltering English, began to mumble about the works of Bosch he had seen in American collections. From time to time Barnes interrupted him to make ironical remarks about American museum directors. Bloch groped his syntactical way through more sentences. Perhaps at the end, Barnes asked him whether he could see any affinity between Bosch's way of handling paint and that of some modern artist. The lecture, the talk, the endurance contest, was over. Though he had in a sense been put on the spot, the young visitor felt, after the ordeal was over, that he had been honored.

The panel was then taken to its appointed place in the gallery, accompanied by the whole class. To Bloch, it must have been in the nature of a triumphal procession: all this, before Barnes had said a word about buying the picture or the price. After the picture was hung, Barnes called him into the office and asked him what he wanted for it. Without a further word, he wrote out the check. From his bookshelf he took a copy of the Barnes-De Mazia book, *The Art of Renoir,* inscribed a pleasant note above his signature, and handed it to Bloch. "Is there anything else I can do for you?"

Elated, exhausted, Bloch wanted only to be driven to the railroad station, and one of the students took him there in his old Ford. "The whole visit," Bloch recalls, "took on for me the colors of a fairy tale."

There was one person who was not altogether pleased with Barnes's purchases, and that was Edith Glackens. As Forbes Watson had written, one could not fairly evaluate

Glackens' work without seeing his pictures in the Barnes collection. Since these were virtually locked up, she may well have felt that there were critics who withheld the recognition due him because they were unfamiliar with these pictures.

One of them she herself especially prized, *Armenian Girl,* she tried to buy back. Of course, Barnes replied, he would be glad to let her have it, and at a bargain price— $85,000! But he consoled her with the thought that the picture was in excellent company, and that in a hundred years, when he "let her" look down on earth with him, she would be satisfied with her husband's position among the stars. . . . It didn't go down too well with Mrs. Glackens.

This exchange took place in 1937. The following spring, while visiting the Charles Prendergasts in Westport, Conn., Glackens suffered a cerebral hemorrhage. The attending physician did not think he could save him. Even at this poignant moment, Mrs. Glackens remained her doughty self. "If you can't bring him back the way he used to be," she said, "please don't bring him back at all."

Barnes had left for Paris the day before his friend was stricken. As soon as he learned of it, he wrote Mrs. Glackens that he had loved "Butts as I have never loved but half a dozen people in my lifetime. He was so real, and so gentle and of a character that I would have given millions to possess."

To the memorial exhibition which the Whitney Museum of American Art quickly got together, in December, Barnes lent *Armenian Girl* and other pictures—the first time he had lent anything from the collection: but when the show went on to the Carnegie Institute, he withdrew them.

Though Henry McBride could cloak an unfavorable

verdict in ambiguous irony, his review of the Glackens show was utterly forthright and damning. One would have thought that Barnes would have vilified McBride and banned him from his domain forever. Barnes *was* furious. In his article in *Art News,* McBride wrote that he was told Barnes "was actually preparing two heavyweight boxers (one would have been enough) to come over to New York to give me a horse-whipping." This was "probably one of those rumors with which Greenwich Village in those days was rife." Forgetting such alleged monkeyshines, one must still assume that McBride's negative verdict on Glackens deeply upset Barnes both as friend and believer in his work. Yet he did not even bar McBride from Merion—he invited him to come again, the only one of the critics in the 1936 group he did invite a second time.

This happened after McBride reviewed an exhibition of Barnes's protégé Angelo R. Pinto, at the Bignou Gallery. Barnes wrote the introduction to the catalog, and McBride quoted "about an inch" of it. "This pleased him inordinately and immediately he wrote me asking me down for any week-end in May I chose, saying I would have the entire museum to myself after the pupils had left on Saturday, and adding that all I wished of the famous Scotch would equally be at my command."

What are we to make of Barnes's uncharacteristic forgiveness of McBride? Is it possible that his judgment of Glackens was shaken under the impact of McBride's authority? Is it significant that he did not get around to writing the monograph on Glackens he had promised himself to do? Was he host to an unconscious resentment of his friend for having started his collection? Barnes made a great point of his having replaced eight of Glackens' purchases with better paintings; and he was loath to tell just which ones Glackens had bought. But all these possibilities may count for nothing against one other interpretation: that the brass-knuckled warrior who had made so many authorities tremble at his approach was really a lonely child seeking and being appeased by just a little love, a little quote.

Barnes was especially active in collecting antiques during these years. Possibly he was first interested in the Pennsylvania German handicrafts of his native region, but he soon went on to Early American work generally. To restore damaged furniture by the same methods the original craftsmen used—"a field in which we believe we have no rivals"—Barnes set up a workshop, which also had the obverse function of taking apart his purchases to see whether they were genuine. "Let one screw, a strip of molding, a replaced bit of wood, be found—and back the [disassembled] article would hurtle to the dealer's shop," his secretary, Mrs. Cynthia Flannery Stine, wrote in a piece for *Harper's* (August, 1956), from which we shall hear more in a later chapter. "If the dealer was humble and contrite, Barnes was back the next day to make a new purchase. But if he asked one question, or offered one explanation, he was instantly blackballed."

As a lover of bargains—though he paid heavily for pictures when he had to—Barnes frequented the auction rooms. But if you buy things at auction, you buy at your own risk and cannot hurtle back mistakes. Once Barnes was boasting of the gateleg table on which he had outbid a well-known local dealer. The man in question, Arthur J. Sussel, overheard him and pointed out that the table was fitted with a new drawer. Even though Barnes had "Mitzi" (Miss de Mazia) do his scouting for him, he fell, according to Sussel, for many fakes.

At a famous auction, that of the Joseph Hergesheimer

collection, Barnes bought some Chippendale silver for
$750—a higher price than he usually paid for antiques—
and a sofa about which he had had endless correspondence
with Hergesheimer until the nonplussed author stopped
answering. At this auction Barnes also bought some five-
dollar items. A bundle of embroidered German towels,
not shown in advance, was started at $2. The bid went to
$15, $16. . . . Sussel, who had managed to get a look at
the bundle, went up to $19 and let Barnes have it for
$20. A few days later Barnes came to Sussel's shop and
the dealer asked him what the towels were like. There was
only one really fine one, Barnes said; the rest were run-of-
the-mill items worth two dollars apiece. "What were you
bidding for?" "The same reason as you," replied Sussel.

Barnes was there that day to shop for early American
glass. "Do you know anything about it?" said Sussel. "No,
I want you to teach me." The first lesson cost $450.

Barnes asked him whether he would take a check. "Got
any credentials?" "Don't you know who I am?" "I know
you hang around auctions." Of course Sussel was pulling
his leg. The transaction completed, Barnes drove Sussel
to Merion for a look at the collection and then saw him
home.

Going out every day immediately after lunch, Barnes
accumulated antiques as he had paintings. "The best
furniture, of course, went to the gallery," wrote Mrs.
Stine, "the next best in Barnes's house, and after that in
the homes of two of his staff and in our city office. Each
morning when I arrived, men were carrying in new pieces
and hauling out replaced ones—a pine cupboard, perhaps,
pushing my typewriter desk into a corner, or a dry sink
forcing files into the hall and an adding machine into the
bathroom. China was installed on shelves that had held
reference books, wrought-iron hinges replaced calendars,

and my posture typing chair gave way to a squat milking stool."

To accommodate his antiques more appropriately, Barnes finally, in 1941, bought a place their own age, a twelve-room house (1775) on a 150-acre farm. "Ker-Feal" he called it, which is Breton dialect for "Fidèle's house," i.e., doghouse. He paid $40,000 for his joke. Besides setting off the antiques, the house served as an annex to the Foundation, where Mrs. Barnes and several members of the University of Pennsylvania faculty held classes in horticulture, botany and landscape architecture.

The Barnes farm at Rapp's Corner was not far from the Sussels country place at Birchrunville, and the Barneses often dropped around. Mrs. Barnes was particularly interested in their garden and shrubs. Barnes criticized their mantel in their living room as being out of place: white marble didn't belong in that setting. "Have you seen the Washington house in Valley Forge?" "Well?" "The mantel is of white marble, from a local quarry. There are three places where white marble was found: Valley Forge, West Chester and Germantown." "Just the same, I wouldn't have it. I don't like it."

He was a collector of mantels, though. There was a row of them at the farmhouse, all whitewashed. Standing so, uninstalled, they looked like so many pieces in a storeroom.

Barnes often came to Sussel's store and they had many amicable tiffs. Barnes liked a bargain and Sussel wasn't offering any. He knew his stuff and he stuck to his price. At the George Horace Lorimer sale, another event in the world of antiques, Barnes didn't get any of the best pieces—Sussel got them all. Afterward Barnes wanted to buy them from him, but he was unwilling to pay the price. Another time Sussel offered him a Pennsylvania

German painted chest in good condition for $1,500. Oh no, that was a lot of money. He bought instead, for $150, a chest in which the painted design was almost worn off. If he couldn't beat Sussel down, he just wouldn't buy. However, Mrs. Sussel observed that Barnes often argued for the sake of arguing, and he must have bargained sometimes in the same spirit, just for the fun of it.

Barnes made the rounds of the antique shops in New York as well as in Philadelphia. He bought quite a few pieces at Ginsburg & Levy's, where he always showed up attended by a retinue . . . to advise him? to be witnesses of what he said or did, in case of court action? It hardly seemed necessary: both the partners were reliable, honorable men. Whatever caused his displeasure, Barnes one day told Ginsburg never to come around again or he would befoul him.

Browsing at the Carlebach Gallery, Barnes found a pair of Swedish tankards to his liking and bought them for $30. When he identified himself, Julius Carlebach, knowing of Barnes's interest in African Negro sculpture, showed him some of the work of primitive peoples from his diverse stock. "Much to my surprise," Carlebach said later, "when I showed him an Alaskan item he thought it was African, and when I showed him an item from the Philippines he thought it was from the Congo. Everything I showed him he mistook for something else."

Well, Barnes didn't pretend to be an expert on all primitive art, but perhaps Carlebach exaggerated the case for cause—in part payment for an atrocious letter Barnes wrote him. When those Swedish tankards were slow in arriving at Merion, Barnes queried him about them. Carlebach checked his records and found that a clerk had misdirected the package, and he so informed Barnes. This was the answer he received: "Your letter of

July 7 confirms my belief you are so *dumm* that you should be put into a concentration camp for imbeciles." Reversing (without the obscenity) the Ginsburg & Levy situation, Carlebach told Barnes to stay away from his place; he didn't want any of his business.

Barnes did not confine his collecting at home to antiques. To supplement the masterworks he purchased abroad, he was constantly exploring for new native talent; and this is the best evidence against those who declare that he had no judgment of his own. In 1939 Milton Avery was having his first one-man show at the Valentine Gallery. Although the dealer had already selected his paintings, he was willing to include some other canvas the artist especially liked. Avery brought in a fairly large canvas he had just finished of a standing figure and child on an expanse of beach. Dudensing took a look at it and said, "I'll hang it, but of course I could never sell a picture like that." All of Avery's work was painted in flat, simplified forms in delicate color. His work was not calculated to draw mobs to the gallery. The latest canvas was only somewhat more austere than the others.

The day after the exhibition opened, Dudensing telephoned the artist excitedly to tell him that Barnes had been around and liked his work, especially the beach scene. He was willing to buy it if he could have it for $150. The asking price was twice that, but Dudensing let his commission go and Barnes made out his check to Avery directly.

After Robert Carlen opened a new gallery in Philadelphia in 1937, Barnes always dropped in at the exhibitions (some of them by his own students). One of the artists he became interested in was Paul Wieghardt. The fact that he was a refugee from Germany did not prevent

Barnes from trying to buy him at bargain rates. One picture he liked was priced at $300. "How much is it to me?" said Barnes. Carlen offered to waive his commission. Not enough; Barnes offered $100 and the dealer had no alternative but to accept. Barnes bought seven Wieghardts all told.

But his greatest find at the Carlen Gallery was Horace Pippin. Untrained, without any knowledge of other painters, Pippin had the vision of a born artist. He came out of the First World War with a crippled right arm and his left hand had to support the right wrist in order for him to be able to paint at all. In his home town, Chester, near Philadelphia, friendly shopkeepers hung his pictures in their windows, but they found no takers at $5 apiece. Pippin gave a picture to a barber friend, but the man's wife wouldn't let him hang it in their home. To the untutored eye, his paintings were uncouth, nor could the untutored eye perceive their imaginative quality. But it was in a shoemaker's window that the art critic Christian Brinton saw *Cabin in the Cotton* and discovered Pippin. Brinton brought his work to the attention of Carlen, who scheduled an exhibition for mid-January of 1940. A few days before the opening Barnes and Miss de Mazia dropped in. Although the pictures were set out on the floor facing the walls, they partially revealed themselves, for Pippin used a home-made canvas so porous that the paints bled through. Curious, Barnes asked to have a look at them right side up, and he was so excited about them he bought five on the spot and reserved another for Charles Laughton. Miss de Mazia also bought one.

Barnes asked whether the catalog for the show contained some foreword. It did not, and what was more, it was already in press. Barnes insisted that it should have a foreword, for Pippin was the most important folk painter he had ever come across. Of course he was too busy to write one himself. . . . Carlin felt that he was eager to do it, and he was and he did. Working at it seriously, writing and rewriting, he achieved an excellent characterization of Pippin's work.

It is probably not too much to say [Barnes concluded], that he is the first important Negro painter to appear on the American scene and that his work shares with that of John Kane the distinction of being the most individual and unadulterated painting authentically expressive of the American spirit that has been produced during our generation. To hold against Pippin his present inability to make pigment express his ideas and feelings with refinement and finesse, is equivalent to finding fault with Andrew Jackson because he never went to college.

The Pippin show ran for a month and every one of the fifteen paintings for sale (six were loans) and the five burnt-wood panels were sold at an average price of $150. Carlen got the picture from Pippin's barber friend for Mrs. Juliana Force, director of the Whitney Museum of American Art, and when he turned over $75, half of the purchase price, to him, the man couldn't believe it. "Do you think anybody was a goddamned fool to pay that much money for Horace's picture?" he asked.

Barnes had Carlen bring Pippin out to Merion. The artist strolled through the galleries by himself for a while, and when he returned Barnes asked him how he liked the pictures. "Very nice," said Pippin. If he had been impressed, he had not been so overawed as to suppress his true judgments. In his monograph on the artist, Selden Rodman reports that Pippin said of a Matisse painting: "That man put the red in the wrong place." Rodman did not set down another comment he knew about. When Barnes asked Pippin which artist he liked best, he said it was Renoyr (so pronounced), because his pictures were "full of sunlight . . . and look at them there tits!" Rodman is careful to explain that Pippin was not referring to Renoir's skill in painting flesh.

Barnes also invited Pippin to attend Miss de Mazia's lectures. Did he expect that this would help the artist rise above "his present inability to make pigment express his ideas and feelings with refinement and finesse," or to help him "see"? ("We do not teach students how to paint, for that would be like teaching ducks to swim. We teach them how to learn to see.") In either case, it was not a happy idea, for it is the essence of a folk artist to lack refinement, and an analytical method was the last thing in the world a *naïf* could benefit from. Instinctively feeling this, Pippin dropped out of the class after several weeks.

Bignou gave Pippin an exhibition that fall. The following year Carlen held a second show and Barnes wrote a second foreword for it. Thereafter, he wanted to see all of Pippin's work before it was put on the market, but there came a time when the dealer felt it was unwise to limit himself in this way. He began to offer the pictures to other buyers. Barnes didn't like it, and when Carlen obtained a commission for the artist to illustrate a special cotton issue of *Vogue* magazine Barnes accused him of exploiting Pippin. Later on, he allowed Carlen to bring Rodman for an interview, but when they arrived he told Carlen, "You stay outside."

As in the 1920's, people kept applying for admission to the gallery all through the following two decades, and most of them stayed outside. The pattern of acceptance or rejection was the same. Those who were admitted—at least those who had status in the art world—often had to pay a small charge, but not in money: they had to listen to a lecture demonstrating the Barnes approach to art. Thus, Harry B. Wehle, then curator of paintings at the Metropolitan Museum of Art, was "compelled" to listen to a talk by Miss de Mazia on the French Primitives, a field in which he was quite at home. Though the exaction of such tribute was, in principle, condescending if not insulting, the actual lecture was not, in this case, too burdensome; Wehle even picked up a pointer from it.

When *The Man Who Came to Dinner* booked in at the Forrest Theatre in Philadelphia in the winter of 1939, the dramatic-critic-turned-actor Alexander Woollcott was playing the title role. Perhaps he was taking advantage of his native city in this, but it was in all simplicity that he sent Barnes a wire asking for permission to see a certain dozen-odd of the paintings. A reasonable request? An intelligent one, implying that it took a great deal of time to see the whole collection? This was the reply Woollcott received at the theater the next evening:

I was alone in the house this morning when a telegraph-office employee telephoned that she had a telegram for Dr. Barnes, charges collect. I explained that our financial condition made it impossible for us to assume the additional responsibility and I declined to accept the telegram. She explained that it was from such an important man that I should call Dr. Barnes to the phone to take the message. . . . My reply was that Dr. Barnes was out on the lawn singing to the birds and that it would cost me my job if I should disturb him at his regular Sunday-morning nature worship.

The telegraph-office girl is evidently a person either very sympathetic to my lowly station or an individual who knows that to thwart a man of your eminence would be flagrant lèse-majesté, for she read the telegram to me.

I write you thus, frankly, so that you will understand the

dilemma I was in, and in the hope that you will forgive my
not knowing what a distinguished person you are.

The letter was type-signed "Fidèle de Port-Manech,
Secrétaire de Dr. Barnes." The French was not effecta-
tion, for the "secretary" was born in Port-Manech. She
was none other than the ingratiating mongrel he had
brought many years before, whose *personal* signature was
a paw mark.

Woollcott's biographer, Samuel Hopkins Adams, says
that Barnes was being facetious in writing as if the telegram had been sent collect. Though the stunt seems very
much in smart Alec's character, Barnes, too, could allow
his fancy free rein. Woollcott's offense was that he dared
seek admittance in a hurry. Didn't he realize that there
was an immutable order of things at the Foundation, a sun
and planets moving in a harmonious relationship, not to
be broken into by a maverick meteorite?

Barnes sent a copy of his letter to the *Record* (he was
always sending carbon copies everywhere to multiply his
protests or his triumphs) and began another verbal battle.
. . . When Woollcott tired of it, he wrote Barnes that it
would be impossible for him to continue the correspondence after he left the city and that he would come to see
the pictures the next time he passed through Philadelphia.
It was, he thought, a clever last word; and it was clever
but not the last word.

Barnes labeled Woollcott's withdrawal a case of cold
feet. As for the plump Woollcott's dropping in some other
time: "I must warn you that thousands of birds inhabit
our park and they swoop down on every visible lump of
suet and peck it to pieces." In its savage wit, precise terse
wording and exultant rhythm, the sentence is superior to
the occasion which evoked it. And still the bulldog in

Barnes did not let go. When Leonard Lyons wrote a résumé of the mock battle in his column in the New York *Post*, Barnes sent him a note with a supplementary batch of clippings: *he* had to have the last word.

Impudent would-be actors, no! Real artists of the stage and screen were as welcome as ever. One day it was Greta Garbo, to whom he discoursed on Pennsylvania German handicrafts; another time it was Edward G. Robinson, himself a collector of French moderns. At lunch they talked affably about art and the theater: Barnes was particularly curious about actors. Robinson spent the whole day in Merion—it was a Sunday, with music by the Bordentown chorus—and left with a copy of *The Art in Painting* (no charge). The two men exchanged letters and this might have gone on indefinitely, Robinson thinks, if he were not such a poor correspondent.

There were students at the Foundation who found Barnes "gentle, generous, unassuming," and whom Barnes treated as equals. He often dropped in informally on one such young couple. What if he lived in a mansion and they in a $10,000 suburban home? Looking out of their living-room window, he said, almost enviously, "You have all that beautiful park and you don't have to pay for the upkeep." On one occasion the young man came to see him, wearing a Palm Beach suit. Feeling the fabric, Barnes said, "What a nice suit. I'd like to get one like that." The young woman frankly asked Barnes why he didn't write the story of his life, to which he answered, "Because I wouldn't tell the truth, that's why." (Was it more than repartee?)

One day, as Barnes was slouching about the gallery, hands in pockets, she approached him.

"Are you in a good mood now?" she said.

"Why? You want money?" He jingled the coins in his pocket.

No, she wanted him to let a refugee friend see the collection. What was the refugee like? A very nice fellow.

"Let him come."

Barnes was there when the visitor arrived and in fact found him to be a nice, intelligent man. After his tour of the gallery they had a pleasant talk, Barnes doing his best with what he himself called his "bad German," which he thought was the cause of the visitor's misunderstanding. For the man reported to his student friend that Barnes had told him he could come again any time he pleased. When she mentioned this to Barnes, he declared, "I didn't say that—I wouldn't give Jesus Christ that privilege!"

Barnes had given a French musician whom he met in Paris a standing invitation to see his collection. The man got to this country during the war, in 1944, and was staying near Merion with a friend, who sent a message to Barnes asking him to redeem his promise. Back came the messenger with the one-word reply: "Nuts." Had Barnes forgotten the man, or—this was soon after the Battle of the Bulge—did he think it too good a joke to pass up, this echoing on his own toy parade ground of General Anthony MacAuliffe's reply on a bloody battlefield to the German demand for surrender?

Another refugee from France had got in touch with Barnes before this: Jacques Lipchitz. He wanted to see the collection or, more accurately, to see his work installed in a great gallery; he was possibly even more interested in obtaining a commission, for, fleeing the Nazis, he had left behind him not only all his sculpture but also most of his belongings of value. Plainly, he needed money. But all the reasons put together were no help. Barnes the anti-Fascist would not even receive the refugee who had committed the unforgivable sin of making him confound art and philanthropy.

21

"Carry Me Back to Old Virginny"

WHILE THE PIPPIN EXHIBITION WAS GOING ON, THE FOUNDA-
tion's annual affair with the Bordentown chorus took place.
Among the guests was Carl Van Vechten, who had first
seen the collection in 1933 and who was exhorted many
times thereafter by Barnes to come for the annual affair.
Van Vechten knew the spirituals too well to care especially
about hearing another amateur group do them, nor was
he tempted by Barnes's promised demonstration of their
kinship to the paintings of Renoir and the Pennsylvania
German handicrafts.

Van Vechten had visited Merion at other times and
had taken photographs of Barnes; once Barnes had sat
for him at his New York home. He was so enthusiastic
about Van Vechten's camera work that he had him photograph members of his staff, his protégés and his famous
friends. For once he was angry with John Dewey when he

did not join their number; for once he was angry with himself when he forgot to ask Vollard to sit for his friend.

In January, 1940, Barnes invited Van Vechten once more to the Foundation's fiesta, this time tempting him with the prospect of meeting Thomas Mann and Albert Einstein, who had attended the previous year's. They "were almost garrulous in their expression of appreciation and asked to come again. It is possible that they may be there on Sunday." Van Vechten accepted because his wife, the actress Fania Marinoff, wanted to see the collection.

After the chorus had completed the program of spirituals, Barnes asked the director, Frederick Work, to give "Carry Me Back to Old Virginny" as an encore, even though it was not a spiritual and the composer was not, he thought, a Negro. He knew a more poignant song of return, of the sweet chariot "comin' for to carry me home," but he shared the universal love for the heavily sentimental song of the Old Dominion. Alma Gluck's rendition was the first Victor Red Seal record to find a million buyers, and the most musical people in Europe were singing *"Heimweh nach Virginia."*

Later in the day Van Vechten told Barnes that the composer, James A. Bland, *was* a Negro, and a famous one. Ashamed that he should not have known this, Barnes would not admit the fact; he appealed to Work, who confirmed it. When Van Vechten added that he had an idea that Bland was buried in some potter's field, Barnes was horrified. He urged him to check on the matter and let him know. And when Van Vechten telephoned him soon after that Bland was indeed buried in an unmarked grave, and *in Merion itself,* Barnes moved energetically to redeem the dishonor, to have a monument erected in the composer's memory.

He did not know anything at all about Bland except that he had written the words and music of one of his favorite songs. Bland was not born in the South but in Flushing, N. Y., in 1854; both parents were born of freemen for generations back, and his father, Allen, was one of the first Negroes to receive a college education, at Wilberforce University, of which he was later president. The family moved to Washington after the Civil War, where Bland's father became the first Negro examiner in the Patent Office. His son entered Howard University as a law student.

Young Bland was no student, but he was a good singer and banjo player; he was writing songs; and he began to entertain around town. His serious-minded parents were not amused. Neither were the authorities at Howard, conscious as they were, in those difficult post-Civil War years, of its high purpose as a center of Negro education. They didn't flunk him out, but they turned down cold his frivolous proposal to put on a musical at the school (which he then "secretly" staged downtown). He was only twenty-one years old when he wrote "Carry Me Back to Old Virginny." (Barber shop quartets are still singing another early composition, "In the Evening by the Moonlight"; and "Dem Golden Slippers" is said to have sold 100,000 copies in a few years.)

By then Bland had graduated from Howard, joined, though they did not require a degree, Billy Kersand's (later Haverly's) Minstrels, a top Negro troupe, and became nationally famous as an entertainer. In 1884 Bland went to England with the Callender Minstrels, scoring such a great personal success as a singing, joking end man that he decided to stay on when the company completed its engagement. Bland was a star in an otherwise white English minstrel show. He gave a command performance in Buckingham Palace before the Prince of Wales. Earning $10,000 a year, he remained in England twenty years with only a few brief trips home. One commentator said he had composed "Carry Me Back . . ." in a "fit of homesickness for his native land."

He returned to Washington in 1901, flat broke. During his long stay abroad, the name of "the best Ethiopian song writer in the world," as he called himself, or, as others called him, "the Negro Stephen Foster," had been all but forgotten. He had taken out full copyright on only thirty-eight of the some seven hundred songs he is said to have composed, and his works were used freely in all the minstrel shows without his receiving either credit or royalties. Bland moved to Philadelphia to try to improve his position, but without success. He died penniless in 1911 at the age of fifty-seven.

"The news about Bland," Barnes wrote Van Vechten soon after he had learned of the composer's pauper's grave, "is indeed exciting. I began immediately to see if I can get the best of the local Negroes to organize a movement to push the matter [of a monument]. One object of this would be to see that the race gets the main share of the glory, instead of, as usual, having it fall in the lap of go-getting whites."

Two weeks later, he reported his dissatisfaction with the way a local committee was handling the matter. Its chairman, Dr. J. F. Cooke, had told him that the only thing they wanted to do was to put a stone on the unmarked grave. Barnes opposed this "because the cemetery [on Rock Hill and Bryn Mawr Avenues] is the most dilapidated, ramshackle affair imaginable" and because it was likely to be moved since fine homes were going up in that area. To make his opposition more effective, Barnes agreed to become a member of the committee.

What he wanted was to transfer the composer's remains to one of the small parks of the township and erect a monument there. He proposed to rally all Negro organizations to back the project, under the leadership of his former protégé, Dr. Hinkson.

Barnes had already discussed his plan with an old friend, "the most forceful political figure in the Township," who had endorsed it and was going to bring it up at the next meeting of the Township Commissioners.

Barnes had also won over John J. Cabrey, publisher of a local weekly newspaper, *Town & Township,* who agreed to publish a series of articles favoring the memorial. To expand the publicity campaign, Barnes asked Van Vechten if he knew of a top-notch newspaperman who could do a feature article which would be syndicated throughout the country. (Nothing came of this.) Finally, he was going to ask Horace Pippin, the Negro painter who was then a student at the Foundation, if he would undertake to model a suitable figure. "We *must* have a Negro sculptor." (Characteristically, Barnes used someone he knew, even if he was a painter.)

Two days later, on February 22, Barnes wrote Van Vechten that "there's a fine buzz of excitement here about Bland and I believe the Memorial is a *fait accompli.* Today Hinkson and [Dr. Charles A.] Lewis, another local Negro star, [will] come to see me in the forenoon. At 3 P.M. Cooke . . . comes to the gallery for a talk. Cabrey . . . will be present and so, I hope, will [W. C.] Handy [the blues composer]. By this time next week the ball will be rolling and kept going until Bland is where he deserves to be."

The day was not finished before "the fine buzz of excitement" mounted to a nasty explosion. For the second time, on February 22, he wrote to Van Vechten:

I could scarcely sit through the session. I left it with the
decision that either that pompous ass [Dr. Cooke] or I disappear from the scene. He is prominent in unanalyzed musical
circles and made a speech at the first meeting at Bland's grave.

He had his photograph taken at the time and reproduced in
a journal with a large circulation. He said then and told us
today that he's the guy that traced Bland and brought him
to light but the evidence is against him.

He passed us his card . . . as the President of a high-sound-
ing something or other. He told us that he holds ten honorary
degrees, that he is an ace in raising money, that he writes
a poem every Christmas which he sends to his friends . . .
and he happened to have on his person enough copies [of his
latest one] to pass out one to each of us. At this point I had
an almost irresistible impulse to piss in his ear. . . .

In his dislike of Cooke, Barnes slurred over the fact
that he was president of the Presser Foundation and
editor for more than thirty years of *Etude,* a magazine
published by this foundation that once had the largest
circulation of any music periodical in the world (it
ceased publication in 1957) and included among its
contributors Ravel, Damrosch, Melchior, and their like.
This was in fact the "journal with a large circulation" in
which his picture had appeared, and quite properly so,
if, as Dr. Cooke informs me, he carried out the first researches on Bland. They led him to Dr. Kelly Miller,
professor of mathematics and astronomy at Howard University, who had entered it only a few years after Bland
left. It was Dr. Miller's article in *Etude* (July, 1939)
which told of Bland's "lately discovered" burial place;
this was the reference which Van Vechten had seen or
heard about.

The cemetery was about a mile from Cooke's home,
and when he saw the grave covered by a jungle of weeds,
he formed a committee to seek contributions from pros-

perous Negro entertainers to mark it. Before this, the Virginia legislature had appropriated funds for a monument to Bland to be erected in Richmond, but when it was discovered that he was a Negro the project was dropped.

At the time Barnes met Cooke, his committee had accomplished nothing more than to suggest the formation of another committee. "Many of the names proposed are more or less professional figureheads, quite a number of them limelighters and stuffed shirts," Barnes wrote on February 23 to Handy. Explaining that he would have nothing more to do with such an unwieldy committee of eighteen members, he proposed to establish a Bland Memorial Association, for which he would nominate John Dewey as president, Handy and Van Vechten as vice-presidents, and Hinkson, Lewis and Cabrey as other officers. All they needed was the consent of Bland's aged sister, Mrs. Irene B. Jurix, to have the body removed, and an ordnance passed by the township to set aside a place for the monument. Some leading citizens had already endorsed the project and the money was guaranteed, though he suggested again the desirability of Negroes contributing their pennies, nickels, dimes and dollars, to show that they themselves, and not only a few rich white people, were wholeheartedly for the memorial. To dispose of Cooke, Barnes assigned him certain tasks which made him withdraw from the new group.

On that day *Town & Township* printed its first long article under the headline:

Men Knew—but in Shocking
Anonymity They Left Him

On February 24, Edna Thomas, Acting Secretary of the Negro Actors Guild of America, to whom Barnes had sent a carbon copy of his letter to Handy, answered, warmly endorsing the memorial.

On March 1, Barnes, in another note to Van Vechten, exulted, "the biggest shot in the local musical world— Herbert Tily—says he's with us to a cinder. He's a resident of the Township, rich, fine, influential." On that same date *Town & Township* reported that the Virginia legislature had that week, after several months' deliberation, voted "Carry Me Back to Old Virginia" (*sic!*) the official anthem of the state. Could little Merion fail to be influenced by this act of the great Old Dominion?

On March 4 Barnes finally met with Handy, Mrs. Jurix and her son-in-law Clayton French, who was a lawyer. Barnes took them on a tour of the gallery, and then to the proposed site of the memorial in the park at Manayunk and Bryn Mawr Avenues: "a hill in a sylvan dell of exquisite beauty." They were all pleased with it, but there was a hitch: Mrs. Jurix had given the agent of a new local cemetery for Negroes power of attorney to remove Bland's remains; but her son-in-law said that he could have it revoked.

"When everything is set," Barnes wrote Van Vechten, "the Barnes Foundation will establish two James A. Bland Fellowships for Negro artists who in our opinion show promise of individual achievement. The recipients will live in Philadelphia, attend one class per week at the Foundation and be absolutely free to work in the field each selects. The stipend will be $1,000 per year for each. Pippin will get one of them. Negroes as a rule are dilatory —hence, if you can work on Mr. French to do the necessary, you'll be a positive benefactor."

By April 1 the family authorization had not come through. Mrs. Jurix had had to obtain authority from another sister, Mrs. May B. James, before giving her own. Barnes was afraid that the community's enthusiasm would fade. Cabrey had been running an article every week; Pippin's sketch was ready. Two weeks later, the required affidavits came through from French, but they were not in proper legal form; and two more weeks were lost. Then, for the final drive, Barnes suggested that Paul Robeson, whom he had once known, be named Honorary President of the Bland Memorial Association.

On May 31 Cabrey's newspaper ran a headline: "Township Commission Turns Down Bland Memorial." The reason? The proposed site was acquired "for rest and recreation, as well as for its natural attractions" and the commission ruled that it had no power to authorize its use for other purposes. The fact that the memorial would have occupied only about twenty square feet of the park's one and a half acres was immaterial. The commissioners suggested that the Association could buy some of the private land adjacent to the park, in which case they "would probably be inclined to accept the finished project as a public trust." But the adjacent land was not desirable, and the repudiation was wrong in principle. In a long editorial *Town & Township* quoted J. P. Morgan's dictum that men always have a "good" reason and a "real" reason for their actions or failure to act, and that most of them prefer to advance only the "good" reason. That was as far as the paper would go in hinting that race prejudice motivated the commissioners.

Several years later the Philadelphia edition of the Pittsburgh *Courier,* the Negro weekly, published a series of articles urging its people to set up a tombstone for Bland. Nothing came of it.

It was the Lions Club of Virginia which finally placed

a granite headstone and slab on Bland's grave, on July 15, 1946. The dedicatory address was made—according to Cooke, at his suggestion—by the governor of Virginia, William M. Tuck. Several persons, black and white, spoke briefly, while the recorded voice of Marian Anderson sang "Carry Me Back. . . ." Among the two hundred people present, mostly white, were Lions from Cuba, South America and Europe; Mrs. Jurix; and Dr. Cooke. Among those conspicuous by their absence were the governor of Pennsylvania, the mayor of Philadelphia, and Dr. Albert C. Barnes.

Nor was he on the committee which, five years later, bought the old cemetery for $50,000, renamed it Merion Memorial Park, and rededicated it as a permanent memorial for distinguished Negroes (and Chinese). Barnes had not lost his battle altogether: Bland had his monument in a park.

In 1940, when his own project failed, Barnes was so angry that he banished all thought of a memorial from his consciousness—especially since he already had another "cause" to be enthusiastic-indignant about. He forgot the Bland fellowships, broke off communications with Van Vechten. In all the seven years of their friendship they had never had a falling out. Yet when, some time after the Bland memorial fiasco, Van Vechten asked him to admit the Negro sculptor Richard Barthe to the collection, he did not even answer. Barnes was simply running away from Van Vechten because he associated him with his failure. About a year later they met by chance in Paris in Kahnweiler's art gallery. Barnes greeted Van Vechten amiably and said to another man present, "Carl is a great friend of mine." It was the first time he had called Van Vechten by his first name—the last time he was to see him. In the end, he placed a higher value on his pride than on their friendship.

Barnes's new cause was Bertrand Russell. Since it led to Russell's joining the Foundation, let us first see something of Barnes in relation to his staff.

22

Barnes and His Staff

ONE MORNING IN 1936, MISS CYNTHIA FLANNERY, A VASSAR
and business school graduate, came to the house on Spruce
Street to serve as Barnes's secretary. She had been interviewed and hired by Miss Nelle Mullen the day before:
Barnes would see her in the morning. Miss Flannery's
first contact with him was oral: a stentorian voice calling
her from the floor above. She went upstairs, was con-
fronted with four doors. She tried one, then another. . . .
" 'Mi . . . i . . . iss Flannery!' bellowed from behind
me. 'I'm here. What in heaven's name are you doing?' "

"Here" was the bathroom. Barnes was taking a steam
bath in an electric cabinet and he began to give her dictation as naturally as if he were in a swivel chair. From
time to time, as a surgeon calls, "Scalpel!" Barnes called
"Towel!" and Miss Flannery mopped his dripping face.
Enough of steam bath. In the middle of a sentence he
cried out: "The shower. Lukewarm. Instantly!" Miss

Flannery had trouble achieving lukewarm: the water was either scalding or freezing. Impatiently Barnes emerged, his body "a brilliant red." . . . . " 'You fool, I'm coming, you fool. I'm coming!' "

The abashed virgin of Vassar hurried down ("tumbled down") the stairs to a bathroom of her own, where she locked herself in to have a good cry and compose herself. " 'Anything I can do for you, Miss Flannery?' " she heard Miss Mullen say. "And many were the times later on she would sit in our adjoining office listening to my sobs—or I, in there, suspecting hers." It was Barnes's delight, reducing people to tears. Miss Flannery stood up under it for five years, and twenty-five years later related her experience in *Harper's*. "My Private War with Dr. Barnes," the article was called. Alas, the artillery was all on one side.

During her first week, Miss Flannery learned something that was not taught at either college or business school. Every day, for twenty minutes, Barnes had her copy his signature carefully, so that she could sign a libelous letter with a reasonable facsimile of his name. He was thus protected by a legal loophole: *he* had not signed the letter!

Miss Flannery described a dictation session in graphic detail. At first "his mood was mellow and his letters were well worded. . . . He talked faster now, longer words, more complicated thoughts. . . . Dr. Barnes's words became short-tempered, his thoughts erupted in wrath and resentment, his first businesslike letters were supplanted by savage, rabid ones. . . . Repeatedly he snapped 'towel' at me." And this pattern was repeated every day. "As perspiration began to roll from his forehead and vituperative words from his tongue, apoplexy would stalk, and every phrase he dictated would be libelous. Half an hour

later, showered, rested, relaxed, he would nod at the invec-
tive I read back to him, but never once did he mitigate
his abuse or hesitate to add still more defamatory words."
(Perhaps Barnes's increasing irritability was due to the increased temperature or dehydration of his body by the
electric cabinet—an apparatus no longer used.)

One of these scorching letters was addressed to George
Biddle, in reply to a passage in an article the artist had
written in the September, 1940, issue of *Harper's* called
"Can Artists Make a Living?" The answer was No, and the
reason implied in the passage: "And I am convinced myself that the outlook for a vigorous flowering of American
art, integrated and scaled to the hopes and tastes of count-
less millions of Americans, rather than to the pocketbooks
of those who still continue to buy French Impressionists
from Fifty-Seventh Street [the art center of New York], is
still more hopeful."

Biddle had expected to get a rise out of Barnes—he sent
him the article for that purpose. Reading it, Barnes must
have thought it hogwash. What did it have to do with
him? Hadn't he just bought Wieghardt, Avery, Pippin . . . ? And he let Biddle have it. As the artist recalls
the letter, which he did not keep, it called him "a fake
artist, always seeking publicity, trying to achieve notoriety
by clinging to the coattails of my successful friends. Something of the sort. I sent him back what I considered a
withering letter. By return post I received my own unopened letter." Unopened, but maybe not unsteamed
open for a quick reading, for in large letters across the
envelope was written—luckily the postmaster of Croton,
N. Y. did not know basic French—*merde!*

Miss Flannery told of the staff's luncheon consisting
always of orange juice and tomato salad. Even though there
was a house cook, no one dared order anything but the

master's orange juice and tomato salad, served without dressing. No choice of tea or coffee? Never mind—revolt was brewing. Miss Flannery reached her twenty-fifth birthday. "Powerfully egged on" by father, two sisters and husband-to-be, she decided to show the stuff she was made of. She would *not* have orange juice and tomato salad for lunch—she will have peas. She orders peas. The Cézannes did not tremble; the master did not rebuke her. She ordered peas and she got peas. Ah, but who ate them? Barnes leaned over and helped himself to a forkful. "They're absolutely delicious," he said. "Let's change." Four days in a row Miss Flannery ordered peas and Barnes ate them, and for the next three years she had orange juice and tomato salad, without dressing . . . without demur.

In the dozen years since Barnes had begun to appoint teachers from his best students, the policy had worked out well. There were more firings than resignations, but most of the teachers lasted several years: not a bad record, considering that the curriculum, the number of teachers and opportunity for advancement were all limited, considering also the nature of the principal.

By 1939 neither the number of teachers nor the number of students had increased appreciably: half a dozen teachers, less than two hundred students. Apparently Barnes did not wish to cope with a larger staff and student body, for there was a waiting list of several hundred eligible students.

It is curious that he did not envisage an increased scale of operations even in the future. Quite the contrary: on March 16, 1939, he had by-law number 37 amended to read that after his own and his wife's death the Foundation was not to employ—or at least not pay the salaries of—more than *three* teachers (and the maximum salary was to remain $5,000). It was not a question of funds—more money would be available, since there were to be no further purchases for the collection. Did Barnes think no one else could operate on a bigger scale than himself?

Prospective teachers did not have to pass formal examinations any more than prospective students did. All they had to do was to satisfy Barnes that they understood and sincerely believed in his system. He had ample opportunity for observing them in the ranks before elevating them. Edward T. Dreibelbies, John Condax, Fred Geasland and Jack Bookbinder had all studied painting at the Pennsylvania Academy before attending a class at the Foundation. Geasland, a reticent, earnest young fellow, had been there three years when Barnes sent him abroad with the group of twelve in 1934. On his return he was offered an instructor's job and was delighted to have it. Bookbinder had a broader education than the rest of the staff: he was a graduate of both the Academy and the University of Pennsylvania, which he had attended at the same time. In 1935, when he was awarded a fellowship in psychology and social work at the university, he became a student at the Foundation.

He was delighted with it as only an artist and enthusiast can be. The masterpieces were there to be enjoyed week after week; he had Geasland for teacher, with whom he had been friendly at the academy. Bookbinder stayed on the next year and the year after that. During all this time Barnes never said a word to him, nor he, naturally, to Barnes. He would often see the master sitting in the great central hall, smoking his pipe or cigarettes (it used to be cigars) as he contemplated some new painting or one offered to him for purchase. (Nobody else was allowed to smoke in the gallery—it might damage the paintings!)

The young man never approached him—he was scared to death of him.

One morning Bookbinder was coming from a room on the second floor. On the rather dark stairway he startled Barnes going up, and covered his embarrassment with a hello. Since the master did not snub him, he afterward got up courage to join the group clustered around him. And Barnes spoke to him and said: "I understand you're studying psychology. I'd like you to read a book. . . ." Neither the name of the author nor the title came to his mind. It was absurd—he knew the book as well as any of his own. He thought of its companions on the shelf upstairs: Santayana's *The Sense of Beauty,* Rignano's *The Psychology of Reasoning* and his other favorites, but it was no use. Annoyed at his lapse of memory, Barnes went upstairs to look for the volume. But it wasn't there.

"It's by a doctor," Barnes called down. "Don't be misled by the title—it's a damned good book."

He still couldn't find it, and Bookbinder asked him if it could be Dr. Bernard Hart's *The Psychology of Insanity.* It was, and Barnes was very much impressed with a student who had read Hart, though it was written for laymen and had been widely acclaimed since its publication in 1912.

Not long after, Dreibelbies, with whom Bookbinder had studied the year before, sounded him out on his interest in a staff position. Barnes thus avoided the disagreeable experience of possibly having someone say no to him. Bookbinder was curious to know why he had been singled out. It was, the intermediary told him, because he was the most attentive student in the class. Barnes had often observed him as he sat on the edge of his chair, as if he could not bear to miss a word of the lecture. Actually, Bookbinder used to force himself into an uncomfortable position in order to keep awake. Neither the subject nor the teacher was responsible for his sleepiness—it was simply the bad ventilation in the classrooms, in which one sat for an hour and a half without moving. Bookbinder was so deeply interested in the program of the Foundation that he felt honored by the offer and, although he was employed elsewhere at a good salary, accepted it. Dreibelbies told him to see Barnes about his pay, but Bookbinder didn't care what it was.

Beginning teachers received a salary of $35 a week for one day's work and attendance at a Thursday morning seminar. Theoretically at least, the rest of the time was their own. (By way of comparison, one may note that teachers at the Pennsylvania Academy received a flat $1,000 a year for one day's teaching, no matter what their term of service.) With paid vacation, the teacher's minimum annual pay at the Foundation came to $1,820.

At the Thursday seminars the major business was usually an analysis of some painting, sculpture or piece of handicraft. This was a means of testing both the applicability of the Barnes method and the teachers' grasp of it. In a more informal way, Barnes got their reaction to a painting set up in the central hall as he contemplated it and they came by one by one. By integrating their piece-meal appraisals, some of the teachers felt, he arrived at "his" decision, without giving them any credit. "Though he might argue a point, his contradictions merely served to cover up his eagerness to learn from us." This seems like an overstatement of the case. We have seen Barnes buying pictures himself in many places. Even when he lent a keen ear to the opinions of others without seeming to, he did make his choice himself. Possibly it was the particular pictures about which he was in doubt that he presented to his teachers.

The most onerous part of the teachers' job was Barnes's close supervision. To judge their competence, it was his privilege to drop in on a class to listen in or to take part in a discussion. But he would also listen in without entering the classroom, taking up a position outside the door. Knowing this, and not knowing when Barnes might be eavesdropping, kept the teachers in tension. Just before the session was over, Barnes would hurry back to his chair in the central gallery, where teachers and students filed by in homage, as if he had been sitting there all along. (Some stopped to chat with the master, some to flatter him, in the hope of being rewarded with one of those free trips to Europe.)

Besides passing on the teachers' competence, Barnes also checked them to find out whether they were observing the purity of his doctrine. Perhaps the prime purpose of his eavesdropping was to detect heresy. While few of the teachers had any wish or the ability to depart from his scripture radically, they did now and then stray into the margin. Geasland, for example, once made a reference in his class to Leo Stein's *The ABC of Aesthetics.* Anything wrong with that? Geasland was a friend of Stein's; Barnes was a friend of Stein's; and they both admired his book. But when Geasland cited it to his students, Barnes didn't like it. Nor did he like it when Bookbinder, in discussing Venetian painting, brought in the historical background to explain the sumptuousness of the settings and the styles of the artists. Social history was "adventitious" to Barnes in his concentration on plastic form.

The Foundation almost invariably had one effect on all the artist teachers: they stopped painting. The strain of Barnes's inescapable scrutiny was only one cause: some teachers complained that he never encouraged them in their painting, and that he made them feel inferior in

general. It was as if he were saying, though he may not
have been aware of it: "I stopped painting. Who the hell
are *you* to go on with it?" It is difficult to generalize, but
most likely those who stopped painting lacked sufficient
drive. The fact is that several of them—the Pintos and
Condax—took the easier road of commercial photography.
And one must note that there was a stronger deterrent
influence to painting in the gallery than Barnes: the
masterpieces themselves. Seeing them all the time, did not
most of the young painters feel, if only unconsciously, How
can I ever paint as well as this?

The teachers also suffered from a common anxiety: the
fear of losing their jobs. Anyone who is not self-employed
has the same fear in some measure, but nowhere was the
danger so ever-present, so ever-threatening, and not because there might be, as in industry, a decline in production, but because the master might indulge in some
arbitrary—or at least hasty—action. They had seen what
he could do.

With his passion for relating art to life and music,
Barnes was half-looking for the equivalent of a unified
field theory relating art to every human activity. Considering the beautiful arboretum in Merion (he once told a
teacher that he was not really interested in it), he conceived the idea of relating arboriculture to art; he passed
on the happy word to Professor Schrepfer, who was about
to lecture at the arboretum. Appearing at his first class,
made up largely of students in the art courses recruited
by Barnes, Schrepfer found a painting of a tree by Renoir
among his demonstration materials. He knew his trees;
he apparently knew nothing about art; and he was an
honest man: he was doomed. What, from his great store of
knowledge, could he say about this Renoir tree? Obviously,

that it was a sick tree. . . . His diagnosis was reported to Barnes. To the distress of Mrs. Barnes, who asked one of the teachers why the remark had to be passed on to her husband, the professor was dismissed immediately and the class disbanded.

If this could happen to a member of the University of Pennsylvania faculty, what could an ordinary teacher at the Foundation, without status, expect? It was true that Barnes was beginning to make provision for the oldest members of his staff on all levels, and in 1950, their loyalty long proved, he greatly liberalized his terms. Before that, as of January 1, 1940, Dewey was granted a stipend of $5,000 a year for life. As of April 1, Laurence Buermeyer, who had early begun to suffer ill health and was perhaps already unable to work, was given $600 a year for life, to be paid in monthly installments. The niggardly sum was increased, two months later, to $1,800 a year. (Some years ago he suffered a stroke which affected his speech; he had to be cared for in a nursing home outside Philadelphia.)

An early provision of $2,500 a year for life granted the Mullen sisters, Miss Geiger and Nulty as "consultants" if they retired after the death of Barnes and his wife, and the same sum to the Misses de Mazia and another teacher, Jeannette Portenar, after their retirement, were subsequently increased. Miss Nelle E. Mullen was to receive $12,000 a year for life even if she was unable to work actively, Miss de Mazia $10,000, Miss Mary Mullen $5,000, Nulty $5,600, Paul B. Hogans $2,400, and James Gray, who helped him about the building, $2,800. Their wives, if the husbands predeceased them, were to receive the same pension until they remarried. Angelo Pinto was to receive $4,800 a year as long as he remained in the service of the Foundation; on his death his widow, Frieda, was to receive $3,600 a year for life or until she remarried. Ten other employees were continued at their current salaries indefinitely, with the provision that if they were permanently incapacitated for work they were to be granted $200 a month for the balance of their lives, with the same safeguards for their wives as given above. Wages and salaries of gallery attendants, watchmen, caretakers, stenographers and clerks were increased on an average about 50 per cent. One of the most bizarre by-laws stipulated that no changes in the amount of compensation to employees could be made after Barnes's death.

Although the $5,000 maximum salary allowed a teacher was no mean sum for the job, few of the teachers in 1940 were getting more than half of it. These were the fearful ones, having neither tenure nor severance pay. One teacher suddenly felt strange crisscrossing pains apparently in the region of the heart, and hurried to his doctor. After a thorough examination, in which he found nothing organically wrong, the doctor supposed his patient was suffering from gas pains of nervous origin. "Where do you work?" he asked. . . . "That's it. You'd better get another job."

The next day this teacher was having lunch with three colleagues, and he couldn't resist telling them of his experience. To his astonishment, they glanced at each other in amusement, then each confessed that he had had the identical experience.

Barnes dropped in one morning at a class of Miss de Mazia's which Geasland was attending, and at one point began to discuss the influences in Picasso's early work. Picasso took this from El Greco and that from Piero Della Francesca, this from Toulouse-Lautrec and that from

Cézanne. . . . As a painter, Geasland was well aware that an artist did not work entirely deliberately. He thought to himself, Isn't it possible that Picasso was, at least in part, unconsciously influenced by these artists?

When, at the end of his exposition, Barnes asked if there were any questions, Geasland spoke what was on his mind. Barnes seemed to be annoyed. At any rate, he asked Geasland to commit his question to writing so that it could be discussed at the next Thursday morning seminar of the staff. (It would also be a record of Geasland's heresy: Barnes's litigious mind invariably sought a document which could be placed in evidence.) Geasland wrote out the question, showed it to his colleagues in advance to make sure that it was clear.

The Thursday morning discussion never took place. Barnes called together all the staff but Geasland, to ask them their opinion of him as a teacher. Ostensibly he was consulting them in democratic fashion as if he would allow himself to be guided by the majority opinion. Actually he had made up his mind to fire Geasland and simply wanted their ratification *pro forma.* It was near the end of the school year; he could have let Geasland go then without renewing his contract; but heresy was heresy and had to be immediately punished. The teachers were placed in a cruel position. Not to chime in with Barnes was to invite an entry in one's dossier. But they all liked Geasland; he knew his art and he took his teaching seriously. They were aware, too, that he was perhaps not as articulate or fluent as he might be. But hadn't Barnes known that all along? Why should they point to it now when Geasland was being put on the spot for quite a different charge? Barnes was there with his inexorable question: What do you think of Geasland as a teacher?

If Bookbinder was still afraid of Barnes, he prized his integrity above his job. (In a small way he had asserted his independence as soon as he received his appointment. Student or teacher, he still was exposed to the stale soporific air of the classroom. As a student, he could only save himself by sitting on the edge of the chair. As a teacher, he had the authority to take the class—yes, the duty to take it—to any room in which there was a painting which could profitably be compared with the one under study in their classroom. This was not idling; this was not waste; this was applying the Barnes canon zealously. Look at the line in this picture. Now let us compare it with the line in so-and-so's picture. If the latter was 140 yards distant and one managed to get some fresh air enroute, where was the harm?) What did he think of Geasland as a teacher? Bookbinder said that it was impossible to answer the question without taking the total situation into account. Geasland had been, he said, working under adverse conditions, and he respectfully suggested that he would be glad to discuss these conditions with Barnes if he wished.

Without a word, Barnes turned to the next teacher. . . . In the end he asked them all to sign a statement that Geasland's question was stupid: this they refused to do.

The Thursday morning discussion never took place because, as soon as Geasland had written out his question, he was informed at his next class that Doctor wished to see him. In the office with Barnes were Miss Nelle C. Mullen, Miss Mary Mullen and Miss de Mazia. It looked to the hapless teacher like battle array, but the three members of the staff were there only as witnesses.

Without ceremony Barnes asked Geasland to resign, and handed him a paper, presumably a release, to sign.

The teacher ignored the document—he just resigned. But, to compare great things to small, and it was not so small a thing for an employee of Barnes to do, Geasland asserted, with Galileo, But the earth does move . . . the question is still valid.

Barnes followed him downstairs and, as if he expected Geasland to put up his fists, summoned his gardeners and guards to bounce him out if he did. . . . And then Barnes was angry with him for not saying good-by.

Barnes gave up the house on Spruce Street for an annex in Merion. There came a time for Miss Flannery, now Mrs. Stine, to say good-by. When one of the Foundation's teachers was called by his draft board, Barnes hysterically dictated a letter directly to the typewriter, "explaining that teaching art at the Foundation was of greater importance to the world and of greater value to the United States than the young man would be in the Armed Forces." To close the letter, he merely said: "the quotation from Dewey"—she had used it many times; and he pulled the sheet from the machine.

The next morning Miss Mullen informed Mrs. Stine that Doctor wouldn't be in until ten, and that he wanted her gone before he arrived. . . . Why the abrupt dismissal? Doctor wanted another secretary, one who could type without making mistakes. What mistake had she made? At the end of the passage from Dewey she had left out the quotation marks. . . . (But it is possible that he had let her go because, the draft board having ignored his appeal, she was witness to his humiliation.)

Despite Miss Mullen's instruction, Mrs. Stine did not leave before Barnes arrived. Although he did not call her, she went into his office. " 'I just wanted to say good-by,'

I said, then stared at him. Tears, yes, tears were stream-
ing down his cheeks. I dug in my bag for a handkerchief.
Tears were dropping from my eyes too."

This was the staff of which Bertrand Russell was to
become a member; this, its headmaster.

23

Mr. and Mrs. Bertrand Russell

ON FEBRUARY 27, 1940, THE NEW YORK BOARD OF HIGHER
Education announced the appointment of Bertrand Russell
as professor of mathematics and logic at the College of the
City of New York for the following academic year. There
were immediate protests by various religious groups, by
Bishop William T. Manning, by members of the City
Council, and by several newspapers. A Brooklyn housewife brought a taxpayer's suit to have the appointment
rescinded, and by March 30 Justice John E. McGeehan
of the Supreme Court of New York so ordered. The essence of the judgment was that Russell was an avowed
enemy of religion and morality and therefore a potential
corrupter of youth.

If the court could hardly adduce as evidence the fact
that the sixty-eight-year-old Russell had been three times
married and twice divorced, it could cite the book which

had created emotional storms a decade previously, *Marriage and Morals,* a collaboration of Russell with his second wife, Dora. This book advocated companionate marriage (and elsewhere, in print, Russell had declared that the trouble with companionate marriage was that it did not "go far enough"). The success of the opposition in New York encouraged someone to try to have Russell put out of the University of California in Los Angeles, where he was completing a year's course of lectures, while another zealot called on Harvard to cancel the series he was scheduled to deliver in the fall term of that year. Both of these efforts failed, but in New York the judge would not even grant Russell a public hearing.

He was not without his defenders. Youth, as represented by the senior class of the Columbia University Engineering School, voted him their favorite author. Prominent liberal professors spoke up for him—for the right of any teacher to his own private beliefs provided he did not violate the law. Forming a Committee for Cultural Freedom, they began work on a symposium on the Russell affair. Edited by John Dewey and Horace M. Kallen, it was published the following year—for the record and for the guidance of purblind judges in the future—as *The Bertrand Russell Case.*[1] Perhaps because Barnes had agreed to pay the $2,000 cost of publication, he was given the honor of writing the foreword. "The book," he said, "is simply the record of an inquiry into the *facts* of the case—an inquiry conducted by specialists qualified to examine its manifold aspects and to relate their findings to the principles of justice, law, humanity, and common decency, as these

[1] The book was made up of essays by Dewey, Kallen, Morris R. Cohen, Sidney Hook, G. E. Shepler, Richard McKeown, Y. H. Krikorian and Carleton Washburne.

are set forth in the Constitution of the United States and in the Bill of Rights. . . ."

Characteristically, the sentence reflects both his objectivity as a scientist in stressing the facts and his unscientific tendency to draw conclusions from them based on value judgments—in this case, moral judgments. For his heart was in the right place, though it was concealed somewhat by his relentless logic and rationalism.

Barnes got along well with all the authors. Kallen found him "a scared little boy, who looked up to Dewey as his (intellectual) father."

While the manuscripts of *The Bertrand Russell Case* were still being written, and an appeal pending before a higher court, Barnes considered the possibility of bringing Russell to Merion. Having developed his art system about as far as he could go, he felt it was time to broaden the course of instruction to include the philosophical and social background from which the diverse art forms had emerged. A man of Russell's breadth of mind, author of such diverse books as *Education and the Good Life; Mysticism and Logic; An Inquiry into the Meaning of Truth;* and *The Principles of Mathematics* seemed to be the ideal person to give such a course.

In thus enriching the curriculum of the Foundation Barnes would also be helping Russell out of his financial difficulties—and capitalizing on his name. He consulted Dewey, who endorsed his plan and agreed to sound out Russell. This was a tribute to the philosopher's decency, for Russell was the man whom he most disliked personally. "Dewey's feelings about Russell," Sidney Hook wrote in his memorial piece, "began in China when Russell insisted upon calling on the Christian missionaries with, at the time, his unwed secretary, then in an advanced state of pregnancy, in order to broaden their cultural horizon. What concerned Dewey was Russell's insensitiveness to other people's feelings. He believed that there was a streak of cruelty in Russell and an aristocratic disdain for the sensibilities of other human beings outside of his class." Furthermore, Dewey was offended time and again by Russell's description of pragmatism (of which his own philosophy was a variety) as a form of commercialism, though he knew better.

Sounding out Russell was a simple matter. At this moment he was first of all concerned about making a living. In the ensuing correspondence, Barnes was all magnanimity, Russell all gratitude.

June 18, 1940. From Bertrand Russell in Los Angeles to Dr. Barnes in Merion.

Thank you for sending me an account of the Barnes Foundation. I am deeply grateful to you for the suggestion that I should join it. . . . Could you also let me know whether my appointment, assuming that I am free to accept it [i.e., if he does not win his appeal], would be for a definite or indefinite period? I cannot tell you what an immense boon your offer is to me. One is almost ashamed, at such a moment, to think of personal things, but when one has young children it is unavoidable.

July 20, 1940. From Bertrand Russell in Lake Tahoe, Calif., to Dr. Barnes in Merion.

Thank you very much for your letter of July 13. Your suggestions are entirely agreeable to me. . . . All that you say about the work sounds most attractive, but it certainly needs conversation [about the details]. I do not know whether you want me to lecture on philosophy or on social questions. I should be very reluctant to lecture on sexual ethics, which have quite wrongly been supposed to be my special field. Actually the subject interests me much less than many others and I should be sorry to be diverted from philosophy and history to sociology. I could, if it suited you, lecture on different philosophies of the past, and their influence on culture and social questions: for example, Platonism and its influence, or the Romantic movement of the nineteenth century. . . . We should be delighted to see you here at any time before the end of August, though I am afraid we could not offer you hospitality, as we are living in a tiny log cabin. There are however hotels all around. . . .

P.S. My very best thanks for your beautiful book [*The Art in Painting?*]

Barnes flew out to California to discuss with Russell details of his engagement. They came to an understanding quickly on August 8, and on his return home Barnes embodied it in a five-year contract dated August 16. But he had written Russell before then.

August 17, 1940. Bertrand Russell in Lake Tahoe to Dr. Barnes in Merion.

Thank you very much for your kind letter of August 11. . . . As for a possible house: we are both immensely grateful to you for the trouble you are taking. It is, I think, rather essential that we should be not less than fifty miles from Philadelphia and quite in the country. Social life takes up time which we can ill afford to spare; I want to be able to concentrate on serious work. What is even more important, my wife's health needs care; she must live as quiet a life as possible, and ought, if at all possible, to be at some altitude above sea level. She intends to devote the first part of my time at Harvard to the question of a house. We shall need six or seven bedrooms and two other rooms: one living-and-dining room, and one not very small study. . . .

I am glad to hear . . . that I can start with you at the beginning of January. . . . It was a great pleasure getting to know you and thanks to you I look forward to much more of the same pleasure in the future.

August 24, 1940. From Bertrand Russell in California to Dr. Barnes in Merion.

Thank you very much for your kind letter of August 21. It is very good of you to be taking so much trouble on our behalf, and when we come East your preliminary search [for a house] will be a great help to us.

There are, however, some points that I should like to put to you, as I am afraid that your enthusiasm for lovely places may lead to your not quite realizing my circumstances. In the first place, it is *impossible* for us to buy: I cannot get money from England, and have here only what I have saved during the last twenty months. In the second place, I shall, out of $6,000 a year, have to keep my two older children at the university, and perhaps spend money on refugee children; I must therefore have a house which not only has a low rental, but is cheap to run and requires little service. I should not know what to do with 60 or 70 acres of farmland. It is much more important to my happiness to live within my means than to live in a beautiful house; and it is essential both to my wife and to myself to reduce the machinery of life to a minimum.

Choosing a house is a very personal matter, like choosing a wife. I know that in China the latter is done by proxy, but although people make mistakes, we are apt to prefer our own folly to the wisdom of others. We should neither of us wish to decide on a house until we have seen a considerable selection. I am deeply touched at your even contemplating spending $35,000 on the matter, but I am sure we can be happy at very much lower cost, and we could not possibly pay a rent corresponding to such a price, so that, in effect, you would be paying me a bigger salary than was agreed upon.

Your offer to pay the fare of one of us to fly East is, again, extraordinarily kind. But we are leaving here very soon, and my wife, at least, will be in Philadelphia about September 13. . . .

Buying furniture is great fun and I hate to disappoint your kindly impulse, but we have enough furniture coming from England. . . .

I am very much afraid all this may sound ungracious, but it is not so intended. . . . What you have already done in giving me the post is so much that no more is needed to secure my life-long gratitude. . . .

P.S. . . . When my wife first gets to Philadelphia, she will be staying with some very old friends of ours.

November 1, 1940, A. C. Barnes in Merion, Pa. to "Dear Russell" in Cambridge, Mass.

. . . I'm in a quandry [*sic*] about your classes—we're swamped with applications from outsiders, some of them of the right sort. What I'd like you to tell me is—how many students do you prefer to have? We limit our classes to 20, but prefer 15. I'll leave the decision entirely in your hands. Another question: would a rapid-fire stenographer to take down what you say, help you in the later job of the book? If it will, I'll engage one. [Russell was not to repeat a course of lectures each year of his engagement, but to extend a single course over the entire five years; and the Foundation was to publish the assembled lectures in book form.]

All set for tomorrow's meeting in N.Y. [of the Committee of Cultural Freedom]. Each of the prospective contributors seems to be enthusiastic. . . . I'll tell you what happens tomorrow.

P.S. I had to fight with Peter [young Mrs. Russell's pet name]. Kiss her for me and tell her I hope to make amends for all the crimes I've committed.

March 13, 1941, A.C.B. in Merion, Pa., to "Dear Russell" in Malvern, Pa.

My associate Angelo Pinto told me of his conversation with you and asked if I had anything to suggest to facilitate your wish to get a "closer contact with the students" in your class.

I know of nothing better than what you are doing but if you would like to try any other plan, you have only to do it without consulting anybody here.

One thing I can say in all sincerity is that your lectures are doing more for those students than you think, or what I thought anybody could do—it's no easy job to jump into a group of mixed and very different backgrounds and create in all of them a genuine interest that makes [them] go into the subject further on their own in an effort to link up what you give with what the other teachers put over in their own classes. Moreover, you've endeared yourself to all of them and if I were a Frenchman I'd kiss you on both cheeks for the benefit you've brought to our efforts to do something worthwhile. Don't you worry about your work here: take it in your stride of living a peaceful, carefree life, and if I can further that wish in any way, you may count on me to do it.

December 28, 1942. From N. E. Mullen, Secretary, The Barnes Foundation, Merion, Pa., to Mr. Bertrand Russell, Malvern, Pa.; delivered by hand.

For a long time past, our Board of Trustees has had under consideration certain events which have occurred since your contract with us was executed, and which seem to bear directly upon its validity. One of these events concerns the conditions which determined the modification of the terms of original contract with you.

The details of the matter referred to have been carefully studied in their legal and ethical aspects by properly qualified, disinterested persons. The legal factor in the situation— breach of contract—is the basis upon which our Board decided that the existing contract with you be terminated as of December 31, 1942. . . .

We regret. . . .

Four days' notice! Why, after all the warm, open correspondence, this creaking, cold-blooded, legalistic mumbo-jumbo? How had this deterioration come about in a relationship which began with Barnes's constant and sincere solicitude and Russell's "lifelong gratitude"? What of the kiss for Peter?

Alas, it was the thirty-year-old Mrs. Russell—red-headed Patricia—lively and pretty Peter—who was made to appear the prime cause. Intelligent enough to have been Russell's secretary-assistant, she was promoted, in the divorce action brought by Dora Russell, to the rank of co-respondent. The kiss Barnes mailed to her in Cambridge in care of her husband seems to have been his last. Perhaps if he had been allowed a few in person he would have been more tolerant of her behavior. Soon after she arrived in Merion, he later complained, she began to give herself airs. A decade previously, Russell had inherited his father's title to an earldom, but he still preferred to be called Mister. Yet his wife was strutting around calling herself Lady Russell.

On one occasion [Barnes wrote], she burst into the building and created a scene by a loud and imperious command to one of the members of the Board of Trustees. This tantrum was one of a series of disturbing events which began soon after Mr. Russell's course started and recurred frequently. A rising tide of complaints from members of the class testified that the normal management of the Foundation's affairs was being disrupted by her disorderly conduct— to put it mildly. A written report given to Mr. Russell called his attention to recorded details of this impossible situation and its lamentable incongruity with an educational program designed to embody equal rights for all. His reply was that he had not shown the complaint to his wife and that he hoped the matter would go no further—a reply which gave the impression that fear of his wife's reaction to the complaint deterred him from informing her about it, and that no remedial action could be expected from him.

In sum, "the series of disturbing events" apparently consisted of Mrs. Russell's encounter with the trustee and her "indulgence in knitting" at Russell's lectures. The "Board of Trustees" convened to write her a solemn letter on the subject, at the same time virtually telling her that she had no business being at the lectures at all: "The Foundation has never been a place where people may drop in occasionally, at their own volition . . ." Russell himself answered, calling the letter "astonishing by its incivility." To which the Board replied by return mail that, under the circumstances, it had been "inordinately courteous."

Violating all rules of pedagogy as well as common sense, Barnes had one of the letters complaining of Mrs. Russell read in the classroom, in the presence of Russell himself. As the philosopher was leaving the room, one of the maturer students, to express his indignation, started to follow him.

Barnes called out: "Where are you going?"

"I don't like this sort of thing."

"Neither do I."

Mrs. Russell undertook to sum up the situation, in her letter of November 1, 1941:

The first sentence of your letter of October 1st has seemed to me incomprehensible. My husband has, however, recalled to me an occasion when Miss Mullen appeared to him to have been annoyed by me; and so, fantastic as the charge appears, I must suppose you are referring to the following incident: On a particular day last winter my husband asked me to be not a moment later than 3:45 in calling for him, as he had an important engagement elsewhere. When, therefore, I called at 3:45, and was told indirectly that my husband was busy talking to a reporter and did not wish to be disturbed, I knew that someone had presumed to interpret my husband's wishes, and that in fact he could not have been told of my arrival. I therefore went into the building and spoke to a white-haired lady who approached me, and whose name I did not know, saying in a normal voice, "Where is Mr. Russell? Will you please let him know that I am here?" I then left the building. If this seems to the Trustees of the Barnes Foundation a disturbance of the peace, may they long continue to enjoy the unreal paradise where such trifles may be so accounted, for I cannot suppose that they would have the fortitude to endure a true disturbance of the peace: for example bombs tearing through the roof.

As for my occasional attendance at my husband's lectures: I have always acted as his assistant in research for and preparation of his lectures, and when, as is usually the case, I am familiar with the subject he is to speak about, he does not desire my attendance. On other occasions, when the subject is not one that I have studied, he has wished me to be present, not for my own sake, but for the sake of his lectures, since I cannot assist him adequately with the preparation of any one lecture without a thorough grasp of the whole course. In every other institution in which my husband has taught since I was his assistant, it has only been necessary for him to mention that he would like to have me present at some of his lectures, and the permission has been most readily and courteously granted. I had understood that my husband had arranged this with the Barnes Foundation, but if he forgot to do so, or understood that permission was granted when in fact it was not so, we can only apologize for my unintentional trespass.

It is in any case necessary for me to drive my husband to his lectures, as he cannot drive himself, and he had not supposed that the Trustees could wish me to wait outside.

I cannot imagine anyone regarding the Foundation as "a place where they may drop in occasionally."

As for my knitting: it was with some hesitation that I took it with me—on two or perhaps three occasions—to the Barnes Foundation; but when I consulted my husband he remarked that I had disturbed no one by knitting at far more difficult and technical lectures at the Universities of Oxford, Chicago, California, and Harvard, and that therefore I might assume that I would be giving no offense. I am distressed that in fact I did disturb someone, and would be glad if you would convey to all the students my sincere apologies.

It would only have been necessary for you to say to me, "Mrs. Russell [not "Lady" Russell], would you mind not knitting" just as you only need to have told my husband "If you want your wife to come to your lectures it will be necessary for her to obtain permission of the Trustees."

My knitting is in no sense an "indulgence" and I would not have run the risk of annoying anyone by it, however slightly, but for a purpose that seems to me serious, the wish to diminish the number of those who suffer from the cold.[2]

If I am sometimes a little cold myself in future, when, having no errands, I wait for my husband outside the Barnes Foundation (outside the *grounds* of course), I will knit with more zest from a nearer realization of what it must mean to be cold and really without shelter; and I will marvel that in such a world anyone should be willing, deliberately, to make one fellow-human cold even for one hour. And I will marvel, too, as I do now, that anyone should wish, in a world so full of mountains of hostility, to magnify so grandiloquently so petty a molehill.

Barnes answered sarcastically what he later called her "tirade composed of arrogance, rage and self-pity": his unfair characterization allowed him to overlook her most significant charge, that he had made a mountain of a molehill. (If she were not stopped, might she not go on to charge that the cloistered inmates of the Foundation were developing a touchiness which bordered on paranoia?) Barnes also told her that if she ever showed up at the doors of the Foundation she would be ejected. At the same time

---

[2] Mrs. Russell's knitting was presumably for victims of the war.

he wrote Russell that everyone liked him personally and his lectures, too, but "that when we engaged you to teach we did not obligate ourselves to endure forever the trouble-making propensities of your wife."

Mrs. Russell's actual behavior toward Miss Mullen may not have been as inoffensive as her own version of it makes out. Her gift for understatement may have been as great as Barnes's for exaggeration. She might very well have been less than polite to a white-haired lady she may have mistaken for the attendant of the powder room. Even a philosopher friend of Russell's who is accustomed to express his complex thoughts, and even his simple ones, in rather involved carefully qualified sentences, described her in one short libelous word.

Barnes's attempt to split husband and wife showed a lack of understanding of human beings. If this were any attractive young woman and any husband more than twice her age who had been married to her for only six years, and who had an infant son with her, no one with any insight would have expected to have at her with a shotgun and still retain her husband's friendship. And Russell was not just any old man. Quite apart from his fame, he was, with or without title, an aristocrat. If he was self-centered and took for granted people doing things for him, he also had the aristocratic virtues of independence of mind and courage. As a pacifist during the first World War (though twenty-five years later Hitler made him accept war as a necessity), he spoke out and pamphleteered for his beliefs, with the result that he lost his job at Trinity College and later went to jail for six months. From such a man, Barnes could not have received any other answer but the one he did:

. . . I shall continue to do all in my power (including utilization of my wife's valuable help in research) to make my lectures as good as I am able to make them; but, so far as any personal relationship is concerned, you are mistaken in supposing that there is no quarrel with me, since whoever quarrels with my wife quarrels with me. [And he signed it, not "Sincerely," but "Yours truly."]

To close the incident, and perhaps to insure his job, Russell did in person what his wife did in her letter: he apologized to the class for his wife's knitting. But he went on to repeat what his wife had written—that no one at the various universities he had lectured in had objected to her knitting and so they had assumed it would be inoffensive in Merion. Possibly Russell said this in all innocence, but Barnes sensed innuendo. In the discussion period after the lecture he stood up to ask the first question: Did Russell mean to suggest that there was something wrong in the way the Foundation was run? "Oh, no," said Russell hastily. Whether or not he had spoken in all innocence, he must have been resentful of being held so rigidly to account.

For nearly a year there was an uneasy truce. . . .

On his arrival at the Foundation, Russell had been interviewed by Carl W. McCardle for the Philadelphia *Evening Bulletin*. Barnes granted him the privilege, despite his professed contempt for all newspapermen, because a telephoned statement he had given the reporter a few weeks before on the ultimate disposition of the collection had been printed on page one, ungarbled and uncut. Finding him an alert, agreeable and good-looking young man in his middle thirties, Barnes invited him and his wife, who was also a journalist, to see the collection at their leisure. Four years previously Archibald MacLeish, then an editor of *Fortune* magazine, had proposed to do an article on the Foundation and Barnes had turned him down on the ground that publicity only led to a heap of applications for admission. "What would happen if a really first-rate intelligence like yours let itself go, God only knows. I imagine we'd need the State militia to protect us." Nor did MacLeish's offer to reproduce some of the paintings in color tempt him, for even the best of reproductions was to the original what "a hearsay version of a honeymoon narrated by an octogenarian" was to the real thing. Having foregone the potentially provocative response of a poet to his work, Barnes now succumbed to the proposal of a journalist to write it up. He was to know poetic justice.

Not taking any chances, he had the reporter agree to two conditions: to write primarily about the educational work of the Foundation (and pledging himself to read certain books which would familiarize him with scientific method), and "to submit his copy for approval before it was offered for publication in any magazine." Thus protected, as he thought, Barnes opened his files, his heart (in part) and his imagination to the writer. Despite what he had said to MacLeish, he even had the Pinto brothers prepare color photographs of some of the paintings.

The article appeared in *The Saturday Evening Post* in four installments beginning with the issue of March 21, 1942. The one-sided title, "The Terrible-Tempered Dr. Barnes" (suggested by a comic strip, "The Terrible-Tempered Mr. Bangs"), was a promise of worse things to come. Barnes had seen portions of the script as McCardle prepared it and had "protested repeatedly . . . the distortion and falsification of facts, the overemphasis of sensational elements of events at the expense of their true meanings, and the whole spirit of his treatment of the subject, [which] was a flagrant violation of the agreement."

Barnes did not see a complete copy of the text until he

threatened legal action, and what he got then was not the manuscript but galley proofs. Making photostatic copies of them, he wrote across the first sheet: "Every one of the twenty-eight (28) sheets of these galley proofs contains statements which are false and misleading and some of which I saw for the first time in this copy." He wanted to have the magazine enjoined from printing the articles, but he was powerless since it was not a party to his contract with McCardle. He tried to argue that it had no moral right to publish the articles. The editor disagreed. Barnes and his staff got to work on the proofs, but "all we could do was remove the most glaring of the falsifications, distortions and fabrications, and let the rest of his imaginative ramblings go."

In short, the articles were an example of "feature writing" at its best (worst?)—even Barnes, unhumorously calling the title of the articles a "plagiarism," thought they were written "in a breezy, swiftly moving style that entertains and amuses the reader" (and pointlessly analyzed that style).

If he felt that he emerged from the text "too much like a warrior-hero with boots licked too clean," he must have been pleased by the accompanying photograph of himself: the head so vigorous that at first one did not notice the white hair (he looked to be in his middle fifties rather than his actual seventy years), with a straight-stemmed pipe jutting above a strong jaw matching the boldness of his shrewd eyes. The caption might well have been: "I can look any man in the eye and tell him to go straight to hell."

Even a spot check of the articles shows their "distortions and falsifications." But not all of them were McCardle's and it is difficult to distinguish them from those of Barnes. McCardle's first anecdote told of Barnes replying to a titled refugee who wanted to see the collection that it was impossible to accommodate her on the day she mentioned because on that day a strip-tease contest for debutantes was being held in the gallery. . . . Barnes denied that he had ever written such a letter. McCardle gave several examples of our hero in action buying pictures. On internal evidence, these were clearly pepped up for the benefit of an audience which only knew about art what they read in the papers. McCardle wrote that Eva Le Gallienne had been put out of the gallery when she began to smoke a cigarette. The actress informs the author of this book that she had simply asked if smoking was permitted. The answer was no, and she had refrained. That was all.

McCardle had Barnes haranguing Waldemar George in the Louvre for four hours on end until the critic fainted dead away. It never happened, says George. . . . McCardle stated that Barnes was intimate with the French composers known as "The Six." One of the survivors of the group, Darius Milhaud, who is now teaching in this country, says that he cannot recall the name. McCardle wrote that as one of the few men of wealth who supported the New Deal, Barnes had access to the most prominent French politicians of the Popular Front, that he often met, for example, Edouard Herriot, then president of the Chamber of Deputies, and Yvon Delbos, one-time foreign minister, regaling them with the lingo of the smoking car. As mayor of Lyons, a leader of his party and as a scholar, Herriot was a busy man. Since the writer of this biography could not call on him, he requested Herriot as a biographer himself to write his recollections of Barnes. Shortly before his death Herriot replied that he would be happy to oblige, but that he had never met Barnes.

A feature writer's imagination could have had Barnes receive his inspiration for Argyrol as he sat in a beer gar-

den, but could hardly have been equal to inventing the
rest of McCardle's account of Barnes in Heidelberg, to
wit, that he completed his studies for a Ph.D., that he
wrote his thesis in German, that on reading it Professor
Paul Ehrlich offered him an assistantship, and that Barnes
did not take the doctoral degree because he refused to
pay the $50 fee required.

It is hardly worth noting that the fee was actually nearly
twice as much and that the rector of the university had
the power to lower or waive the fee for a gifted but needy
student in view of the fact that Barnes never wrote a
thesis at all. He was not even formally qualified for an
undergraduate degree in chemistry. If Ehrlich was already
experimenting on the first hundred of the 606 compounds
he was to try out before hitting on Salvarsan, a specific
for syphilis, he needed a large staff of assistants. As director of the Institute for Experimental Therapy at Frankfort
on the Main, only a short distance from Heidelberg, he
must have been in touch with Professor Gottlieb, with
whom Barnes was studying; and if the latter had shown
resourcefulness in the laboratory the professor might well
have recommended him. This was at least plausible; and
so was Barnes's reason for turning down the offer: he was
in a hurry to get home to work on his own invention. But
the allegation that it was his (nonexistent) thesis which impressed Ehrlich makes it more likely that in retrospect
Barnes magnified a possibility into a positive offer.

Following the Heidelberg pattern, Barnes told of having refused to pay the University of Pennsylvania a $20
fee for a diploma—as if he would have dared open an
office without that standard medical mural—when in fact
medical school graduates were not required to pay the fee.
Evidently Barnes was trying to build up a nonconformist
past to prove that he had scorned the accolade of a degree,

especially of the Ph.D. degree which had been beyond his reach. Yet he was in reality a devout believer in Ph.D-ism.

What McCardle wrote about Hermann Hille—whom he, whom Barnes, did not mention by name—was surely the most imaginative part of his story, and again, could hardly have been his own invention.

Barnes told him that he had asked the University of Heidelberg (through his former teacher, Professor Gott-lieb?) to recommend an assistant to him, that he got a job for this man in the laboratory to which he was "consult-ant," and that he made him his partner when he was ready to manufacture Argyrol. This contradicts the assumption made earlier in the book that Barnes met Hille at the University, and would, if true, eliminate the need for speculating as to whether Barnes double-crossed him when he first asked his colleagues at Mulford's to become his partner.

The university was large; not every student knew every other student; even a student in pharmacology might never meet a student in chemistry, especially when the one was merely there for a summer course while the other was im-mersed in study for a Ph.D. How, then, could one account for Hille's sharing the credit for the research on Argyrol, as reported in the *Medical Record?* Even if, during his first few months in this country, he had a hand in the final stage of its development, was it likely that Barnes would have allowed him equal credit, as if he had assisted at its birth? It seems more reasonable to find that Barnes did meet Hille in Germany and that Hille, with his superior chemical knowledge, played an essential role either in proposing the direction of the research or in planning its execution, or both. That Barnes did not see fit to tell McCardle Hille's name may only reflect the fact that they parted on bad terms, but it would have been all too human or all to Barnesian if he had not, when he could do so with impunity, minimized to anonymity the role of his partner in order to imply that the achievement was all his own.

A local radio station gave Barnes a half hour to air his charges against McCardle, and he took such further satisfaction as he could from writing and publishing a pamphlet, *How It Happened*. This referred only to the articles themselves: it did not tell what happened when the promotion crew of the *Saturday Evening Post* began to distribute posters along the Main Line announcing the forthcoming series. Tipped off, Barnes was on hand with car and chauffeur to trail them from drugstore to drugstore and tear down or take away the posters as fast as they were distributed. "Hot on his heels was another car filled with promotion men who would tear into the drugstore and put up new cards." Samuel Hopkins Adams gives it in his biography of Woollcott as coming from one of the magazine's crew. But that second car? It makes the affair look like a collaboration! Some time afterward, in a jocular spirit, Barnes himself admitted only that he had reproached the owner of a Merion drugstore for selling those issues of the *Post*. (Later on, James Michener had Barnes dashing "from one [news] stand to another pitching offending journals [after paying for them] in the gutter.")

The McCardle articles and the chase gave the Philadelphia press cause for comment. In turn, Barnes urged his teachers and students to reply to their editorials. In acknowledging the letter of Jack Bookbinder, the editor of the *Record*, Harry T. Saylor, declared that he had received eleven letters, only two of which were not "boorish, vituperative and utterly intolerant. Therefore, I think your honest letter deserves an honest answer." Reviewing the history of the relations of Barnes and the *Record* since the episode of 1930, when Barnes refused to grant its reporter an interview and insulted its publisher, Saylor declared that over the years, whenever the Foundation was in the news, his paper, and the others as well, never received "anything remotely resembling courtesy from Barnes."

When Barnes told McCardle about the origin of Argyrol, he evidently thought that no one remembered Hille. A dozen years before, at the hearings in the tax case, he had said, "I invented Argyrol." McCardle had no reason to doubt his word, and readers of the *Post* were not likely to browse in back numbers of the *Medical Record*. No one did remember clearly, but fragments of fact were in circulation which, infused with hatred of Barnes, emerged in wondrous distortions. If the name of Hille was lost, these stories sustained a suspicion that he had been more than merely a "German assistant." In one version, Barnes bought the formula from him; in another, he stole it. In a more elaborate third account, Barnes was commissioned by a Philadelphia syndicate to buy the formula in Germany. Once there, he bought the formula for himself.

The most charitable version of all was advanced confidently by a man who still claims to be Barnes's friend. According to him, Barnes got the formula for nothing from the United States government when it released German patents during the First World War. When the author pointed out that Barnes was manufacturing Argyrol in 1902, he said casually, "Oh, in that case I'm wrong."

Barnes told McCardle that he had bought out his partner for "several hundred thousand dollars." It seems like a lot of money for a small business, however profitable, not half a dozen years after it was established.

Barnes was especially aggrieved that McCardle had

said very little about his method of studying art. He was displeased in another sense when an extended analysis of his method was made in an essay, "A Critique of Art Criticism," written by the author of the present book. The article appeared in the 1942 winter issue of *The Virginia Quarterly Review*. (Chapter 14 of this book is based on it, though more weight is here given to the value of the method as an elementary means of instruction than in the original.) Barnes thought the piece called for rebuttal because of the caliber of the magazine which sponsored it. Since *The Virginia Quarterly* did not favor polemics, the editor, Archibald Shepperson, agreed to consider a piece which would present the Barnes method favorably and which would only incidentally be a reply to the article. Well satisfied with that, Barnes sent Shepperson an autographed copy of *The Art in Painting* and promised to have John Dewey present his case. The editor and I (I had not then read *Art as Experience*) were of course delighted.

One issue of the magazine appeared, and another, and then Shepperson informed me that he had received a manuscript, not by Dewey but by Barnes himself, and that he had rejected it. Perhaps because *The Virginia Quarterly Review* did not have the circulation of *The Saturday Evening Post* or its promotion crew, Barnes did not trouble him further.

Unfortunately I did not ask Barnes to let me see his rejoinder because I had written the essay many years before and was then involved in war work. Miss de Mazia would not let me have it now because it is being included in a book of Barnes's unpublished papers and she did not wish it quoted before it was in print.

For nearly a year there had been an uneasy truce between the Russells and Barnes. On their side, forbearance was dictated simply by the need of an income, yet they could hardly accept with grace restraints which were self-imposed only by economic necessity. Barnes later alleged that Russell's lectures deteriorated after his wife had been ordered to stay off the premises. During his first five months, when he spoke extemporaneously for the most part, he had been "fluent, vivacious and witty," holding the attention of the students unfailingly. Now "his manner in the classroom lost its animation and grew perfunctory, even apathetic. More and more he merely read from his manuscript, and more and more of what he read consisted of matter accessible to all in standard works of reference. Often he spoke so fast that a skilled stenographer could not take accurate notes of what he said. During the discussion period after the class he was increasingly disposed to answer questions with a chuckle, a wisecrack or a reply which subjected the questioner to ridicule." As a result, absences multiplied, and the better students began to drop out altogether. "By December of 1942, of the sixty selected students originally admitted, only eleven were left." So Barnes wrote in a later pamphlet.

If the thought inevitably occurred to Barnes to let Russell go, he was deterred by the contract and, more strongly perhaps, by what Dewey and his friends might say of him: either he had been a fool to rescue Russell from his legal persecutors in New York or he was a knave to dump him now. Seeking a peaceful solution of their conflict, Barnes entertained the idea of making Temple University a present of his services. He tentatively sounded out a member of the faculty, but seems not to have gone beyond that.

Russell was talking, too. At a tea at his home he said that the Barnes Foundation was set up expressly to keep the public from seeing the collection. In New York he was telling friends who asked him to get them in that it was impossible because "that man's crazy."

Such an attitude on both sides could have led to strained social relations, but Russell in a recent letter said: "I accepted his invitations and invited him in return. The amount of social contact was regulated by his wishes." At these meetings Russell found Mrs. Barnes "a thoroughly nice woman, but I wished she had been less submissive when he treated her as servants were treated a hundred years ago. . . . At first, I was sorry for Barnes because he suffered tortures from an inferiority complex. I thought I should be able to reassure him and get on good terms with him, but he made this quite impossible. He could only get on with dogs and colored people, because he did not regard either as equals."

Was Barnes subtly aware of Russell's opinion of him? He unwittingly, and foolishly, invited an almost open expression of it when he undertook to summarize Russell's lectures, perhaps for the benefit of the average members of the class. The first time he did so Russell was forced to interject: "That was not quite right." Week after week Barnes persisted, drawing nearly every time that same correction. If Russell's assumption was true, Barnes's mind could have run on unconsciously: That was not quite right. You don't follow me. You *can't* follow me. You're wrong. You don't understand. You are an inferior fellow. . . . And he would have sought relief for the humiliation. As it happened, Barnes first sought cause for breaking off relations on a high intellectual plane.

When it was announced that Russell was to give a lecture on India at Temple University, Barnes called together his faculty. "We've got to put him against the wall," he said. Writing down some loaded questions, he handed them to Jack Bookbinder. The answers would prove, out of his own mouth, that Russell was an aristocrat and an autocrat and that he disdained the common man. Bookbinder did not relish the role of stooge. In all his college years he had never heard as brilliant a lecturer as Russell, and he felt it was a privilege to ask him questions in class, and a pleasure, for his replies were always fair and to the point. But to put questions to him at a public meeting for the sake of entrapping him was another matter. Bookbinder attended the lecture, Barnes's notes in his pocket. The talk over, the floor was thrown open to questions. Barnes's went unheard by pocket veto. And Bookbinder was not fired.

Barnes then tried to make something of Russell's reservations on pragmatism. Barnes was impressed by the critical questions which one student frequently put to Russell, and so he was dismayed when this student raised an objection to Dewey's pragmatism with which Russell agreed. Instead of cutting off his head, Barnes invited the young man, to his astonishment and delight, to have dinner with Dewey, Russell and himself to discuss the matter further. (Barnes had often invited this student for a drink before dinner—he always had two stiff drinks himself, but only two, and always two, at exactly the same time. As the student entered the room one evening, Fidèle rushed at him yapping and nipped him. Barnes was aghast. "She really nipped you?" Picking up the dog, he shouted, "You son of a bitch!" and hurled her across the room. Fidèle fell heavily and began to whimper. There were flecks of blood on her muzzle. Immediately Barnes's fury vanished: he took her up remorsefully and fondled her.)

The dinner with Dewey and Russell was not a cold sober affair entirely dedicated to the pursuit of truth. It began with whisky for three and sherry for one, and at the end Barnes gave full throat to one of his favorite

Methodist hymns. Remembering more of the words than
Barnes did, the student joined in. Russell stared. Perhaps
a little high, Barnes kept ribbing Dewey—whom he
called "Jack"—about one thing and another, until at last
even the patient philosopher was tried. He said, "What's
the matter, Al?" Barnes at once subsided.

During the serious talk, Barnes did not have much to
say, and Russell, who could have talked rings around
them all, gave Dewey his head. Before the evening was
over, the student had a clearer understanding of Dewey's
pragmatism. (Barnes later gave him a copy of a volume of
essays published in honor of Dewey on his seventieth
birthday, inscribing it "To My Friend ——— ———." Although to the young man Barnes was always gentle and
kindly and their relationship was in every way pleasant, he
did not regard it as deeply rooted; and it did not in fact
last beyond the period of his study at the Foundation. The
inscription touched the young man, giving him the feeling
that a lonely man was reaching out for friendship.)

After Russell left, rather early, Barnes said that he
didn't want to fight, "but if anyone starts a fight I'm going
to give it to him." It must have been soon after this that
Barnes held a faculty meeting away from the Foundation.
Triumphantly he announced that he had finally caught
Russell with his pants down: he was an empiricist, deny-
ing the validity of pragmatism and therefore undermining
the Foundation. The thing to do, he said, talking straight
to Bookbinder, was to corner him and make him confess
his heresy publicly. This time, because he was curious
about the point himself, the teacher did ask the question
and. . . . After all this rationalistic maneuvering, Russell
gave Barnes, as he thought, legal cause for expulsion.

In the original letter of contract Barnes—not his lawyer

—drew up, Russell was to have received $6,000 a year salary. About a month after it was signed, Russell expressed his disgust at having to deliver popular lectures because he needed the money. These lectures brought him about $2,000 a year, and Barnes offered to make his salary $8,000, so that he could discontinue them in the spring when he would have completed his current engagements. Now Barnes learned that Russell was scheduled to deliver weekly lectures of a popular nature at the Rand School in New York from October 7 to December 23, 1942.

With this gross breach of contract [he later explained], we began to consider the question of his dismissal from the staff, but delayed action for several months while we submitted the entire evidence to a group of distinguished authorities in ethics and law. The legal experts' opinion was that he had broken his contract by popular lecturing and by his upholding of Mrs. Russell's disorderly conduct. The ethical support of the legal opinion was based upon Mrs. Russell's performance. . . .

The authority of the distinguished authorities in ethics went unchallenged, but when Russell brought suit for $24,000 (for the three years the contract was yet to run), Barnes found out that his distinguished authorities in law were no authorities at all. As soon as both sides had presented their briefs, Russell's lawyer, Thomas Raeburn White, asked for a summary judgment—that is, an immediate verdict for the plaintiff—on the ground that there was no issue as to the material facts; and the court granted it. The only purpose of the ensuing trial was to fix the amount of damage Russell had suffered.

But before it took place Barnes insisted, against his lawyer's advice, on appealing the verdict. "You signed a contract with Russell without consulting me," McCracken wrote him, "drew up a supplement without consulting me, got yourself into trouble, and now want me to bail you out. I can't; no lawyer can." Barnes, who had often visited McCracken informally at his home in Chestnut Hill, dropped him both as counsel and friend, and retained (Gerald A.) Gleeson & (Edward J.) McGrath. The appeal was denied on the ground that it could not be heard until the amount of damages due Russell was fixed.

At the trial, Russell testified on his earnings from sources other than the Foundation. He got $30 for an article in *Free World*, $100 for one in *Glamour*, $150 for one in *Vogue*, $1,050 for several long articles in Haldeman-Julius's *Monthly*, $75 for a lecture at Vassar, $100 for one before a private group in Phoenixville, $50 for one at the South Norwalk Foreign Policy Association. . . . In all, he had earned from his lectures and writings some $2,400 in 1941, $3,200 in 1942, and $3,000 in the eight months since his dismissal. He had now used up his best prospects and had not succeeded in obtaining a regular teaching appointment.

Barnes was ill at ease on the witness stand, even under direct examination by his own attorney. He was bewildered when White repeatedly objected to his answering the common-sense questions Gleeson tried to ask and in which the court sustained him. He was puzzled when White did not bother to cross-examine him. There were moments when, compared to the rules of evidence, the laws of chemistry seemed childishly simple.

In a poorly calculated effort to prove that Russell had scanted on his work at the Foundation by taking on outside assignments, Barnes reviewed the subject of every last one of his lectures (he had himself attended every one the first year)—on Thales, Bacchus, Orpheus, Dionysus, Anaximander, Anaximines, Pythagoras ("an important early man"), Empedocles (Russell says he pronounced them Pythagóras and Empedóckles), Democritus, Gorgias, Protagoras, down through the Cynics, the Skeptics the Epicureans, the Stoics, and so on. If the case had been tried before twelve good men and true—the defense asked for a jury trial too late—they would probably have deduced from the parade of imposing exotic names that Russell had been underpaid. After the roll call of lectures was over, Judge Guy K. Bard ruled that it was irrevelant.

The verdict, handed down in November, awarded Russell $20,000,—$24,000 less $4,000 for his probable earnings for the unexpired period of the contract.

Legally, the gist of the case was this: that an oral agreement can be binding, that the conversations amplifying a casual memorandum of agreement may also be binding, but that a contract as specifically drawn as that which Barnes and Russell had signed was all-inclusive and therefore did not permit supplementary oral agreement to be admitted in evidence. This was the letter of contract:

We confirm herewith the verbal agreement made with you on August 8, 1940:—

We agree to engage you as a member of the teaching staff of the Barnes Foundation at a salary of eight thousand ($8,000) dollars per year, payable in twelve (12) equal monthly installments, on the fifteenth day of each month.

The agreement is to extend for a period of five (5) years, dating from January 1, 1941. If, during the period of the aforesaid agreement, your personal affairs should make it necessary or advisable to terminate the contract, we agree that such a termination may be effected at the end of our school year; namely May 31st.

Your service to the Foundation will consist of one lecture

each week during the school year which extends from October 1st to May 31st inclusive, each lecture to be delivered in the gallery of the Barnes Foundation, at Merion, Pennsylvania.

The particularity of this agreement, the court ruled in effect, superseded any oral agreements because it presumably included them. Therefore Barnes's explanation of the change from $6,000 to $8,000 in salary was not admitted as evidence, and all statements about the deterioration of Russell's lectures, lack of cooperation with the rest of the staff, and failure to communicate with the students were irrelevant.

Nevertheless there is no doubt about why Barnes increased Russell's salary. In his affidavit in support of the motion for summary judgment, Russell admitted as much, but he contended that "it was clearly understood" that he was under no *obligation* to discontinue his popular lectures.

On the face of it, this was unconvincing. Why should Barnes have increased Russell's salary by one-third if Russell had not forthrightly stated that it would enable him to give up the popular lectures he detested? If he was to give them up only if they proved to be too burdensome, why should Barnes have anticipated that they would be and raise Russell's salary in advance, and for a five-year period?

Furthermore, when *The New York Times,* in its report of Russell's engagement by the Foundation, stated that he would have to give up *all* outside lectures, Russell, thinking that this came from Barnes, corrected him; for they had agreed that Russell was to have the right to give scholarly lectures occasionally, say at a university level. Barnes in turn so informed *The Times,* and in the course of a long humble letter of explanation to Russell said:

"When you told me that you were sick and tired of delivering popular lectures I wrote a new contract at an increased salary to provide the amount which you said you expected to get from these popular lectures. I never told anybody—not even my closest friend, Dewey—of this change in the contract and I certainly would think it was no business of the public." If the first sentence of the quotation was incorrect, why didn't Russell take exception to it, as he had to the statement in *The Times?* It could only be because it was true.

If Barnes was morally right, he was legally vulnerable, and lost a second appeal. He talked of carrying the case to a higher court, but in the end he settled for the less costly and less hampered appeal to the court of public opinion in a pamphlet, *The Case of Bertrand Russell versus Democracy and Education* (from which several passages have been quoted). Here were no confining rules of evidence, no judge to stop his mouth: he could assert his spites as well as his reasoned judgments. In his summing up he held that Russell "had no conception of democracy as a sharing in significant experience" and that if the students "learned anything whatever of democracy in education from him, it was because he presented them with the perfect example of its antithesis."

Returning to an allegation made by his attorney at the trial, Barnes took exception to Russell's assertion in one of his lectures "that issues involving ultimate moral or social values could not be settled by the use of scientific method, but only by a 'bash on the head'—by violence or terror." The arch-rationalist Barnes, forgetting all recorded history, the terrible war then in progress, and the violence of his own nature, was aghast. He was on the verge of assuming the position of those who had condemned

Russell as an enemy of religion and morals, a corrupter of youth. It was a bitter retreat from the higher moral position he had taken in *The Bertrand Russell Case*. But that was an act of faith. The deed, the doing a great man a good turn, involved conflicts of will and pride. The postscript to a lofty book was a recriminating pamphlet.

Russell had the better of him there: he turned his lectures into a book, *A History of Western Philosophy*—and gave the Foundation credit.

24

"Me Imperturbe"

DEFEATED BY RUSSELL IN COURT BATTLE, RIDICULED IN PRAISE in one magazine and his contribution to art diminished in another—it was nothing: Barnes absorbed all these blows delivered in one year. His resilience, at seventy, was unimpaired. He seemed, indeed, to have achieved self-knowledge and with it a measure of serenity when he delivered, at the turn of the year, the annual guest lecture before the Rhode Island Philosophical Society meeting at Brown University.

The announced title was "Art and Education," but this was no formal academic address; his own title for the lecture was "Having a Hell of a Good Time Playing with Art, Education, Science and Philosophy." It was in this talk that Barnes told of his having known hunger as a child, of his having tried desperately to learn to paint before settling for the lesser role of collector, of the time he

53

criticized Soutine's painting and Soutine, acting on that criticism, ruined his work. When he could tell a joke, not only on himself, but on his system, he was very far from the hypersensitive Barnes who could brook no opposition. Throughout the talk he was not only candid, as G. Y. Loveridge observed in a full-length report in the Providence *Journal*, but "spoke in a quiet voice."

And he faced up to every question from the audience calmly, even to the explosive one of why he restricted admission to the collection, or, as it was put this time: How were ordinary people going to get to appreciate great modern art if he kept it locked up? Without bristling, Barnes explained the work of the Foundation and the need for reserving the collection for those who could get the most out of it—his students. On what basis did he select his paintings? Barnes replied that some people considered him the anointed of God whose judgment was infallible, while others thought that "he didn't know a damned thing." The truth, he said, was somewhere between. (Was he aware that still others, including a person who had seen a good deal of him in France, felt that he did not genuinely care for art or artists? *"Il a été un bon client pour les marchands de tableaux—et les serruriers"* —he was a good customer for art dealers—and locksmiths.)

He sounded like a well-balanced man. His battles with the outer world—with academy, museum and magazine, with Ingersoll, Kimball and Russell—forgotten; he seemed at last inwardly at peace. No need now for theories to explain the worse part of his behavior, to attribute it to the residual anxieties and inferiority of childhood poverty (most poor people do not develop inferiority complexes), or the beatings he suffered in childhood (most kids survive them without trauma), or his snubbing by society folk (which he denied). He had outgrown all that:

it was only a passing phase. Now he had come through, had a right to his serenity. No longer did he have to wear frayed pants or rent cap and gown: he had the best of all the goods of this world. And he had not lived only for himself: Argyrol had relieved millions of sick (forget about the profits: Argyrol was still selling a million units a year; Ovoferrin, too, was selling 25,000 units); and his successor company found it worth while to perpetuate his name.[1]

Still better, he had given millions—well, multitudes— a true insight into the spiritual riches of mankind. If access to his paintings was still as restricted as ever, art lovers could now see paintings to match them in piecemeal exhibitions at art galleries and in the new museums. His influence was exerted through *The Art in Painting*. Especially popular in the University of California, the book had sold 15,000 copies, which was not an index of either the actual number of readers or the number of people who had benefited from it. At the Museum of Modern Art in New York, his protégé Abraham Chanin was guiding visitors and he talked the idiom of Barnes. At the Cleveland Museum of Art, his man Thomas Munro was curator of education and in his writings never failed to acknowledge his debt to his master. James Johnson Sweeney frankly said that what he learned in Merion determined his whole outlook on art, and he was to be in a position, as the director of the Solomon R. Guggenheim Museum of Art, to perpetuate the Barnes influence.

Was there ever a time when he did not face an adversary

[1] The A. C. Barnes Co. was a division of Zonite Products Corp., now called the Chemway Corp., until it purchased the Crookes Laboratories in 1956 and created the Crookes-Barnes Laboratories, Inc., as its ethical pharmaceutical division. The figures cited are current sales. Probably some time in the 1920's gelatin replaced vitellin in Argyrol.

calmly?—when, having him on the ropes, he could not, for God's sake or the Marquis of Queensberry's, back off but had to smash him through? Was there a time that he nursed grudges? Years after he had put out the group of Bryn Mawr students from the gallery, he is alleged to have responded to another request for admission with a letter which made all the faculty blush unto the third generation. Yet there he was again, after many years, having dinner with Miss Katherine McBride, president of the college, telling her what was wrong with it and she taking it with a smile and both of them enjoying themselves. Was there ever a time when he always thought in terms of legal action (though seldom going beyond the threat), looking for "evidence" in personal conflicts which called for common sense rather than a court of law for resolution? No need to consider now whether it was the effect of his endless litigation in the legitimate protection of his rights in Argyrol or some antecedent need which found expression—and relief—in such aggressive police work.

In another frank mood some years before, the patient made a jovial diagnosis of himself. On one of his many transatlantic crossings in the company of Ralph Evans, a lawyer friend, Barnes—apropos of a tiff with museum or university?—gaily exclaimed, "I guess I'm a son of a bitch, but I was born that way." Could you accuse him of being a willful egoist when he shared a common opinion of himself?

Then, on January 14, 1943, talking to his audience in Providence, he was a bit more considerate of himself. Still, he was completely honest, disarming; ready, if pressed, to strip off the last thin layer of pretense and say, after Goethe's Faust:

> I've studied philosophy,
> Psychology and chemistry,

> Art, medicine and legal lore—
> Studied them deep and ardently:
> Poor fool, with all my store,
> No wiser than I was before.

Had he really, at seventy-one, become a mellow teacher, a laughing philosopher? As of January 14, he had. Could he hold his emotions in balance for much longer than an acrobat can sustain his partner on his head? He could, for a month. But on February 15 he read in the *Record,* under the headline "New Echo of Barnes-Russell Spat," a letter signed by "A Former Student," which concluded: "The Barnes Foundation, from attic to cellar, including all tributaries and annexes, boards and committees, is but one A. C. Barnes. There must be no debates, no heretics. Mr. Russell is final proof that new or different ideas cannot be tolerated by that 'educational institution.' Certainly democracy in thought has never been a member of its classes."

Though these were sharp words, a laughing philosopher would have acknowledged them to be true and shrugged them off. Yes, but that was a month before and this reminder that he had lost the second appeal in the Russell case was most annoying. Certain that "Former Student" was an employee of the museum, Barnes charged it with having egged him on: Kimball actually checked the minor members of the staff and obtained their denials of authorship of the letter.

That outburst done with, Barnes had fresh cause for resentment in a booklet written by Earl B. Milliette, director of fine and industrial arts of the city's schools, called *Art Annals of the Central High School of Philadelphia.* This was designed to show the caliber of the school's faculty (Rembrandt Peale once taught there) and of its graduates (Thomas Eakins and Glackens among profes-

sional artists; Peter A. B. Widener, John G. Johnson and
Barnes, among collectors). Although Milliette made a
just statement of Barnes's work in his introductory text,
he later quoted from an article in *Art Digest:*

> The scientific training of Barnes prevents him from seeing
> the soul in art. . . . *The Art in Painting* remains a cold
> recital of causality, behaviorism, mechanism and descriptive
> medical journal writing. Dr. Barnes has been caught pausing
> too long at the word "modern." . . . Time marches on, and
> . . . ideas change.

Why did the author single out this one unperceptive
critical comment in a booklet whose whole purpose was
panegyric? Barnes wrote a stinging letter to the board of
education and Milliette apologized.

Provocation and more provocation! First a booklet,
then a book. This was a memorial to the artist Henry
McCarter, an unpretentious little book made up largely
of quotations from his own letters that revealed him as a
witty, observant lover of life, a true artist nature whatever
the measure of his talent. The author was the same R.
Sturgis Ingersoll with whom Barnes had clashed over
The Three Sisters, and he was therefore enraged when
he read: "A patent medicine manufacturer, Albert Barnes,
had been accumulating some contemporary paintings under
the advice of Mac's friend Glackens." Although there
was a handsome tribute to his collection on the next
page, Barnes could not let this statement pass.

"I challenge Ingersoll," he wrote, "to refute my claim
that the sentence quoted above is false in every particular:
Argyrol, which was never patented, is a definite synthetic
chemical and is listed as such in the scientific annals of all
nations." Although Ingersoll avows that he used the phrase
"patent medicine" innocently, one can understand that

Barnes should have taken it in the derogatory sense it has in common usage and felt, perhaps, that Ingersoll was paying him off for past grievances. A laughing, smiling or even grim philosopher would have been justified in his challenge.

But Barnes did not stop there. Ingersoll was not only Ingersoll but a symbol of the museum crowd, and Barnes could not resist the opportunity to mount an attack of his own. It took the form of *A Message to Students at the Pennsylvania Academy of Fine Arts,* where McCarter had taught all his life. Born in anger, it was for the most part a masterly piece of distortion. It asserted that Ingersoll "garbled and flagrantly exploited" the story of McCarter's career, and gave "the names of rich snobs and bad painters who hang on the coattails of art. His snappy stories of gay drinking parties fail to mention the sexual orgies which, according to current legends, often followed these sprees. McCarter was never present at these orgies." "Current legends" can hardly be counted as reliable evidence; quite a few are circulating about Barnes himself which are not true. Furthermore, not all the painters mentioned by Ingersoll were bad painters, nor did Ingersoll record especially "snappy stories."

"Some years ago," Barnes went on, "Ingersoll tried by flattery, to entice me into joining this local band of artistic and mental cripples, and into allowing them to contaminate our gallery by their presence; for example, he wrote me: 'It [*The Art in Painting*] comes so close to being the only intelligent book on the subject that it should have a wide and useful scope. Your contribution to life here is immense.'"

Does the letter sound familiar? It is the very one Barnes quoted in the tax case hearing as evidence of the beneficent influence of the Barnes Foundation!

Once more he resorted to the curious sophistry which he had used in his article in *The New Republic* twenty years previously. This time he put it in this form: "I never bought a painting 'under the advice of' Glackens or any other person." Did not Barnes himself asknowledge on more than one occasion that Glackens had bought the first pictures for his collection? That's it—*Glackens* bought the pictures. Barnes did not buy them on his advice!

Barnes concluded his "Message" with this parting shot: "I also challenge Ingersoll to refute the statement that a painting for which he paid a high price, and which he exhibits as the work of a famous foreign artist now dead, was painted by a man now living in America." Whether this was true or not, what did it have to do with Ingersoll's book on McCarter?

A week after the "Message" went out, the two men met by chance in a trolley car. Each gave a very different report of the encounter. According to Ingersoll, he said that he had not received a letter which Barnes was supposed to have sent him together with a copy of the "Message," and that Barnes said he thought he was lying; and then as Ingersoll moved away from him toward the door, "his face developed literally a demoniac expression, and he hissed, 'You son of a bitch.' "

In Barnes's version, he had not only called Ingersoll a liar but said that he stank of bad whisky—a charge which he elaborated in a subsequent letter saying that Ingersoll forced his attention on one of the passengers, who declared, " 'You're drunk—if you bother me, I'll sock you in the jaw.' "

Barnes saw to it that Ingersoll got his letter: "Come on, Sturgeon, you poor fish, toe the scratch by any means you choose—law, public press or fists. I'm ready to meet any legitimate demands to name the fake painting, the forger,

the fornicators. . . ." Still swinging his fists, still thinking in terms of legal action, where was the philosopher of
the serene mind who spoke in Providence?

Where indeed, when the printing presses continued to
turn out provocations? After the Milliette booklet and the
Ingersoll book, a brochure called *Invitation to the Arts*
came to his desk. Unopened, it pleased him, for it was
written by Jack Bookbinder, now in his seventh year as
instructor at the Foundation. Barnes had recognized his
merits as a teacher. Only a couple of years back a group
of students had quit rather than accept a substitute.
Barnes had put him in charge of advanced classes, steadily
increasing his pay. More than that, he liked the young
man, had often dropped in at his apartment, had paid his
transportation for two trips abroad, and had enjoyed
running into him in Paris and in—Audierne, was it?—
where he was painting with eyes the Foundation had
trained to see.

Against this *prima facie* evidence in favor of *Invitation
to the Arts* was its sponsorship by the board of education,
whose most recent affront—the Milliette study on Central
High—he was not forgetting.

He opened the brochure; he read the brochure, with
steadily increasing displeasure. A man who had been
teaching at the Foundation writing this stuff? He took
notes, more notes, and when the docket was complete he
summoned the author to his office. . . .

Since the early days, Bookbinder had come to fear
Barnes a shade less, and he had lost an illusion or two
about him. He was disturbed, for example, when Barnes
dismissed some students in his class on the ground of
absence but actually because they worked for the museum.
As against this, Bookbinder was naturally flattered when
Barnes began to visit him informally. It was the period

when Barnes was filling office and home and farmhouse with antiques, and he sold a mantel, a hutch table, arrowback chairs and pottery to Bookbinder at cost. As he kept on offering to sell more and more pottery, the visits seemed less like socializing than unloading of surplus stock. When Bookbinder was constrained to hint gently that enough was enough, the master came no more.

Although the Foundation paid well for the time it required, the income was insufficient for Bookbinder's needs. With Barnes's consent, he was also teaching in the city's evening schools, and Barnes even allowed his class to see the collection. Again, Barnes did not object to Bookbinder's working at the board of education's Summer Workshop, in which teachers were given an opportunity to try their hand at the arts. After his third year with the project, the school authorities asked Bookbinder to prepare a brochure about it for distribution to the professional personnel of the city's schools. His 15,000-word *Invitation to the Arts* aimed to free adults from the fear of attempting some art expression because of lack of talent or unsureness of technique or taste. The material was not radically new, but it was presented with spirit for the intended audience.

When Bookbinder responded to Barnes's summons, he found him seated at the end of a long table, flanked by Miss de Mazia and Miss Mary Mullen, each equipped with pad and pencil. Before him lay a detailed analysis of the brochure which seemed, to its author under fire, longer than the brochure itself. What was wrong with it? In the first place, it stated that Bookbinder had been lecturing at the Barnes Foundation on art appreciation. Barnes had not given permission for the use of his name.

The teacher replied that he had not thought it necessary, since the Board of Education knew that he taught there. In fact, the statement about his connection was not made in the text but in the introduction written by C. Leslie Cushman, Associate Superintendent of Schools.

The second count of the indictment—which gave point to the first—was that the brochure did not represent the teachings of the Foundation. As proof, Barnes cited several passages. For instance, leading a "Miss Meek" beginner to learn to paint still life, the putative instructor of the brochure "instead of explaining how to blend colors . . . raves about the flowers. And to tell the truth, those flowers begin to live." At the Foundation one did not *rave* about flowers or painting or anything. Here was another passage: "To 'appreciate' a work of art is to feel its pulse and throb, to commune with its maker. Other than that, appreciation has no meaning." At the Foundation they called this "literary rhapsodizing." Did a teacher of seven years' standing have to be told that to appreciate a painting is to know it in terms of color, line, light, plastic unity? Bookbinder said it was misleading to take sentences out of their context. As Barnes continued, he could afford to listen with seeming respect, for he was sitting there with an ace in the hole. When Barnes finished, Bookbinder produced it.

"That," he said, "is your opinion against that of someone we both honor."

"Whom do you mean?"

"John Dewey."

Like Barnes, Dewey had received an advance copy of *Invitation to the Arts*. In acknowledging it, the philosopher implied that it derived from his own ideas, and suggested that a copy be sent to Robert M. Hutchins, then president of the University of Chicago and an ardent advocate of the humanities as the primary basis of education.

Barnes wouldn't believe it. Bookbinder offered to take a cab home to fetch the letter. Barnes, his face red, did not take him up. What he insisted on was that Bookbinder request the Board of Education to recall the brochures already distributed and withhold the rest from circulation until the reference to the Foundation was deleted. Either that, or resign.

So far as Bookbinder could see, the two witnesses—reluctant witnesses this time, for they had both been friendly with him over the years—had not written a line in evidence. Gratefully he shook their hands and left.

Barnes went after him and cried out, "You son of a bitch!"

Bookbinder turned back. What had he done now?

"Somewhere in your pamphlet," said Barnes, "you mention a warm handshake. You shook their hands, but you wouldn't shake mine."

Usually the rejected and humiliated think of a brilliant retort hours later, perhaps during a sleepless night. This time the victim's mind was keyed up and he flashed back, "Doctor, read the pamphlet again. Nowhere does it say to shake the hand of a Hitler."

Barnes continued the controversy by mail. Interpreting one statement to mean that he would attack the Board if Bookbinder did not ask it to modify or withdraw the brochure, the latter consulted his attorney, Robert D. Abrahams.

On August 1 Abrahams informed Barnes that he "would take such steps as the situation warrants" if Barnes said or did anything harmful to his client's business relationship with the Board. Furthermore, he had advised his client that his employment ran until September 30 (August and September were vacation months), and that "you have no right to demand the withdrawal of a publication which contains a statement of fact concerning his employment by you, merely because you do not wish to have such a statement made."

This was a challenge very much to the taste of the old warrior. First, he presented his case straightforwardly to the Board of Education (with a carbon copy to Abrahams). On the tenth Barnes wrote the two again. On September 1, he wrote Bookbinder; on the sixth, Abrahams. A month later Abrahams thanked him for his pamphlet on the Russell case, which he had read with interest. "What I should read with even more interest would be a check . . . for the balance of wages due Mr. Bookbinder." Barnes replied—the very next day—that if Bookbinder "had brains enough to stay away from you, he would have received the $450 as a *gratuity*—the result of a kindness which, to save his face, gave him the opportunity to put in a formal resignation *after* he had been officially, legally and justifiably fired from a job which his brochure proved he was totally unfitted to hold." Since he hadn't resigned, Barnes had fired him and therefore he was not entitled to any pay. . . . Is the logic clear?

Having been appointed consultant by the Board, Bookbinder[1] thought it best to sacrifice the money and spare them Barnes's further attentions and unpleasant newspaper publicity.

But Barnes having taken steps and Abrahams having threatened to take steps their bout continued. Barnes be-

[1] Bookbinder has been named (1959) Director of the Division of Fine and Industrial Arts in the Philadelphia school system.

gan his letter of December 7, just cited, with the information that Abrahams had misdirected his thanks. "I did
not send you the pamphlet about the Russell case. The
list was prepared and the enclosures mailed by an addressing company. I did not know that their lists included
inhabitants of the intellectual slums."

A writer himself, Abrahams could give as well as take
blows—words. Climbing into the ring with his antagonist,
he explained that the pamphlet gave the sender's address
as "Albert C. Barnes, Merion, Pa.," and added: "I thought
I detected a faint stink of Argyrol thereon, so that I
assumed that the contents were one of your Imperial
Rescripts sent directly from the Palace."

That proves, Barnes replied—the next day—that "the
addressing company *does* reach denizens of the intellectual
slums," because "Argyrol is entirely free from unpleasant
odor. The 'stink' you refer to is obviously attached to yourself. . . ."

Abrahams executed a Barnesian maneuver, by having
his secretary write Barnes the rules for entering into an
exchange of invectives with him, e.g., "Only the choicest
A No. 1 invectives must be used. No old or stale material
such as you recently submitted is desired. . . . A stamped
addressed envelope must be provided if a reply is expected."

Perhaps Barnes enjoyed the parody on his own manner.
The best he could do by way of reply—the very next day
—was to address the secretary, as it were contemptuously,
by her first name, asserting that "when a stuffed shirt
realizes he is thoroughly licked he often shoots from
behind a pair of rayon panties."

Abrahams replied the following day, as follows:
"Hebrews 13:8."

It referred to a current joke about a boardinghouse

guest who, fed up with the daily hash, when called upon to say grace, said: "Hebrews 13:8"—which reads: "Jesus Christ the same yesterday, and today, and forever."

The following day, Barnes delivered a quick jab: "The devil can quote Scripture for his purpose." He twisted the lawyer's quotation of it to mean that he was identifying himself with Jesus Christ, and closed his letter by quoting Hebrews 14:1 (try and find it): "And verily I say unto you: Abraham begat Isaac; Isaac begat Jacob; and Jacob begat the illegitimate INVITATION TO THE ARTS which got him into such a disgraceful mess that he had to call on his granddad for succor; and Abrahams obligingly made a sucker out of Jacob."

Pitying a sick man, Abrahams sent him a "Get Well" card. Barnes replied with a strained joke addressed to "Dear Abie." Three days later, he (that is, Miss Nelle Mullen) bethought himself (herself) to challenge Abrahams all over again to bring the fight into the open. What fight? Why, the case, the near-case of Barnes vs. Bookbinder or Bookbinder vs. Barnes or. . . .

Well, enough was enough. From the end of July to the end of December was enough. December meant Christmas, good will on earth, and New Year was Happy New Year and good cheer and enough was enough. The little feud seemed over.

But it revived at the end of April, when Miss Nelle Mullen informed Abrahams that there were five prints belonging to his client in the storeroom. On written order from the owner within ten days, they would be delivered to a messenger. Meanwhile they were being kept "at the owner's risk." A simple courtesy? A simple matter? Owner writes note; prints delivered; matter closed. Oh, no! Nothing of the sort! A facetious touch by Abrahams invited a solemn letter from another secretary, setting

forth that a woman presented Bookbinder's request for
the prints, typed on "a very small piece of paper," to a
gallery attendant. This was not the "proper official" to
handle it, and the whole matter had been turned over
to an attorney, not in Philadelphia or Merion but in
Norristown, the county seat. What the hell, has an author,
critic, educator, millionaire—has a man seventy-three years
old nothing better to do with his remaining years? Well,
he had had his philosophic fling in Providence; now, perhaps, he thought there was nothing better than a couple
of rounds of sophisticuffs or an opera bouffe battle of
scraps of paper, winner take all and a handful of lichee
nuts.

Halfway through a long letter to Abrahams which re-
pudiated his client's effort to get his prints through a
student at the Foundation—no, sir! that was not the prescribed procedure—Barnes went regal: "For your services
as counsel for a member of the personnel of the Philadelphia Board of Education you are entitled to the decoration of Knight of the Order of the White Feather. . . ."
Clipped to the letter was a pure white, genuine chicken
feather.

Abrahams accepted "with thanks your kind invitation
to join the Knights of the Order of the White Feather,
of which I understand you are Past Master. I assume that
the duties of the Knights involve jousting at windmills,"
and he hoped that they did not include "pottering about
in a tax-free gallery. . . ."

Battling Al sank to his knees, but he recovered and
let loose a mighty wham which struck down the lawyer,
his client, the Board of Education ("the educational sewer
on the Parkway"), and, by association, the museum ("the
house of educational and artistic prostitution"). "It would
seem from this alliance that the status of your client is

about on a par with that of a piano player in a whorehouse. . . ."

Miss Sarah A. Stewart, an employee of the Doubleday
bookshop in the Broad Street Suburban Station, was
browsing through the French periodicals, when she became aware of a "somewhat nervous and apprehensive"
seventyish-year-old man, approaching. He engaged her in
conversation, but he was not buying right now: simply
passing the time until the Merion local arrived. The
young girl interested him because she was reading French.
Any harm in that, just because she was pretty? Miss Stewart thought not. She was only twenty, and she was just
back from more than a year's sophistication in France.
She knew that Philadelphia had "its share of characters,
particularly in the suburbs, and had learned to pay
little or no attention to eccentric requests and conversations." Not that this old man—"Dr. Barnes," he called
himself—was eccentric, not at first. She was reading
French magazines: what was more natural than that he
should talk about France (pronouncing place names
with a typically American nasal accent)? She had spent
eleven months in Brittany; he was an honorary citizen of
Port Manech: they had things in common, scope enough
for pleasant, uneccentric talk several afternoons a week.

But one day the old man went wacky: he began to talk
about his art collection, "in a rather guarded fashion,
with considerable pride, however, somewhat as if the
collection were a secret." He talked about his Cézannes
and Renoirs, El Grecos and Titians, his Egyptian and
African Negro sculpture. . . . Such names, such abun-
dance, the young woman associated with public museums,
not private collections; and she listened skeptically: there
were queer birds in the woods fringing the Quaker City.

What was his game? After a year and a half of his acquaintance, she didn't especially care. In that time she had heard him complain about the high price of the books he wanted, heard him ask, foolishly, why they were not sold over the counter at book-club prices. He gave all the salespeople a hard time and they detested him. What was his game? She didn't know, but she couldn't imagine its being anything but innocent, for when he invited her to see his imaginary collection he included her husband. She never tried to find out. She never went to Merion.

Leo Stein was more grateful for Barnes's attention. In 1947 he published his second long-awaited book, *Appreciation: Painting, Poetry, Prose.* Barnes read it immediately and wrote the author: *"Appreciation* is a knockout! I have never read any other exposition so clear, so sensible and accurately descriptive." He agreed with Stein's discussion of cubism, which was better than his own treatment of the subject. "What I have said above is but a feeble expression of my enthusiasm for the book and the deep admiration [I have] for its creator." *Appreciation* would be required reading for students of the Foundation.

A week after the book appeared Stein wrote his cousin Fred Stein in New York (the book was dedicated to him and his wife, Beatrice) that he had not heard from anyone but Barnes so far. With dead-pan complacency he quoted Barnes verbatim, adding: "Barnes is a competent person and no flatterer." Apparently Stein felt safe in assuming that Barnes could not put on an act as he himself had done in praising Dewey's book for Barnes's benefit.

It goes without saying that I am pleased with your letter [he replied]. We have had divergences, but there has always been, I think, a mutual recognition that neither of us liked twaddle about art instead of hard-headed commonsense. We have both of us brains enough to know that aspiration is not inspiration, that until one has reached intelligibility one hasn't really said anything. . . .

Barnes's enthusiasm must have been genuine. He certainly could not have been logrolling, for this is all that Stein said about the method of art appreciation which Barnes and his collaborator had so arduously developed through five thick volumes, in behalf of which he had fought so many battles with the infidels who did not accept it wholeheartedly: "The degree of accuracy possible when one deals with art does not amount to science in any rigorous sense. What is possible is rather intelligently discriminated description, of which there are good examples in the books of A. C. Barnes." Not *analysis* of paintings but *description*—the very thing Barnes detested; and he had written analysis. Stein wrote further: "[Appreciation] means taking things for values found in them directly, and not as the result of analysis. Analysis may, of course, be used for purposes of preliminary study, to prepare for a more intimate acquaintance; but appreciation always deals with wholes."

One has the feeling that if Stein were not a friend of Barnes, he might not have mentioned him at all. Yet Barnes did not raise hell with Stein over his handout of "intelligently discriminated description" (awful afterthought: could he have been flattered by being called *intelligent?*)—he took the bare, misleading mention of himself as praise enough, and praised Stein for his overall performance.

The intimacy of two strong egotists is always in delicate balance. The scale is the more sensitive, responsive to the weight of a single hostile word, when they are self-conscious intellectuals, unsure of themselves, constantly re-evaluating themselves, and hoping other people will have a higher opinion of them than they really have of themselves, no matter how boastful they may seem to be. Such people are not made for stable friendships. Though Barnes's relationship with Stein was as uneasy as most of his friendships (only one of them rooted in boyhood), it endured. It had wavered and broken but it had healed, and it ended on the happy note of their mutual pleasure in *Appreciation*. Stein died the year it was published.

25

The Kill

THE PHILADELPHIA MUSEUM OF ART WAS PLANNING A comprehensive Matisse exhibition for the spring of 1948. Ignoring all of the previous skirmishes between Barnes and the museum, its curator of paintings, Henry Clifford, wrote him on February 3 to request the loan of *Joy of Living* and, if possible, two other paintings. To fortify his request—modest enough, and what did he have to lose?—Clifford stated that he had recently seen Matisse in Paris and the artist had expressed the hope that the Foundation would consent to such a loan.

Three days later he received a reply from N. E. Mullen, pointing out an error in a parenthetical remark in his letter. . . .

Barnes himself replied on March 23. Just back from a trip, he had before him a newspaper clipping which referred to the museum's show as "the most important

exhibition of Matisse's work ever held anywhere"; he had
before him a telegram from an editor requesting an article
on the show; and finally there was Clifford's letter. (The
telegram was from Alfred Frankfurter, editor of *Art News*.
To tie in with the exhibition, he wanted an article on
Matisse for the April issue from Barnes "as foremost
Matisse connoisseur in America . . . any length you like
for the benefit of the many thousands unable to attend
your lectures. . . . I still remember that wonderful
Scotch when Vollard visited . . . never tasted anything
near it since." Barnes ignored the telegram, flattery and
all; to Clifford he wrote an essay.

In the course of it he stated that the collection now
had sixty-five works by Matisse, exaggerated his intimacy
with the artist (whom he met "each time I have gone to
Paris," but, he did not say, met only in his studio, never
at home), and suggested that the knowledgeable, subtle
and witty Matisse had been pulling Clifford's leg when he
told him that he hoped Barnes would lend his pictures
to the exhibition. For Matisse knew about the Benson
and Cézanne incidents—he even knew all about the
Academy exhibition in 1923 and *The Three Sisters* controversy in 1934, apropos of which Matisse had said,
"Plus ça change, plus ça reste la même chose"—a sage
quotation but irrelevant, since Ingersoll and the museum
were not responsible for what the critics and doctors had
said a dozen years previously.

While Barnes was writing as if he had Matisse in his
pocket, Clifford had before him a letter which he had
received more than a month previously: "Dear Mr. Clifford: I hope that my exhibition may be worthy of all the
work it is making for you, which touches me deeply.
. . ." The body of the long letter was concerned with the
harmful effect the exhibition might have on young paint-

ers. What he was afraid of was that they would not understand the years of hard labor which had given him the
ability to produce pictures with "apparent facility."

. . . My dear Mr. Clifford, here is the end of my letter. I
started it to let you know that I realize the trouble you are
taking over me at the moment. I see that, obeying an interior
necessity, I have made it an expression of what I feel about
drawing, color, and the importance of discipline in the
education of an artist. If you think that all these reflections
of mine can be of any use to anyone, do whatever you think
best with this letter. . . . Please believe me, dear Mr. Clifford,

> Yours gratefully,
> Henri Matisse

Clifford did not send a copy of this letter to Barnes—
he had it printed in full in the foreword to the catalog
of the exhibition, with the prefatory statement: "We are
fortunate in having the blessing of Matisse himself."

Did Barnes realize that he had made a fool of himself?
Was he squelched? Watch the great psychologist perform a
switcheroo. During a week's gestation, he hatched himself
a fine piece of gallows humor: he imagined himself invited
to talk at the museum on the day the Matisse exhibition
opened, and, on the pretext of answering a question from
the "audience," he carried out a violent attack on the
museum. "What puzzles many of us artists," his putative
listener asked, "is—How can a man of Matisse's culture
and artistic stature put his 'blessing' upon an institution
which has frequently been named [by whom?] as a place
where both art and education are prostituted? Does
Matisse dispute another published charge [by whom?] that
'the main function of the Museum has been to serve as
a pedestal upon which a clique of socialites pose as
patrons of art and culture,' or does he not know of such
charges?"

Why, from that pontifical letter Barnes wrote Clifford, we thought that *he* had kept Matisse thoroughly informed, that Matisse knew all. . . . Never mind that: Barnes answered the question, and answered, and answered, and mimeographed choice excerpts from his sardonic joke for distribution to his mailing list.

That was not all: he was only warming up. Barnes had packages made up, each one containing a carbon copy of Clifford's letter to him and his reply, a carbon copy of his letter to Kimball, a carbon copy of the Frankfurter telegram (marked: *Telegram Ignored*), a carbon copy of the Ingersoll telegram of 1931 requesting Barnes's advice on *The Three Sisters,* carbon copies of his and Valentine Dudensing's letters of 1934 on the same subject, a copy of *A Message to the Students of the Pennsylvania Academy of the Fine Arts*—the whole sandwiched between the leaves of *A Disgrace to Philadelphia.*[1] A couple of days before the exhibition opened, Barnes had the packages placed at strategic points in the museum for the benefit of visitors: one on the sales desk, one in the print gallery, one in a telephone booth, one in a passenger elevator, two each in two ladies' rooms. One set he handed in person to a guard. A couple of days after the exhibition opened, his demon drove him to dispose of six more packages at the Philadelphia Art Alliance, frequented by many art lovers.

Punishment enough? Vengeance enough? Barnes was still only warming up. From low comedy he turned to high drama. The announcement that Kimball would lecture on Matisse at the museum on April 13 gave him his cue. Kimball had been trained as an architect, and Barnes was convinced that he knew nothing about painting and

---

[1] By this time the Barnes Foundation had become the second largest consumer of carbon paper in the United States.

would prove it in his talk. He awaited the occasion—
prepared for it—with glee.

If it would be too much to say that Barnes packed the
audience, and it may not be, he surely had a hand in the
composition of "the intelligent portion" of it which, he
said later, became restive after a half hour of Kimball's
"futile rambling" and began to ask questions. For, as
Barnes's stenographic transcript and comment put it, the
audience included "distinguished artists, educators and
writers from New York, Philadelphia, Baltimore and
Boston." In the context, "distinguished" signified that
these persons were or had been associated with Barnes.
Among them were Laurence Buermeyer and Abraham
Chanin, who said with a straight face that he had come
"from a distance of ninety miles [from New York], hoping
to add to my knowledge of Matisse." From the excerpts
which follow it is plain that the old matador had sent for
him to act as his banderillero and picador in one, and
even, perhaps, to dispatch the bull.

Chanin: What makes a still-life a masterpiece?
Kimball: The *life* with which the artist has impressed it.
Chanin: Can you give me an idea of what you mean by that?
Kimball: Do *you* know the secret of organic life?
Chanin: There are no specifics that make it a Matisse?
Kimball: I think there are, but they are not the ones that
     give it life.
Chanin: What does 'life' mean?
Someone: That's a mystery.
Kimball: Yes, that's a mystery. . . .
Chanin: I have come . . . hoping to add to my knowledge
     of Matisse, but I find myself deeply disappointed with
     the talk.
Woman: So do I, and I came all the way from Baltimore. . . .
Chanin: You have not made a single statement that would

enable a person of average intelligence to learn what makes a painting a work of art, or what makes a painting by Matisse different from the work of any other modern painter.

Kimball: Young man, art can't be explained like that. The only specific thing about Matisse is his being Matisse. What is the difference, for instance, between Shelly and Keats? . . .

Chanin: But one *can* explain the difference between Shelly and Keats.

Barnes: You mean Kelly and Sheets, don't you? [laughter]

(Kimball kept coming back to the phrase, "the life in a work of art.")

Barnes: Wouldn't you point out what that "life" in Matisse consists of?

Kimball: Yes! Wouldn't you tell us, Dr. Barnes?

Barnes: It's you who are here to talk about Matisse; *I* came here to learn. . . . (He mentions having sixty-five works by Matisse.)

Kimball: I wish you would interpret them to me.

Barnes: I would if you would come out there [to the Foundation] and enter as a student in the first-year class. . . .

(And so on and so on. Chanin finally stood up and began an analysis of *The Blue Window* in the Barnesian manner.)

Kimball [interrupting]: My dear boy, I'm sure we have all enjoyed—

Barnes: You can't interrupt him. He has the floor. That's not very polite, and you know, Mr. Kimball, that *I* am *never* impolite.

Kimball: I am director of the museum.

Barnes: That doesn't mean you own the museum. It's tax-supported and you are expected to serve the tax-paying public. Besides, you asked the man to speak and he has the right to finish what he wants to say.

But Kimball left and Barnes closed the meeting by reading an example of obfuscated, pretentious and meaningless writing quoted by William James in *Principles of Psychology*, Volume I, pp. 263, 264 (which he happened to have handy). This, Barnes said, was "a fitting epilogue to Kimball's demonstration of the 'Progressive Decay' of the Philadelphia Museum of Art. . . ." Buermeyer saw in this question-and-answer period "the spirit of ancient Athens . . . a memorable demonstration that democracy and education, put into practice, provide the means of intelligent living."

Was Barnes so determined to get Kimball because of his hostility to Kimball himself—which he had often denied—or was the one-time fox-hunter still striking back through him at the higher social class which had forced him, through indifference if not direct snub, to abandon the chase? In his pamphlet on the museum, Harry Fuiman had written for him:

The trusteeship of an art museum is rarely, if ever, a primary consideration with the trustees. It has become a device for bestowing upon individuals—at public expense—flattery and social prestige masked, of course, behind a pretense of disinterested public service. The public service consists, however, in attending occasional meetings, making occasional donations, and selecting for the director of the museum someone physically and mentally acceptable to the infantile predilections and purposes of the uninformed trustees.

That was written a decade previously. Now, after the kill, satisfied with his bloody work justified in reason, his incessant need for self-justification slacked in the name of education, Barnes could sit back and laugh. Some weeks later, in the name of Bella Donna Van Byttsche, an alleged associate of the museum, he wrote himself a letter (with carbon copies all around):

I want you to know that you are too, too, awfully, perfectly horrid to say all the nasty things about us aristocratic art

lovers who have done so much for the common herd by making the Philadelphia Museum of Art the truly marvelous
institution it is today. . . .

Of course, recent immigrants like you would hardly understand true quality, but I will have you know that my ancestry
is simply unassailable. Our great-great-grandfather was Lord
Costermonger, of Billingsgate Mews, and founded that great
British institution, "The Hulks." Another ancestor was the
Earl of Droolingtoole, of Houndsditch Manure, Sluppinton-
on-Slops, Herts. And besides Herts, many of the great nobles
of Harts, Nerts and Tarts are my relatives. There the old
traditions are still preserved, with tea and strumpets served
every afternoon. . . .

On the continental side, there is the great Graf Lakmir im
Arsch, of the small but potent principality which has supplied
so many royal partners, Saxe-Schaffner-und Marx. You profess
to know France, so you must have seen the art treasures of
another close and noble relative, le Comte Trou de Quêne,
whose estate, "Eaux d'Egout" you will remember as *the* most
notable in all Visqueux. That is, if you were actually in
France.

The lady went on to consider the ancestry of her consort, "a direct descendant of that greatest of early Dutch
poltroons, Mynheer Ludwig van Gott Damm, of Spuyten
Duyvil, Weehawken and Flatbush." As for art, she loves
"all of that fellow Matice's works," whose name she
variantly spells *Matis* and *Mattice,* but never once cor-
rectly. . . .

While he may have had certain people loosely in mind,
Barnes was just having a hell of a good time playing
around with low puns, foreign vulgate and Dickensian-
cum-sophomoric extravagance.

26

Reprise

HERE BARNES WAS THE LOW COMEDIAN, BUT HE HAD NOT yet given up the higher role of explorer. When his former student Willi Bruckner came back from service, he brought with him fifteen canvases by Alo Altripp, an anti-Nazi artist who had held an exhibition in Wiesbaden soon after the American Military Government moved in. Barnes bought several. Later on he showed them to Dorothy Norman and even, after much persuasion, to Miss Eileen Talmey, feature editor of *Vogue,* for which Mrs. Norman was doing an article on Altripp. In the August, 1949, issue, two of Barnes's Altripps were reproduced in color, and he wrote a short piece relating one of them to Renoir and the other to Cézanne, without saying whether or why he *liked* them.

There was also an Altripp exhibition at the Ferargil Galleries. Barnes brought the artist to this country, paid all his expenses, and otherwise treated him kindly. After the opening Barnes gave a party to a small group at which, Mrs. Norman recalls, he was entirely amiable and jovial.

Towards applicants for admission to the gallery Barnes was, as before, sometimes gracious. But he stiffened when a rajah and his consort tried to barge into his domain. Didn't they know that no rajahs need apply? Informed that Mme. Krishna Hutheesing was a sister of Mme. Nehru, the Main Line monarch of all he surveyed said, in effect, Well, what do you know? And how are things in old Werinhellanbedad? The answer was still no. They were not so easily put off, these people. They were used to having things done for them, and pulled strings: they appealed to Dorothy Norman to help them. On the death of Alfred Stieglitz in the summer of 1946, planning to edit and publish a memorial portfolio, she had solicited a contribution from Barnes. He had responded promptly, testifying that "the present status of good contemporary painting [in America?] probably owes more to him than it does to any other person," and was delighted to have been asked. When Mrs. Norman called him on behalf of the Hutheesings, they were as good as in.

In London, Cristabel Aberconway, wife of the head of the Cunard Line, had long heard of the Barnes collection. Owning a small but choice group of French moderns herself, Lady Aberconway was determined, as a friend advised her, to see the pictures in Merion *at all costs*. On board the *Queen Elizabeth* bound for New York, she wrote her first note to Barnes. There was no answer awaiting her in port. No answer came within a week. Putting away pride, she wrote again. No response.

Returning from a trip to Washington, she spent a day in Philadelphia and drove out to Merion. When she rang the doorbell of the gallery,

a sympathetic, but firm, employee opened the door. No: no one was ever allowed to see the pictures. No: no matter what hour of the day I came I couldn't possibly see the pictures. No: I couldn't send in a message to Dr. Barnes; he had gone to New York for the day.

Oh! so I had read Dr. Barnes's books on Renoir and Cézanne . . . ? And I had come all the way from England, and one of my great desires was to see Dr. Barnes's pictures? And I wasn't attached to any museum, nor a dealer? What a pity Dr. Barnes was in New York! For perhaps had he been at the Foundation, he *might* have let me in . . . !

She wrote a message for Barnes—and two days later received the standard rejection slip. But, within a week, "I received a copy of a most oddly worded letter which Dr. Barnes had sent to Dr. Vitale Bloch. . . ."

In this Barnes said that

it is only once in a blue moon that we can have casual visitors. However, the moon takes on that hue on Thursday afternoon of this week, March 16th, between the hours of one and four.

If that fits in with your plans, let me know, and I'll make arrangements to have you admitted. While you're about it, you might get in touch with Christabel Aberconway, 14 East 89th Street, New York, at Atwater 9-5092, who has applied for admission several times, apparently without having been informed by her friends in London of our problems and how we handle them. I don't know her from Adam's wife, but she might be young, attractive and interesting, so, if you are still like you were in the old days when we spent so much time together in Berlin, you might find it worthwhile to be her guide in how to reach the Foundation. . . .

Lady Aberconway canceled her engagements for the sixteenth. "With, I confess, considerable apprehension, I called for Dr. Bloch. . . ." She needed not have been apprehensive, for she found Barnes "courteous" and "fatherly." To her letter of thanks after the visit, Barnes replied:

Thank you for the nice letter to me written on board the *Queen Mary*.

Contrary to the suspicions, what you wrote did not go into the wastebasket, but was circulated among the members of the staff and enjoyed by them as much as by myself.

You made a serious mistake when you were here in not telling me that I had the voice of a singer; if you had, I should have had the greatest pleasure, and you probably a great shock, in singing the largest repertoire of Methodist hymns of any person I know. I was brought up in the Methodist Church, and every time I am out in the country, I let loose in my loudest voice of the complete repertoire. Sometimes a friend, a Justice of the U.S. Supreme Court, accompanies me, and he gets as much fun out of it as I do.

I am glad to know that you enjoyed your visit to the Foundation, but it's safe to say that our enjoyment at having you here was equal to yours. When you come again, which I hope will be with your husband, let me know in advance and we'll try to arrange for you to get more time with the collection than you did last time.

The curmudgeon could be charming; the passionate democrat could recognize a human being in an aristocrat.

As they had entered the gallery, Bloch asked whether he might smoke. "Yes," said Barnes, "if you put the ashes in your pocket." Yet, despite such responses, Bloch found that "somehow it was not the old Dr. Barnes any more. On this very day he made some exchanges which I could not understand, of some of his lovely Cézannes against some eighteenth century French pictures." (One of these was a Chardin.) But Bloch had always considered Barnes "unpredictable in his artistic judgments" (Bloch himself had become an authority on seventeenth-century art and was editor of the Dutch magazine, *Monthly for Figurative Arts*), so that he must have sensed some deeper change, an aging perhaps, of the hitherto "boyish" man he had known.

In one thing—and perhaps that was everything—Barnes had not changed: he still rode the hounds of controversy. He was still loving-fighting alma mater. Then he took on in quick succession and partly at the same time two new foes.

A columnist in the *Evening Bulletin,* Paul Jones, made a reference to "a little picture collection kept by an obscure chemist somewhere on the Main Line." Jones knew perfectly well what he was doing—he was looking for free copy. And he got it—anyway, got a reply—the very next day.

Merion, le 11 mai 1950

Monsieur,

J'ai reçu une demande de renseignements au sujet de vos ancêtres et, ne sachant y repondre, je suggère que vous fassiez paraître en votre colonne les renseignements requis.

La demande est exprimée comme suit: "Serait-il possible que John Paul Jones, le Capitaine du *Bon Homme Richard,* soit un ancêtre de Skatole Paul Jones, le feuilletoniste du *Evening Bulletin?*"

Je vous prie de bien vouloir agréer, Monsieur, l'expression de mes salutations les plus distinguées.

Fidèle de Port Manech
Secrétaire du Docteur Barnes[1]

[1] I have received a request for information on the subject of your ancestors and, not knowing how to answer it, I suggest that you

Fidèle signed it, as usual, with her patterned paw mark.

Barnes had picked the right man to show off his French to. Jones understood it and replied in kind, repudiating the nickname and "suggesting that his wits were addled by the fumes of the horse manure he spent his time analyzing." Barnes came back, again on the following day:

Cher ami:

Vous remerciant de votre lettre du 18 courant, je désire corriger une grave erreur de votre part. Vous affirmez que "quant au nommé Skatole Jones, on ne le connait pas ici."-"16-iou!" est ma réponse. Se peut-il que vous soyez victime de fausse modestie?

Afin de vous tenir au courant des choses telles qu'elles le sont, j'ai le plaisir de vous faire savoir qu'une copie de ma lettre du 11 mai, envoyée au "City Editor," vous a appliqué l'indécollable sobriquet—connu partout à present, même parmi les jeunes garçons de course et colporteurs.—Quelle déplorable ignorance de votre part, Monsieur!

Ma bonne-amie, la charmante chiennette d'en face, toujours pleine de bonnes intentions, me prie d'être son interprète et de vous suggérer que vous aidiez le "Evening Bulletin"—si cela vous est possible—a publier de vraies nouvelles et non de ces articles scatologiques qui coulent de votre plume—

> Skatole, oh! vielle commère,
> La plus belle des poubelles,
> Vivra en paix, sure la terre,
> Tranquille et bien loin de Fidèle. . . .[2]

---

have the required information published in your column. The request was expressed as follows: "Would it be possible that John Paul Jones, captain of the *Bon Homme Richard,* is an ancestor of Skatole Paul Jones, columnist of the *Evening Bulletin?*" (The last sentence of the letter is the conventional flowery closing form of French correspondence.) "Skatole" may be freely rendered as "Stinker," but that does not give the full flavor of Barnes's chemical joke. Skatole and indole are two constituents of feces which give it its characteristic smell.

[2] Thanking you for your letter of the 18th, I wish to correct a

This time Fidèle's paw mark was augmented, as the letter says, by her picture.

All this was pleasant foolery for Barnes, but it did not provide copy for Jones; and Jones, like Kimball before him, found that he could not keep up the controversy because he had his work to do and Barnes had all the time in the world for it, or seemed to. . . .

In the April, 1950, issue of *Holiday* magazine, James A. Michener had written an article about the Main Line, describing it as "one of the loveliest areas in the world" and "the home of an aristocratic middle class." "All things considered, the Main Line represents suburban America at its best."

Having painted a good many individuals of the area in rosy hues, Michener refrained from doing Barnes in Picasso blue. Writing of the collection, he merely said that the chances were you could not get in to see it without some kind of alluring trick. And he told of the college student, name not given, who, after applying for admis-

---

serious mistake you made. You state that "nobody around here knows a fellow name of Skatole Jones." "Sez you!" is my answer. Can it be that you are a victim of false modesty? To keep you posted on things as they are, I have the pleasure of informing you that a copy of my letter of the 11th of May, sent to your City Editor, stamped you indelibly with the nickname—now known everywhere, even among the young errand boys and newsboys.—What deplorable ignorance on your part, sir!

My good friend, the charming little dog on the opposite page, always full of good intentions, asks me to be her interpreter and to suggest to you that you would help the *Evening Bulletin*—if you were capable of doing so—by publishing the real news and not those scatological articles which flow from your pen—

> Skatole, dear old scout,
> Most charming chamberpot,
> On earth in peace will dwell,
> In quiet, far far from Fidèle. . . .

sion three times and being three times ignored, became
a steelworker and, addressing Barnes from Pittsburgh, received by return mail permission to come.

Barnes did not allow the sociologizing reporter to have
his sweet say uncontested. Writing to Michener, he said,
among other things, trenchantly and with much truth:
"You glamorize ordinary people, lick their boots *ad nau-
seam,* and comfort the smug complacency of snobs."

Something he wrote concerning Michener's reference
to himself drew the confession of the author that he,
Michener, was

the four-flushing swine who pulled that Pittsburgh iron-
worker routine on you some twenty-five years ago, and I remember the trip to Merion as about the best intellectual part
of my years at Swarthmore with A. M. Brooks, who first told
me of the indecent number of good paintings you have.

I judge from the tenor of your letter that it would do me
no good to apply for another visit. . . . But since the vitriol
of your pen seems to be diminishing with age, and since you
have appeared to mellow with the passing years, do you think
there's any chance that my wife—who is a good artist and
not at all like me—might get a chance to see what you're sitting on, over there behind the wall?

A shrewd letter, but Barnes answered rough and tough.
. . . Soon after, Michener gave a literary talk at the
Irvine Auditorium. When he finished, Barnes walked up
to him, introduced himself, and after an exchange of
amenities challenged him to a debate on art. Apparently
he already had a radio station lined up and made his
proposition seriously and forcefully. Michener, however,
shied away from it "because I realized that I was in the
hands of a madman and could gain nothing" [from the
debate].

How, mad? He had been flourishing that way for fifty

years, and he disarmed Michener some time after their "vitriolic exchange of pleasantries" by writing him "several long and congenial letters in which he gave me carbon copies of his previous bouts with other gentlemen of the Philadelphia area, and he made a great and happy point of the fact that he had scared every one of them to death, and that college presidents, curators of museums, ministers of the cloth, editors alike all quailed before his profanity and personal figure. I look back on my own brush with Barnes as a completely hilarious episode in which a very powerful man quite overwhelmed me."

27

Alma Mater: Finale Quasi Fantasia

HOW, MAD? WHEN, IN THE FALL OF 1945, HE HAD RECEIVED an inquiry from a U. S. Army post for a copy of *The Bertrand Russell Case,* did he not have the sound sense to perceive an unusual quality in the writer? He began to correspond with this Dr. Roderick M. Chisholm; before long he invited him to Merion and introduced him to Dewey. For Chisholm had been an outstanding student of philosophy at Harvard before graduating to the infantry. He had by now worked himself up to the rank of clinical psychologist, and was looking forward to his early discharge from the Army and a position in his own field.

Chisholm and Dewey had some personal conversations and continued them by mail, with the self-taught philosopher alertly listening in. Astonished by Dewey's praise of universities, Barnes wrote Chisholm of his own unsatisfactory experiences in his salad days at the University of Pennsylvania, where he was given a teaching formula which "never got anywhere near meeting the individuality of the students or promoting their growth." Striking out on his own path, he "was in hot water all the time with the big shots." Explicit as this is—and Barnes had testified at the Russell trial that he "taught at Penn for a while" —there is no record of his ever having been on the faculty.

When Chisholm disagreed with Dewey on certain points and the master conceded that he was right in one of them, Barnes was naturally impressed; and when he received a copy of *The Philosophy of Bertrand Russell*, a symposium in which Chisholm was represented, Barnes was ready to give him an appointment at the Foundation. (Barnes most enjoyed one contributor's "lambasting so thorough and so well grounded in common sense" and Russell's reply to all of his critics, of which Barnes wrote:

In soapy thinking and silken language, he proves to my complete satisfaction . . . that he is intellectually dishonest. . . . He is unquestionably brilliant—but in the Goethe sense that "there is no greatness in being brilliant if one respects nothing." What I can't understand is what's the use of having a brilliant intellect   [one] . . . lacks common sense, is an exhibitionist and has the character of a rat. [Could Russell reply, *Tu quoque?*]

Of Chisholm's own contribution, Barnes said candidly and tactfully that he was not competent to judge it, but that he "enjoyed the workings of an acute mind engaged in reflection upon the specific points mentioned," in which, however, he happened not to be interested.

An able young man, optimistic with his first teaching job at a unique institution, Chisholm breezed through a two-page single-spaced letter from Barnes without worrying overmuch about the magnitude of the task it set forth.

He was to present in a one-year course "an objective
study of the organic relationship between art and philosophy" which the Foundation tried to give in four years
—a course which would bring to the students "the essentials of philosophy, psychology, scientific method, orderly
thinking, experience, and . . . put them over objectively
by means of the paintings" in the collection. Barnes had
faith in Chisholm's ability to do this: he regarded him as
Russell's successor at the Foundation.

Chisholm came on to Merion. He lived at the Foundation, had an office in the gallery. Attending Miss de
Mazia's class, he had the collection at his disposal at all
times. Barnes was there to answer questions. For six
months, Chisholm had a wonderful time.

In February, 1946, he began to give his course. Barnes
sat in on the lectures, taking notes. Laurence Buermeyer
dropped around, too ill to hold a regular job, and by way
of rendering some service for his pension, *he* took notes.
The two keen minds sitting there in front of him, writing,
writing, made Chisholm uneasy. He wondered what they
were writing. Afterward, they told him only too clearly
what was wrong with his lectures. He had thought (he
wrote the author of this book) that he was "to undertake
an independent examination of the basic philosophical
questions with which Barnes's program was involved." It
wasn't so. Barnes wanted the lectures to serve as "demonstrations" of his approach to art. Week after week, Barnes
grew more and more discontented, and curbed his expression of it less and less. Chisholm became rattled.
Barnes called on the university people to see for themselves how rambling and confused he was, confusing the
students. . . .

What university?

The University of Pennsylvania of course.

Why, hadn't Barnes broken with it years before?

Yes, but Chisholm was a natural link between them. More than that: foreseeing a great increase in registration, Barnes had proposed setting up a teachers' training course at the university. Investigating the man it suggested to direct it, Barnes found that he had studied at Princeton with Frank Jewett Mather, Jr.—strike one; that he was teaching art with the aid of photographs—strike two; and that at the gallery he proved himself "incapable of recognizing characteristic paintings of either distinguished contemporary artists or old masters"—strike three, and that project was out. But the course began. University students were attending it. Dean Morrow, of the College of Arts and Sciences, even allowed his assistant, Jon D. Longaker, time off to take three courses at the Foundation, for Barnes had found him promising teaching material and was planning to send him abroad for further study, to conduct a class for Penn students on his return. In Chisholm's class—

Who's Chisholm?

Why, he's the Army-Harvard man who—

He's fired!

Barnes had taken over his class after five lectures.

Dean Morrow said that he had not given Chisholm a fair trial. Barnes made him retract his statement, but the president of the university, George G. McClelland, reaffirmed it; and he gave substance to his support by appointing Chisholm to the faculty of philosophy for the following academic year. (He is now chairman of the philosophy department at Brown University.)

On April 10, 1947, in a "Report on the University of Pennsylvania—Barnes Foundation Experiment," Barnes wrote: "Thus ends a melancholy record of inertia, lethargy, disorder, blindness and futility on the part of

Penn officials. . . . By their torpor, the authorities have forfeited for the second, and last, time one of the most valuable gifts, educational and material, ever offered to a university. . . ."

So he was finally, not semifinally but finally-finally, finished with alma mater?—*16-iou!*

Along came Harold E. Stassen—candidate for the Republican nomination for the Presidency? The same.

How did he get in on the act?

Ex-governor of one state, ex-aspirant to head all the states, Stassen became president of the University of Pennsylvania in July, 1948. Informed of "one of the most valuable gifts ever offered to a university," he was not reconciled to Penn's loss of it. Like Marceau when he joined the Pennsylvania Museum, Stassen said to himself: The people around here didn't know how to handle Barnes. Tactfully, skillfully, Stassen made his approach under cover of Fogg. Vice-provost of the university as well as professor of botany and curator of the herbarium, Dr. John M. Fogg, Jr., also advised Mrs. Barnes on the arboretum. Barnes had the greatest respect for him.

Dear Jack [Barnes wrote him]:
When I got home from Europe, I found your letter of July 26th *qui éclaire la situation plus à travers vos songes qu'à travers la réalitè:*—The first chapter of Santayana's book, *Poetry and Religion,* defines the difference between Understanding and Imagination. I shall draw upon the psychology of that chapter to meet the requirements of reality. . . .

Quite an opening paragraph to fling at a friend on a hot July day. Well, Fogg-Stassen asked for it when proposing that Barnes join forces with those who, with the new president, wanted to bring a New Deal to the university. The whole idea, Barnes said, was a pipe dream.

Stassen was not squelched. He wrote Barnes himself, graciously inviting him to lunch. Oh, not in the first paragraph. As one man of ideas to another, he first touched on world affairs, and most appropriately in connection with the celebration of John Dewey's ninetieth birthday (and with the most delicate hint that John Dewey was sort of close to Barnes): "I am particularly interested in his appraisal of the approach of Prime Minister Nehru of India to the world situation. Do you know whether Dr. Dewey has written or spoken about this? . . . I now have the reported recommendations as to the School of Fine Arts and would like to discuss them with you."

Patiently but firmly Barnes replied that to expect "a man not trained in educational science" and without advisers so trained, to reform the university would be virtually a confession of a belief in miracles. Stassen's job, it seemed to him, was as herculean as the cleaning of the Augean stables.

Stassen thought that one over, thought it over for five months. As he wrote on March 29, 1950: "I appreciated the bluntness of your letter and have given much thought to the situation." Not bad for a man who was still giving much thought to becoming president of a considerably larger institution. "Even though I lay no claim to being a twentieth century Hercules, I am determined to make progress on the task." As for the luncheon invitation, it still stood. And his last word was not of the business in hand: "I think the State Department made a mistake in Picasso's case." This was a liberal-statesmanlike gesture, such as Barnes would approve, deprecating the State Department's decision to exclude a "peace mission" of twelve, including the artist, as Communist propagandists.

Dear Governor [Barnes replied, without thinking it over more than five days]: How to avoid "bluntness" is always the

problem of the person whose painful duty it is to pronounce
a death. In the present instance, the cause of death is metic-
ulously set forth in the documents I have placed in Penn's
official records. . . .

In view of the finality of death, your numerous invitations
to me to luncheon and to discuss with you the situation at
Penn stimulate the imagination. When I received the third
such invitation last week, it recalled a story, ascribed to Abe
Lincoln, about a Negro woman in Georgia who supported her
no-good husband and their children by taking in washing. She
was young, beautiful, buxom and flirtatious—in short, a
potent aphrodisiac. On one occasion, as she was scrubbing
clothes outdoors, a slick-looking black man lingered at her
side. Her husband called out the window—"Mandy, what you
doin' there?" She replied, "Dis man wants me to go over to
his house to do some washin'!" The husband said, "Come on
in heah; dat man don't want no washin' done—I see the front
of his pants move."

Barnes had in the meantime received a letter from Jon
Longaker—

Longaker? Wasn't Barnes through with him when he
fired Chisholm and the university together?

No, for he was a just man. He merely did not subsidize
Longaker's trip to Europe. Now the young man was back,
broke, and asking for a formal statement of his study at
the Foundation, to be filed with his application for a job
in the Fine Arts Department of the university. Barnes
was willing to give it to him, but he pointed out that the
department had not changed its method of teaching art
appreciation and suggested that Longaker ask for a free
hand in selecting his pupils. "Under these conditions you
would be permitted to use the galleries of the Foundation
one afternoon each week for the instruction of the members of your class in accordance with the principles of

the Foundation." Longaker was further to stipulate that he would have no other duties and that he would receive an adequate salary. "Whether you accept this idea, and how you go about presenting it is entirely up to you. However, be assured that I offer it because I have your best interests at heart and certainly would like to see Penn get out of the educational mess in its Fine Arts Department."

A heavy burden to put on a young man just beginning his career? And what did Barnes mean by sending a carbon copy of the letter to Stassen?

A few weeks later Longaker informed him that he had an appointment with Stassen. Barnes replied that his reference to Longaker's possible admittance to the Foundation had prompted the president to give it to him. After vilifying Stassen at length, Barnes asked him whether he was willing to begin his career "under the jurisdiction of a man who shoots at a wooden decoy which he mistook for a live duck." If he was willing to be a party to Penn's prostitution of art and education, let him keep his appointment; if not, "come to see me, and I shall show you how you can get the help that you have told me you need."

Longaker kept his appointment with Stassen. But two can play games: Stassen stalled him off. He called on Barnes, who suggested that he try to get a job at Sarah Lawrence College, and gave him three dollars to get back to New York. Somehow, Harold Taylor, president of Sarah Lawrence, failed to see Longaker and Barnes wrote him a nasty letter. At the same time he proposed that Longaker teach a class of Sarah Lawrence students, who would of course have to travel from Bronxville, N. Y., to Merion to have the benefit of the paintings. On Longaker's second visit, Taylor received him. Perched on his chair, both feet under him, Taylor said, "Frankly, don't you think Barnes is off his rocker?" . . .

Barnes himself hired Longaker for the 1950-1951 school year, to teach a group of students from Lincoln University, the Negro institution in Lincoln University, Pa. Barnes had previously shown a keen interest in Lincoln. "I can only say that I had the highest regard and affection for him," Horace M. Bond wrote me on May 20, 1957, while he was still president, "and that I was more grateful to him for his interest . . . than to any other donor . . . I have known in my twelve years here."

Barnes was not sentimental about the individual students. When one boy asked a good many questions in class, Barnes thought it was because he didn't grasp the subject, and dismissed him—without even consulting Longaker.

This class from Lincoln was symbolic. Barnes's last encounter with Stassen could only have given him a dismal pleasure; and he could not have had any joy of the step he took to cut the connection of the Foundation and Penn, for this was an irrevocable break. Originally, Penn and the Academy were, after the Barneses died, to have named alternately all but one of the successor trustees of the Foundation. (Its treasurer, the Girard Trust Corn Exchange Bank, was to choose that one.) To punish the Academy, Barnes had amended the pertinent by-law to deprive it of its power. To punish his alma mater, he amended the by-law again. On October 20, 1950 he transferred its authority to Lincoln University, with the safeguard that "no Trustee [of the Foundation] shall be a member of the faculty or Board of Trustees or Directors of the University of Pennsylvania, Temple University, Bryn Mawr, Haverford or Swarthmore Colleges, or Pennsylvania Academy of the Fine Arts"—all the educational institutions of Philadelphia and environs, for they had failed to do justice to the Foundation or render sufficient homage to him.

Grant Barnes's genuine concern for Negro welfare; grant his previous interest in Lincoln University in particular. There is no escaping the inference that he was using it to vent his spite. In opposing the small home development near the Foundation years ago, he had threatened to convert it to a Negro institution. If the last amendment did not turn it over for Negro use, it placed the Foundation, though Lincoln has some white trustees, under ostensible Negro control. Humiliating his enemies —the academy, the museum, the university—he was, without apparently realizing it, also humiliating the Negro. For this was to assume the opinion of the enemies of the Negro people that it was unworthy of the honor. Even if it was not his own opinion, he was still favoring the Negro, not as a fellow human being and friend, but as a weapon.

28

The Stop Sign

THAT SETTLED THE FUTURE OF THE FOUNDATION, OR AT least as much of it as myopic man can foresee. What else was there for the master to do? To live in the continuing present of his own creation; to partake, day after day, in the Creation which belongs to every man. Winter comes. A referee—Father Time, calls it year's end, and he goes down for the count of seventy-nine.

But Barnes was on his feet again, fighting. There was spring ahead, and summer; he spent most days on the farm. Probably he did less weeding than antiquing, and not much of that. Whatever it was, he got around on his own, and not every seventy-nine-year-old can step on the gas and go. One day he'd picked up Leo Stein at the station and Leo'd remarked on his new Cadillac. "The Renoir of cars," says Barnes; "And I presume," said Leo, "you are the Renoir of drivers?" Very pretty, but the old man drove his car with more force than elegance. He knew the road from Merion to Ker Feal like the path from his favorite Renoir to his favorite Cézanne. He could drive it blindfolded, or anyway with one hand tied behind his back, and on this July 24, 1951 he seemed to. At least, he drove as if there were no other cars on the road, no intersections to cross. Before he had gone very far a state trooper signaled him to pull over. Sitting beside her master, Fidèle knew something was wrong. Whether the officer recognized her master or simply respected an old man, he let him off with a warning.

Barnes didn't continue on his way—he returned homeward. Wasn't he feeling well, or did he mean to pick up his wife? She, too, had intended going to the farm before, but he'd been too impatient to wait for her. If he was indisposed, he could ride with her. He could, but he wouldn't: she was still getting ready. He'd just come back, but he had to be off again. What was the matter with him? There were times now when he looked as irascible as he'd often felt—looked, indeed, quite mad. And on this day he must have been wildly impatient, unwilling, unable to wait for his wife.

There was no trooper on the road now to stop him. Maybe he wasn't driving too fast this time, but maybe he was. Or was something on his mind which drove him so that he didn't see the end of his country road and the intersection up ahead with Route 29, the through route from West Chester to Phoenixville? The STOP sign was there—he'd seen it a thousand times and had told friends to watch out for it.

A trailer truck smashed into the car and he was flung clear of it. Fidèle was hurt, too, so badly hurt that a trooper relieved her pain with a bullet. Her master needed no sedation: he was down for the count of ten in eternity.

Within the half hour, before there was time to notify her, Mrs. Barnes came by.

When the news reached Merion, there were those who were shocked with pain. When the news reached Philadelphia, Marceau at the museum telephoned Kimball, who spoke with charity for a multitude when he said only, "How natural."

Some years before, returning from a visit to his brother Charley, the victim of a prolonged final illness, Barnes had said, "I wouldn't want to die like that."

Five simple clauses sufficed for Barnes's last will and testament. Filed in 1944, they confirmed the gifts he had made to the Foundation and further bequeathed to it Ker Feal (if the transfer were not made before his death) and a piece of property on Lapsley Road where the courses of the arboretum were held; Mrs. Barnes was given the rest of the estate and made executrix. The estate was appraised at some $2,123,000, of which more than $2,000,-000 were in various municipal bonds. There were no gifts to any other institution or any individual. Had Mrs. Barnes died before him or within six months, the residual estate would also have gone to the Foundation. His only "child" would have inherited everything.

Originally, Mrs. Barnes was to have become president and director of the Foundation after her husband's death. In the final spate of amendments to the by-laws in 1950, she was made president of the Foundation and director of the arboretum, at a minimum salary of $30,000. Miss Nelle Mullen was to become general manager of the Foundation, and Miss de Mazia director of education of the art department.

With the passing of the founder, a great stillness has fallen over the institution which is his lengthened shadow. A school like other schools along the Main Line, it is no longer involved in controversy. The reports of the University of Pennsylvania, the Philadelphia Museum of Art and the Pennsylvania Academy of the Fine Arts which appear in the newspapers are not linked with the Barnes Foundation.

Only twice since Barnes's death has it been in the news, when attempts were made to void his policy of admission and to have the gallery opened to the public. But these cannot be called controversies. Without the presence of Barnes to stir things up, they were quiet, strictly legal affairs. Early in 1952, Harold Wiegand, editorial writer of the *Inquirer*, began a taxpayers' suit to force the opening of the gallery. It was doomed to fail because only the state of Pennsylvania, through its attorney-general, was legally empowered to bring such a suit. Early in 1958 that official did so, contending that the educational facilities of the Foundation and the art gallery were separate and distinct, and that the gallery could therefore be made available to the public. On May 8, 1959, the court denied the validity of the argument. This seems to preclude further legal action. If the doors of the Foundation are ever opened wide, it will be from the inside.

Meanwhile, Barnes's basic policy remains in force. Even if it were not embodied in the charter, his widow and the vestal virgins who attended the altar would have piously preserved it. Although it is still difficult to see the collection on short notice, Miss de Mazia seems to dispense cards of admission more or less routinely to any reasonably interested applicant. There is usually a wait of several months, but a canceled card may be transferred to someone on the list who may be pressed for time.

Barnes had sought to erect monuments in honor of Bland and Pascin. Six years after his death, Mrs. Barnes provided a memorial for him: a small plaque for the fire engine of the volunteer fire company he had walked out of so many years ago. The Foundation is his quasi-public monument.

NOTE. As this book was in press, the state began another action to open the gallery to the public.

Index

Aberconway, Christabel, 382-384
Abrahams, Robert D., 364-368
Adams, Samuel Hopkins, 291
Adult education, experiment in, 96-99
Altman collection, 89
Altripp, Alo, 381
Amato, Fortunato, 249, 250
American Therapeutic Society, 48
Anderson, John, 275
Anderson, Marian, 183, 304
Arboretum: *see* Barnes Foundation
Argyrol
   composition of, 43, 47, 355fn.
   manufacture and sale of, 50-53, 86
   profits from, 52
   properties of, 47-49, 386
   publication of research on, 48
   research on, 42-44, 46-49
   testing of, 47-49, 85
   as trademark, 50, 54
   uses of, de Schweinitz on, 85
Armory Show, 83, 84
Art analysis, Barnes's system of, 192-206
Art of Cézanne, The, 193, 262
Art Digest, 358
Art as Experience (Dewey), 239, 242
Art of Henri-Matisse, The, 193, 237, 262
Art News, 276, 281, 374
Art in Painting, The, 158, 159, 166, 170, 181-183, 193, 198, 205, 218, 219, 227, 238, 263, 264, 270, 355, 358, 359
Art of Renoir, The, 193, 279
Art Students League, 179
Artists' Union, 253
Arts, The, 111, 125, 139
Arts à Paris, Les, 24, 153, 208
Arts & Decoration, 86

Avery, Milton, 286, 308
Ayres, Clarence, 220
Ayres, Mrs. Clarence, 220

Bailey, "Diamond" Lew, 58
Barbizon painters, 75
Bard, Judge Guy K., 349
Barnes, Albert Coombs
   ancestry, 19, 44
   baseball fan, 28, 68
   baseball player, 28-30
   benefactions, 60, 103, 107, 244-248, 266, 315
   birth, 20
   buys first pictures, 39, 74
   childhood, 20-26
   collaborates with Violette de Mazia, 193
   collects antiques, 282-286
   collects paintings and sculptures, 62, 74-79, 81, 84, 111, 112, 116-123, 259, 273, 274, 278-280, 286, 287
   commissions Matisse mural, 224, 227-229
   commissions Wm. Glackens to buy modern French paintings, 78
   death, 15, 17
   establishes A. C. Barnes Company, 54
   establishes Barnes Foundation, 125
   establishes Barnes & Hille, 51
   exhibits acquisitions at Pennsylvania Academy of the Fine Arts, 124-132
   first trip to Paris, 79-81
   goes fox hunting, 63-68, 73
   honored, 174, 190, 191, 267
   internship, 32, 33

405